Our Wild Niche

Our Wild Niche

Laurie Cookson

toExcel

San Jose New York Lincoln Shanghai

Our Wild Niche

Published by toExcel

For information address:
toExcel
165 West 95th Street, Suite B-N
New York, NY 10025
www.toExcel.com

ISBN: 1-58348-368-3

LCCN: 99-64069

Printed in the United States of America

To all the species that shared their wild information

Contents

1. Introduction

What is our true nature? Is it one that can never go wild because of the damage it might cause? Are selfishness, spite and infallibility an inseparable part of our make-up, against which we must always be on guard? Our species seems to think so, and suppresses its wildness. After all, wildness can make people do whatever they want. It can stop the mind from thinking clearly and objectively, to a higher set of standards. The remnants of wildness are often blamed for the violence and aggression that we can still find in our society today. Wildness looks uncontrolled. We need restraint and consideration rather than wildness, if our society is to find any peace within itself. Our inability to control wildness, and the basic instincts that it can call upon, are blamed for many of our ills. What makes people civilised is that we have crawled out of the primal slime, and broken the shackles of nature that once made us just like any other animal.

But wildness is poorly understood. Wildness lives in millions of other species, and they have been using it for millions of years. Do they sense something about it that we don't know? I have been studying how animals read and use the wildness for some time now. In the process I found it to be the key to a daring new world of understanding. It asks a lot, but gives a lot in return. To see the value of wildness, the human mind has to change. You can carry no baggage such as belief and attitude to see it clearly. However, it is worth the change, because with each small gain towards the development of a wild mind, a new insight can suddenly appear. This book explores the biological credentials that animals need to see the wildness correctly, and then uses that view to shed new light on the most pressing biological problem today, the human being.

Wildness conjures many meanings for us. The worst connotations began to appear later in our species' civilisation, when we had lost our direct contact with the wildness. Before 800 AD, wild (or wilde) simply meant in the natural state, uncultivated, free, unrestrained or undomesticated. More recent usage of the word includes meanings such as uncivilised, barbarous, of unrestrained violence, unrestrained by reason, disorderly. This is not wildness in nature, and to be able to associate such additional meanings to the word shows to me how poorly we now understand wildness.

Why study wildness? Is it an actual item or force that needs to be addressed? There are few if any books on the subject yet people intuitively know that it is something found widely in nature. Animals feel 'the call of the wild', and some people feel rejuvenated by the wilderness. What is the best way to understand this elusive force? For a human today to understand the wildness, we will have to see things differently. The change must be a bit like a human reared animal that has to be weaned to the ways of the wildness before it can be released from our care. The artificial and supported mind has to change to a wild mind. So why make such a change? Is the wildness a lost force that can no longer have an impact on modern society? As nature shrinks, does wildness shrink, or does it permeate the universe more strongly?

There are some features to wildness that make it attractive. Wildness explores true natures. This gives its creatures an openness and honesty that I don't think can be found in people. It might not always make animals do what to us seems right, but at least their actions speak for how they feel. Wildness also makes animals more skilful, if they can survive in its domain. Wildness tests them out and strengthens their innate qualities. Animals cannot hold anything back from the wildness, because a part of being wild is to explore their deepest feelings freely. They must live or die upon the strength of their own exposed attributes. In nature, this process brings animals to the point where they learn how to use all of their adaptations to full capacity. Without any artificial support to fall back on, they learn to rely on the true qualities of their nature. They become instinctive in their abilities, as they learn to respond rapidly to the demands of the wild.

Wildness is also easy to use. Life becomes uncomplicated if you can find and trust your own true feelings. Animals trust their instincts, and they survive. This experience gives them a natural confidence. They do not linger on doubt, but stand or fall on their own instinctive abilities. Wild animals adjust until they are on equal terms with their environment, and powerful in their world. They complement rather than destroy their world. We might see some of those animals as threatening and dangerous. But imagine the confidence we would have, if we could live at our full potential. It is something that animals do every day.

In the wild, life is easy to resolve and its pathways clear. Wildness offers no shielding or protection from the elements, and no room for pretence or inaction. It forces everything out into the open, and presses true natures into view, where they must stand up for themselves and be counted. False natures do not last long in the wild, because wildness calls for total commitment. Entering wildness is like entering a test of whether our true nature is able to cope, unprotected, with the realities of nature. Our species has been able to cheat this test and contrive its results, because we have learnt how to change the environment. We have been able to give ourselves the answers we like. We have not been forced to come to terms with ourselves and how we behave. We do not have to feel our true nature instinctively, because we can survive on less. We have been able to hide our true nature, and in the process I think that we have forgotten what our true nature is like. We have not had to put ourselves into the wildness, in a way that would expose what we really are.

However, our control over the environment is coming to an end. Our artificial work is turning sour, and there is a limit to how much change the environment can forgive. Today, the environment is having a stronger say in how our world will run. Its pests and diseases have become resistant to our chemical defences. The rays from its sun have become damaging to our skin, so that we can no longer walk about freely without risking cancer. Ecosystems that took millions of years to evolve are collapsing, and can no longer provide us with buffer against the elements. The reserves of forests and foods in nature are running short. Without these reserves, we will become exposed to the barest and harshest of nature's forces. Those harsher forces will be more difficult for us to control.

When we can no longer cheat and exploit the environment, but must come to equal terms with our world, what will it be like? Will we buckle under the pressure of its wildest and strongest forces? When the problems of our artificial world become unbearable, and we must stare directly at the forces of wildness, is there a part of us that can come forward and shine through?

This question is something that humans have been unable to answer. As a species, many thousands of years have passed since our cultures have had to face the wildness. Since that time, we have forgotten much of what we should know about ourselves. What would wildness ask of us now? What would it be like if we could equalise to its terms? Our species evolved as one, but while it has dominated nature, it has been able to diversify into a host of different individualities, cultures and attitudes. Have these personalities built upon our true nature, or has our true nature become buried within our civilisation and assumed sophistication? We might sometimes feel comfortable with our natures as we live them now, but what is strong enough to last? What would remain if our artificial supports and teachings fell away? Wildness is only interested in true natures, but do we still know how that feels?

If we cannot answer such fundamental questions about ourselves, then we cannot be sure that the life we lead even now is as simple and fulfilling as it could perhaps be. It is important for an animal to know its true adaptations and nature, as only when we understand the basics can we ever hope to build anything that will last. There are many questions that only a proper understanding of our true nature can answer. But in this time of change and trouble, there is no guarantee that our true nature can find its way through our artificial props. True natures evolved for the wildness. A true nature can become lost or pushed aside in our artificial world, unless we understand its strengths. Our species has kept wildness away so long, that there has been no special need for us to focus on our true nature. Within such a vacuum, many other contenders have emerged to claim responsibility for what we do and how we feel. Without our true nature to refer, we have begun to cloak ourselves in natures and understandings that are false.

These false natures might appear to explain the modern realities of life, but they will never be as fulfilling as a true nature would feel, nor will they see reasons as simply as a true nature could see. We are in danger of losing sight of the world where true natures live. We might forget, and replace it with a world of false natures and rushed dreams.

A true nature is within us all somewhere. Amongst all the drums that our false natures would have us play, there is still one beat that can ring true. There are many things that influence us now. There are instincts, emotions, moods, feelings, conscience, consciousness, pleasures, good and bad, the spirit and the soul, and things of weakness and strength. But where do all of these come from? What nature does each influence spring from? Which ones belong in the wildness, and which ones can live only in our artificial world? To uncover our true nature, we must be able to see through all of these things. Indeed, a true nature should be able to explain every influence that affects us. A true nature should understand its beast simply and in all instances.

Wild animals surpass our ratio of development by making full use of their true natures. Of course, quantitatively we know much more than any wild animal. But it is the quality of what we do with ourselves that is poor. In comparison to the wild animal, we fail dismally in the ratio of what we have to what we do. Wild animals as lowly as the beetle have much less knowledge and equipment than we do, but for what they are, the beetle can apply itself brilliantly. It is a complete package that comfortably survives the test of time. They are like little gems. In contrast, human is unsettled and confused. Any species that sends about twenty others to extinction each day is wrong. So I will try to improve our ratio. A wild animal is in us all, and even though it is trapped and forgotten, it is the best potential carer available for human and all the other species.

Wild animals improve their ratio of development by seeing or equalising with 'the wildness'. They enter an arena of interaction that draws the best out of their adaptations. The fear a reader might have with this book is that if I am asking you to become wild, then does that mean we must assume the behaviour of other animals? No. I am not suggesting that we live like other animals and copy their behaviours. The wildness works on each species differently to draw out their unique set of adaptations to their own breath-taking conclusions. I will show that when a human is wild, we become the fairest and gentlest of the species produced so far. We could become what we want to be, while also being skilful enough to do what everyone else and our environment needs us to be.

To make a start I need to challenge many human concepts. It should be fun. The first part of this book will look at 'the nature of nature.' I will try to awaken the natural sense that we have for the wildness, before the human consciousness became artificial. After that grounding, I will show what made us assume, to the point where we began to lose touch with our true nature and fall instead for the various false natures that lead us astray today. That will be the subject of 'the nature of mindrules.' Later, I will look at 'the nature of the universe,' grand indeed, to describe the original strength that lies behind all true natures. Finally, I will identify why our species is changing so rapidly that in its turbulence we can no longer see or feel the obvious: that we are rapidly accelerating through a transitional period towards our wild niche.

2. The nature of nature

To gain an understanding of what a wild nature is like, in theory, we should be able to turn to the science of biology. However, biology is currently teaching that nature is a ruthless and self-serving place. Animals are supposed to develop selfish natures, if they are to find favour in evolution. Many people think that our problems are a consequence of that natural struggle for life. However, I think that biology now fails to understand its subject, and does not even know what a true wild nature is like.

My own study of nature began very early in my life. Ever since I could walk, I was carrying handfuls of worms into the house, and keeping small grass skinks as pets. I had such an interest in nature, that our backyard finished up looking like a small zoo, housing various lizards, frogs, tortoises, insect larvae and so on. Photos of me at a young age holding lizards went into the local newspaper, and my enthusiasm contributed to the formation of a local field naturalist club. Classes of school children would come to our home to look at the animals I kept. I also spent many weekends in the bush exploring, or looking for new insects that I could add to a collection that numbered over two thousand by age fifteen. This later hobby might seem a cruel pursuit, especially for someone concerned with the freedom of nature, but it helped to feed a fascination and knowledge that I thought I could repay one day.

I came to see such contrast between the nature of people, and the nature of the animals I had as pets or saw in the bush. This made me suspicious. One nature could be angry, hurtful, and selfish, while the other held no grudges. One could be sensitive and touchy, the other cool and relaxed. One had a free spirit, while the other was trapped in its establishment and formality. One could live life the way it wanted, while the other didn't even seem to know what it wanted. I had some ten different species of lizards and tortoises living in one large enclosure at home, that in the natural setting provided seemed wild, and yet they caused no harm to each other. Indeed, I found them to be extremely tolerant. So different to the intolerance being reported on our news at night. In nature, animals look to me to be in tune with their surroundings, where they live in harmony. This is something I don't see people doing. A wild animal has a strength and confidence in its eye that I find penetrating. I have never found the same degree of wisdom in people, as I found in the reptiles that I held captive in my backyard. It is hard not to be drawn into the world of something so admirable and inspiring.

If you learned about nature from documentaries that centre on lions bringing down antelope, or killer whales tossing baby seals for apparent sport, then nature must look a bad place. If you learned about nature from text books, before having the fascination to watch and feel it for yourself, then nature might seem a quagmire full of animals pitched in constant struggle. If nature has not touched you, then its wildness will be hard to understand. Our species no longer feels close to nature, and has missed its plot. We think nothing of clearing it away for our own development, or of plucking out minor mechanisms in its domain to justify and perpetuate our own beliefs.

While surrounded by concrete and pavement, humans have made judgements that nature is a dangerous jungle, where there is no place for the weak. It is survival of the fittest, a struggle to survive, a land of selfish genes, dog eat dog, and of red tooth and claw. Most of our nature documentaries feed us this line, and few care to take a closer look to see if it is true. It is a line even used to justify success and ruthlessness in the business world. It must be comforting to think that there is no Garden of Eden to learn from. If there is no precedent, then we must be free to pursue our own mundane thoughts, and focus on trying to make our own little worlds more comfortable within a society of competing demands and shrinking resources. But this line does not match what I have seen. It is false nature, and exists only in artificial mind. The nature of nature is far more beautiful and powerful than a species that is out of tune with it could ever realise.

The signs that nature is a place of struggle were always hard for me to find. Of course, there is life and death in nature, or what might seem like harsh realities, but the way nature deals with those harsh realities shows to me that its creatures have great strength and grace. They have no attitudes or selfish baggage. Instead, they follow a natural reasoning that goes well beyond any self-centred limitations of their own. Far more impressive to me were the signs that life in nature is easy. More often, wild animals seem comfortable with their lot. They are able to trust their instincts and feelings, and fill their every need. Indeed, they live life so well, that they fill their nature with gentleness, fulfilment and harmony. These traits do not suggest that life in the wild is a place of struggle or difficulty. It is important for us to get the right sense and feeling for nature, because that is where our roots lie. Only when we know the nature of nature, will we know if we have improved upon that nature, or let it down.

2.1 Gentleness

When I look at nature, I see a gentle and reasonable place. How does this contrast with what you see? Some animals must eat other animals to survive. They therefore have to catch and kill their prey. This is a parameter that they cannot escape. However, given this constraint or harsh reality, nature's predators seek to go about their task in the gentlest way possible. Their nature is far kinder than the false natures under which we labour. They are gentle in many ways.

Predators have numerous adaptations that effectively minimise the pain that their natural prey must suffer. Widespread throughout the predator world is the use of anaesthetics and tranquillisers. Wild animals invented these chemicals long before our doctors and scientists learnt about their manufacture. Snakes, spiders, cone shells, jellyfish, ants, wasps, scorpions, in all many thousands of different species, have powerful venoms that can quickly immobilise and numb their natural prey.

Most snake bites are not painful. Even receiving the initial puncture marks can go unnoticed, and people will not always realise that they have been bitten. Snake bites usually produce a flaccid paralysis (Lee, 1972). Most animals become drowsy or droopy, or may appear drunk. Some snake venoms are a source of analgesics. Toxin from the cobra can be used to treat severe cancer, as it is a more powerful pain reliever than morphine (Habermehl, 1981). Toxins from the asp viper can be used to relieve arthritis and rheumatism (Habermehl, 1981). The betrayal of the real deadliness behind snake bite may explain why people view snakes with such suspicion. They speak with forked tongue.

As well as producing toxins that paralyse their prey, snakes usually produce it in such high quantity that it almost instantly overwhelms their prey. The bite from one taipan is sufficient to kill 50,000 mice (Sutherland, 1983).

Similarly, spiders produce venom that seems to produce a flaccid paralysis in their natural prey. Some scientists are investigating these venoms as a potential source of relaxants (Walker, 1991). Spiders mostly target their venom against insects and other invertebrates. Perhaps because of the differences in metabolism between their natural prey species and ourselves, we can sometimes suffer unintended even painful side effects from their bite.

The toxins of predators are often only painful when they bite or sting the wrong prey species. While the sting of a cone shell mollusc is excruciatingly painful to us, it quickly tranquillises its intended natural prey. For example, *Nucella lapillus* is a marine snail with a toxin that relaxes the muscles of its natural prey, the mussel (West *et al.*, 1994). While the bite of the funnel web spider is painful and deadly to humans, it is almost harmless to cats and rabbits (Sutherland, 1983). Perhaps the bite is also painless to the invertebrates that the funnel web would normally attack. Jelly fish stings can quickly immobilise fish, but some are extremely painful to humans. The bite of the red back spider is very painful, yet only the female can harm us, as the male's fangs are too small to puncture human skin. Insects and other invertebrates is its natural prey.

Some other venoms hurt because they are used as defence rather than for predation. The venom from these defensive animals is often much more painful to us than is the venom from, for example, snakes. The venom is meant to warn or teach rather than kill.

However, animals that produce pain through their venom usually also find ways to minimise its use. Before they sting, they usually give some visual or olfactory display designed to warn a wizened animal that it should not proceed with its attack or blunder. This seems to me the action of a reasonable and gentle nature, giving signals to those that will listen. The blue ringed octopus will flash a blue warning signal before it stings. Jumping jack ants will jump and jerk if disturbed before they sting. Cup moth caterpillars have brightly coloured poisonous spines that they puff up to display as warning. A rattlesnake will make a characteristic noise if threatened, but not when striking for food. Some snake charmers in India consider the cobra to be of gentlemanly behaviour, because of the hooded display or warning dance they give well before striking.

Other predators use other methods to reduce the struggle and pain that their prey must suffer. Most predators are an order of magnitude larger than their intended prey. The size difference makes them overwhelming to their prey, effectively reducing the stress and pain that a prey must feel. Most lizards feed on much smaller invertebrates and insects, so when prey is seen, it is almost instantly caught and crunched between the teeth. Whales feed on krill, birds feed on insects and many possums and small mammals feed on various invertebrates.

A predator can also reduce the pain suffered by its prey, by increasing the speed and surprise of capture. The speed of a trap-door spider, or the flashing tongue of a chameleon, or the lure of an angler fish demonstrates such adaptations.

Larger prey are often more difficult to subdue painlessly. Predators of vertebrates and mammals must often learn and hone their skills before they can become efficient. They may learn to attack and kill their prey quickly by seizing and attacking the most vital areas like the throat. Such predators might learn their skills through experience, or by further training in play. Play ensures that on balance in the life of the predator, it is less likely to make a mess of its kill. It learns to become efficient, and therefore more gentle. An experienced lion can kill its prey very quickly, and thus minimise pain. But when its stomach is full other animals know that they can walk nearby in safety. A successful and highly adapted predator can efficiently capture and kill its prey. It doesn't let its prey know what hit it. The 'cruellest' behaviours that we see in nature are usually from a few of the less efficient hunters that are untrained or more recently evolved and clumsy.

There is a simple reason why nature makes its predators as gentle towards their prey as physically possible. The more pain a prey feels, the more likely it is to struggle, and the more likely it will escape or harm the predator. There is nothing to be gained in trying to cause more harm than necessary, and there is no hidden desire to do so. Nature in the wild bends to good reason rather than selfish or frustrated desire. The reason for gentleness is widespread throughout nature, and wild animals have abided by that reason for so long that it has influenced their evolution and become a part of their nature.

I am not trying to say that everything is rosy in the way predators collect their prey. They often offend our mind. We cannot help but view them from our background of greater skill. We could collect their prey in nicer fashion, or target prey species less appealing and fluffy. But we should see that there is nothing wrong with the way predators collect their prey. We should not use their actions as an excuse to damn their nature. Nor should we take our moral lessons from their methods of attack. We are a different species, and the way we collect our prey and tackle our life should be in best accord with our own unique characteristics. We should not take our life lessons from predators or other animals; other than to discover how they make such wise use of their own adaptations. They are doing the best they can within their adaptations. If we copied them, we would not be doing our best. We would not be equalising with the test of wildness the way they do. We would fail to achieve their ratio of development.

In the wild, the true nature of predators is to be gentle, within the limitation of the adaptations they have at their disposal. This compares with our own society, where cruelty is not so uncommon. Our methods of death are often much more convoluted and indirect. Many of the films that we make for entertainment centre on people being killed or maimed for various reasons that are more flimsy than good. There are many examples throughout our history where people caused unnecessary pain to others. At least when animals cause pain, they do it for a reason, and they try to make it minimal. Torture is unknown to wild animals. Animals in their natural and wild state are not cruel for cruelty's sake. They might make mistakes, or be unaware of the effects of their actions, but they are not cruel. This compares with our system of life, driven by our current state of nature, which produces torture, revenge, malice, and cruelty.

Nature's parasites and diseases show a similar trend towards gentleness. Here again, the natural tendency of these creatures is to become as unobtrusive as possible. It is a poorly adapted disease that actually kills its host. The best and most highly evolved disease or parasite will enter and leave its host's body almost undetected, without affecting the viability of the host. Many of the deadly diseases or parasites that we know, became that way because we introduced them to new or foreign hosts. For example, the trypanosome protozoan in central Africa is fatal to most livestock animals, and some varieties cause sleeping sickness in humans, while native animals such as antelopes are little affected (Schmidt and Roberts, 1981: 57). The African green monkey is thought to be the natural host of the AIDS virus, and appears to be unharmed by its infection. However, the same virus in humans and macaque monkeys can be deadly. This transfer to humans was a recent event, perhaps occurring through monkey bite, or from eating raw monkey brain (Melbye, 1986; Denning, 1987).

Nature also creates a system where competition is made to be as gentle as possible. Struggles for territory, mates, and food, are usually highly ritualised. Animals assume an enormous variety of displays and threat postures, all designed to try and decide the matter well before any real physical harm is needed. Lorenz (1966) noted that during fights, animals conduct themselves according to highly ritualised rules of conduct, and refrain from dealing the final killing blow. Birds with the brightest dance or song, deer with the loudest stomp or largest antlers, can win the prize without having to battle. Death or injury from direct contest between competitors is rare, under natural conditions. However, our documentary teams will often seek out the rare examples so they can show people what they want to see. Direct competition for territory by our own species, under our system, has led to the death of millions. Our history is full of wars and of colonialism, where efforts were made to wipe out other races or peoples. The production of deadly armaments is one of the largest industries in our society today.

2.2 Fulfilment

A true nature should leave its animal fulfilled. Wild animals in their natural state rarely become depressed sufficient to cause their own death. Yet suicide is a major problem in many of our species' societies, and is particularly common amongst the young. What should this be telling us about our comparative life styles and levels of fulfilment? Of course, we might smugly say that animals are not intelligent enough to commit suicide - as though this was some strange indicator of intelligence. But other species have all kinds of adaptations, none of which leave them with such useless feeling. Our own minds are more likely to become unfulfilled to the degree that allows suicide, simply because it is in such poor state of organisation. It cannot properly express our true nature.

Further evidence that the expression of a true nature should leave its animal happy and content is that most wild animals are unable to cope with stress. It is foreign to them. If they are disturbed or put into some strange surrounding or cage, they often pine and die, or lose their spirit. They simply are not used to stress. Our species can tolerate much more stress, because we are so much more accustomed to hurt and discomfort. Animals are more aware of their surroundings than we are. They can sense even small changes that we might make in their environment that can easily upset them. They might abandon their nest or flee. We can live in barren and polluted cities, and not realise what this does to our spirit. An animal will much more quickly seek a wild place to live, while we have learnt to tolerate so much crap.

There is a drug problem in our society. Many people try to escape the realities of human life through drugs. Perhaps if animals knew about drugs, and they were available to them, they might take them? Many of our drugs occur naturally in plants. If animals wanted drugs that could alter their perceptions, evolution would have long ago found some kind of relationship that made use of this need. If animals wanted drugs, then a plant could provide a drug in its leaves or flowers, and attract animals to it for pollination, to aid in seed dispersal, or provide it with herbivore protection. However, no such basis for a relationship exists. The interactions are instead based on other needs that animals have, such as food, protection from predators, and shelter. Animals do not need to fill the needs in their lives artificially. Their true natures are already free.

Animals live wildly and on the edge of their abilities. They put all that they have into their daily lives. They learn how to do what they want, and bring their full being into play. They can live their true natures honestly. How different to what a false nature must do. If people speak their minds, they often cause pain and suffering to others. If people do what they want, they can lose friendships or cause damage. Our jails are full of people who went too far in pursuing their own wants under our system of organisation. Our natures cannot be so open and honest. Why? Could it be that our natures have not yet developed or matured into a true state that is worthy of honest expression? Or, unlike any of the other 30 million or so species, were we the first to evolve a nature tinged with flaw and evil, that simply has no place in the natural scheme of things? The odds do not support the later view.

All of this suggests to me that animals are happy with their natures. We might denigrate other animals for being able to be fulfilled with their lot of minor adaptations. Perhaps we would be fulfilled also, if we had less and knew their ignorance. Intelligence makes us aware of so much more. But what they do better than us is become equal with their lot, whatever that might be. They can accept and attune their lot to the point where it becomes completely satisfying. They show that if they align their true nature with the wildness, then life for them becomes easy and accomplished. How well organised, or understanding, is our intelligence? Is it satisfying, or do we look for excuses?

2.3 Harmony

Wild animals live in a climate of harmony. They can take themselves seriously, and still be a success. They can do whatever they want, and follow their first instinct or response confidently. When people take themselves seriously, they usually just become more ridiculous or dangerous. Most of our wars arose when someone took themselves or their beliefs too seriously. I have always found people to be at their best when they show wit and humour. But what a strange position for a species to be in, that if they are to be at their best then they should not take themselves seriously. Such contrast to what animals can do. Their natures are such that they can be as serious and single minded as they like, and still function appropriately. They do not need our sense of humour to produce their harmony.

When wild animals do what they want, it fits in with their environment. Indeed, it is usually essential to the environment that they do what they want, if the whole ecosystem is to function. They can do what they want, and still be a part of the harmony of nature. The system produced by our nature is different. Our species has overpopulated and ruined the land, and caused rapid and mass extinction. We have produced dersertifation, global warming, loss of soil fertility, pollution, soil salination, the eutrophication of our waterways, and so much more.

Wild animals can live side by side comfortably. Their natures display tolerance. An animal living in a forest has far more variety of neighbouring species living around it, than a whole suburb of our species could stand. We rid our gardens and streets of its snakes, 'pests', 'bush', spiders, and almost anything that moves or looks unconventional.

The true nature of nature is best seen in pristine environments. In those environments, nature had time to develop without interruption from us or from erratic climatic and geographical changes. The rainforest ecosystem is one example where conditions are relatively stable. Rainforests are amongst our oldest ecosystems. In the rainforest, there is an abundance and diversity of life. That life lives together harmoniously, so that the species are often ancient, and have had time to develop in their own way into an amazing array of forms and behaviours. Wildness in nature favours diversity. It also favours finding value within animals through specialisation, so each species can pursue their own adaptations to become highly tuned to a special niche. Each species can fill their niche so completely, that it can all build together into a stable ecosystem.

An animal's ecosystem can survive with little change over hundreds of thousands even millions of years. Their true natures have built a system of organisation that is much stronger and more successful than the one we have invented. Their proven system works for 30 million different species, and trillions of different individuals. Our system shows signs of failure for just one species, and six billion individuals, after only a few thousand years. They don't have to prop up continually their system with hard work and new inventions. Our system must change rapidly to find solutions to the problems we created a mere decade ago.

2.4 Wildness

Perhaps the most telling difference between people and other animals that are not under our artificial protection, is the relative difference in wildness. What can we read into this? Our understanding of wild behaviour is that it involves doing what we want, by following our first impulse. This would bring us closer to a level of instinctive behaviour that would presumably reflect our true nature more closely. However, it is difficult for us to imagine how our species could follow such wildness, and still maintain harmony and kindness. The problem our species has with such impulsive actions is that they do not leave any room for consideration. Following our instinctive call would not necessarily prevent us from doing harm and wreaking havoc. The instincts of our nature as it is currently understood are weak.

But this is the test or standard that wildness offers. How do you reach a state of organisation where you can be wild and do what you want, and yet be of no harm to your world but instead beneficial? Can we make our first impulse instinctively good? That is the wildness that animals have, and one that I think is worth seeking. Their world is one of harmony, even though they are wild. How do they do it? Is there a position and knowledge for us where our own first impulse could fit in beautifully with every-thing that surrounds? It takes great wisdom and power to be able to combine the two, where we can be wild, and still be someone that we would like and admire.

Indeed, any organism that can be wild must have reached its highest level of achievement. It has come to good and equal terms with all things in its world, and can behave entirely reasonably and in sympathy. People tend to associate being wild with behaving without reason. However, the strongest and fairest reasons I know are to be found in wildness. In the wild, animals must know their reasons instinctively, rather than being something in need of thought. Being wild puts us to the test of how good we are at having our affairs and mind in order. It is a matter of finally sorting out our true nature, getting to its purity, and not settling for anything less or false. It is a test that other species have risen to, which is why they can do what they want, through being wild. We have yet to get our affairs and 'instincts' into such similar state.

Whether our species could still pass the test of wildness, or whether we will always need to shield ourselves from our instincts, will come down to what impression we have about the fundamental qualities of our own true nature. Is it one that we can trust? Is it strong enough to find a place in the natural world without constant artificial aid? Could it give us a new set of instincts that we can admire?

If we look at the natural world, we will find that all of its creatures, before or out-side our influence, are wild. They have been that way for billions of years. In this realm of wildness, they follow their true natures and they survive. It is only our species, and our domesticated pets that can no longer be wild. We have been this way in what for geological and evolutionary terms is a very short time. We now have our problems. Why did we take such a divergent path?

I think that our species' true nature has become buried so that we can no longer feel it directly. It has become buried under a host of civilised individual natures that might seem comfortable and endearing, but when you come down to it, are false in some way so will never lead to the state where we can know true gentleness, harmony and ful-filment. While we are reluctant to turn away from our well meaning but false natures, we will also have to put up with their inevitable problems and pain. Do we fail to look any further, because we feel that if we unleash our true natures, they would not be endearing as well?

Wildness holds the key to seeing a different world. Wildness is the reality or realm of nature where all forces interact directly and honestly. It is where all living things have greatest impact. Wildness is not a specific force of its own, so it cannot be isolated and studied like magnetism or gravity. It gathers its power from other forces when they combine into its system. Wildness is an assemblage of forces. It is an impressive level of organisation that allows the most efficient and direct interactions possible. Therefore, it is the fairest way to organise, because it accepts the best results that can arise from its contributors. It can occur throughout the universe wherever interactions take place. It can be in an environment, or a state of mind. Whatever contributes to the wildness is bravely willing to have its impact determined on the same terms as any other contributor. Other methods of organisation are artificial, and abandon efficient and fair interaction in favour of pretence and self-preservation.

Wildness is not of course confined to living things, but is felt there most strongly because that is where interactions happen with greatest frequency and intensity. If we could become a part of that fabric, we would see reasons much more clearly than under artificial light. Wildness is the most practical and workable state to be in for any animal. The pathways in wildness are so simple yet great, that they can fill the senses. To be wild requires us to be direct and receptive to our surroundings. Therefore, by varying our degree of openness, we could enter or leave the realm of wildness.

Once we can see the wild values within our surroundings, reasons can flow into us easily and sweetly. Reasons will fall naturally into place because of the way the universe is organised. It is structured like a branching tree. Wild animals can use that pattern directly. Our science is still studying this universal structure, and is getting closer to the understanding. We already divide our science into various branches that allow us to fit more and more pieces together. One small branch we see in biology as the evolutionary tree. We perceive that there is a tree of knowledge. Every branch of science, and every fact known, can or should be able to fit together in a way that lets us relate one fact back to another. The laws of physics, mathematics, chemistry and biology all tie in together.

Wildness is dominant and important in nature because it lets life tap directly into that universal structure without that life having to know its detail. Wildness places its creatures within the universal structure, where they can see things most clearly. It prevents them from becoming an obtuse and artificial appendage that has to work hard to breathe. Wildness offers us direct and intimate access to the strongest and wisest assemblage of forces in the universe. It shows an animal how to become simply effective.

This universal and natural structure is what makes things work. It is what supports survival. It makes everything fit and relate together. It is this universal structure, or at least the parts of it that can come down to earth, that each animal must respond to if they are to live efficiently. Whoever can see and touch that structure most truly, will feel first whatever it has to offer. Whoever is most sensitive to it will reap its strength.

Being wild is the best way available for tapping into the universal structure, because you become a part of its assemblage, and can then rely on that structure instinctively.

Wildness can drive the niche containing portions of the structure into an animal, so that its information becomes a part of them. The animal can then read its information without hesitation or precondition. An animal can feel the full forces of nature run through it, and those forces are very supportive and exciting. The structure that wildness can plug into satisfies all wants, and gives greatest impact to anything they do. Wildness gives them speed of interaction. It is like going on a ride.

The most efficient state for an animal to reach is one hundred percent wildness. Then they could fill all their needs most directly because they would be completely attuned to nature's supporting structure. However, such idyllic levels of wildness are probably rare because of alternative needs within nature. Therefore, animals must find a balance where they can most often meet their needs comfortably, but not always. There are various levels of wildness. One hundred percent wildness should be achievable, but because an ecosystem finds a balance within alternative needs, such levels are not always possible. Instead, animals maintain a functional level of wildness where some 'error' can occur. Nature's structure might not always be able to support them fully and fill their every need. Sometimes, animals might find it difficult to maintain harmony, fulfilment and gentleness. However, these variations of support from the wildness are minor. Animals are still wild at a functional level, and are driven by its structure. It remains the best way for them to organise their mind. They remain open. I will describe more fully in a later section on emotions, how animals cope with the variations of support they receive from the wildness.

Each step by an animal towards greater wildness extends their senses and ability to see through nature. The 'spirit' or being of an animal will move into its surroundings to become 'one' with nature. Its intentions will blend with the fellow forces of the wildness. Being wild is like being in a club, non-exclusive, where all the members feel the same. This might seem like an anthropocentric statement to make, yet our inability to get involved at such a level with anything outside our own species category withholds from us the true meaning of this the most powerful force in nature. Wild animals do not have the fears of restricted and individualised minds. They feel the same, even though they are different species. They feel the same because they all feel wild.

The wildness can gain a strong hold over an animal. It makes them efficient, and places them into the fabric of nature. Our science is trying to understand that same structure, but we still find it a very difficult structure to understand directly. We cannot immerse ourselves in it. We still don't see or feel the answers that it holds. Unlike other species, we lack the wildness needed to see our world properly. The morals that science has found for us so far are not inspiring, so cannot grab our enthusiasm. We look elsewhere for fulfilment. We do not have wildness, so cannot see through its eyes, what other animals can see.

Under the conditions of wildness, nature has been able to branch out and occupy almost every corner of the earth. The ecosystems it produces are remarkably strong and resilient, because all of the pieces in them work so well together and can reliably build upon each other. Wildness is a state of organisation that allows the pinnacle functioning of each component or species to combine into a mutually advantageous system.

2.5 Evolution

So why does current biological theory tell us that nature is a place of selfishness and spite, where animals are in struggle? Evolution through natural selection, first proposed by Darwin, neatly explains the process by which the species are produced in nature. The part that I question is whether this natural selection involves a struggle to survive, and a survival of the fittest. These latter terms seem more to do with describing our own lifestyles, than actually describing what nature is about. Anything that must struggle, or try to survive and be fit, will fail in nature and indeed will be selected against. There is more art to 'survival' than merely struggling and surviving. Those that do it well are wild.

Our lack of vision of what wildness entails has led to the belief that evolution can act alone, to produce survival in whatever way it sees fit. Then, those that struggle are more likely to prevail. However, evolution is not at the forefront of nature. There is more to wildness than we know. It is not just a matter of doing what we want. It is a level of organisation. If we could find our own natural wildness as well, we would find it to be a great source of wisdom and power, that makes life simple, not a struggle. Evolution recognises the important benefits of wildness, so selects for ways to better join its creatures into the wildness, in ways that we might not have realised.

There are two approaches that evolution might take to mould its species, with or without the wildness. The first approach is one that ignores the influence of wildness, so produces species that are gifted at struggling to survive. The second approach will produce species that need to be open and comfortable to survive. The difference between these two approaches might seem small at first, but the ideas that grow out from them give two very different views on the ultimate nature of nature.

In one view where evolution acts alone, nature becomes a place of competing individuals, or of selfishness and aggression, where anything that in the end is not self-serving is not natural. Nature becomes a world of survivors, where life centres upon finding conscious or subconscious ways of promoting an individual's genes into the next generation. This becomes the main function and aim of nature, and is what natural fulfilment is supposed to be about. Then, using nature as our model for life, we might implement its imagined principles into our own society. Evolution is used to justify selfishness and competition. Those who want to get ahead should trample on whoever stands in their way. Anything less would be like trying to hold back, and will fail to relieve our most basic and primordial instincts.

Under this scenario, people might use evolution to justify conscious selection, and the division of people into fit and unfit groups or races. An extreme example of the extent to which evolution can be misread was when Hitler tried to develop his master race. Today's view of evolution is preoccupied with struggle, selfishness and fitness. Evolution has been hijacked, and made to conform to the alienated and self-indulging views sought by our society.

As a mechanism, evolution is easier to understand within a climate of struggle. It is easier to visualise how the 'weak' could fall to the wayside, leaving the 'fit' behind. This would give a rapid and clear turnover of the species, in time frames that we are better able to comprehend. No wonder Darwin convinced himself that nature was in struggle. It perhaps helped to crystallise and explain such a groundbreaking theory to his mind. He ignored his sense for 'the glad face of nature', but instead remembered that each animal feeds on the other (Darwin, 1859: 74). I think it is better to trust what we sense than what we think we know, as personal knowledge seems to be very easily persuaded by itself.

The view of evolution I see has natural selection as a process that selects for greater wildness, by exploring intrinsic beauty and simple efficiency. Wildness is the highest state of achievement that any creature can reach. An animal that is highly adapted, responsive, efficient, and complete earns the right to be wild. The primary aim of animals is to achieve the level of accomplishment that will let them break through into this functional state of wildness. Evolution is not survival of the fittest. Evolution is survival of the wildest. Anything that detracts from being wild will only delay that achievement. Wildness might be a lost concept for us, but it remains important to get a feel for what it entails. Nature is not in a climate of struggle, but in a climate that favours creativity and comfort, instinctiveness and the embodiment of wisdom. Such creatures have no need to cheat or struggle beyond what the other participants in the wildness will allow.

We might see the fights of some animals as a sign that they are struggling. However, when animals fight, it is usually because they feel confident and natural. That is why pain needs to be so painful. In the absence of fear or an awareness of struggle, pain makes animals want to avoid damaging themselves. When their battles do become a struggle, they give up, usually fairly easily. Wild animals are usually quite timid, and prefer to stay where they feel comfortable, in their wild and free place. This is also why displays are so effective in nature. At any early sign of struggle, or of being out manoeuvred, one of the contestants will usually give up. They will produce an appeasing display or signal, drop the head or avert the eyes, or simply try to escape. Alternatively, when competing animals of the same species are injured, those injuries are often not particularly harmful. For example, the sea lion may take little notice of the gashes that it receives during its battles, because vital damage penetrating its thick layers of blubber is rare. Similarly, antelope that engage in head butting for displays of strength have skulls that are honeycombed with air cavities, allowing them to absorb their impacts.

The foreignness of struggle to an animal also explains why they rarely deliver the final blow during battle, or pursue the defeated more than is needed. They do not need to take out revenge or cruelty. They do not need to relieve the emotions that would build if there were excessive tensions in their struggles. Their emotions do not overwhelm them and drive them onwards to do more damage than the task at hand demands. They are more methodical and adapted to their battles. Their battles are not struggle to them.

Much of biology today tries to confine nature within the terms of evolution, without noticing the wildness that courses through it. Wildness can be hard to pin down and come to terms with when we do not experience it directly. But while it is excluded, subject biology will fail to stir the animal inside us. We are an animal species, so why shouldn't the subject of biology inform us most? There is something fundamentally wrong with our knowledge if biology cannot even inspire its author. As poor replacement, we have other subjects such as economics and politics dominating our lives, and acting as our main outlets for fulfilment. Wildness could do this so much better. To those who have lost sight of nature, I suggest you step out of the laboratory or from behind the computer, go to a forest or wilderness, open up the senses, and see if you can notice what is really happening and connecting all of the pieces there together.

When you visit a forest alone, and step away from the cars and guided tracks, and stand quietly, the forest can come alive as you begin to notice the life that it has. You can feel the age and strength of the trees, and imagine the time over which such similar scenes existed. The scene can seem ancient and vibrant with life. During these times, the power that you feel coming through from nature is wildness. Each part of nature has a firm place in that scene. They work together, and seem to draw their energies from the same place. Wildness is a most powerful force that has worked its way through all of nature, and touches everything before you. It is ever present, and it dominates the lives and behaviours of everything natural.

Evolution works within this setting, where it is subservient and almost imperceptible, such is the power of wildness. All that evolution can do is to make its presence felt at the barest of levels. It has a cumulative rather than daily effect. It changes species, but cannot affect their 'common soul' or participation in the wildness. Evolution needs millions of years before its effects can be seen. The process of forming a new species takes on average about one million years (Weisz, 1973: 282). This compares to wildness, which is an ever-present force that caters to the daily needs of its creatures. It is the most widespread and important component in any part of nature. All animals in nature are wild, whereas not all of them are evolving. The rate of evolution in some groups of animals that live in stable marine environments, such as horseshoe crabs, lamp shells, and radiolaria, has been virtually zero for several hundred million years (Weisz,

1973: 283). Some other creatures such as the crocodile have barely had to change at all. They are like living dinosaurs. Wildness is the dominant game, and evolution tries out different and new pieces that might be able to join in the main game. Evolution has to go through wildness, before it can touch an animal.

Wild animals do not have to struggle against a tide of selection pressure and change, because for them their niches barely change at all. They have little tolerance for struggle and stress. They have so much freedom from struggle, that they can instead feel natural and do whatever they want by being wild.

The changing or splitting of niches is normally a very slow process. Therefore, the accompanying natural selection required to better fill those niches is also slow. Over time some species become extinct. Does this mean that they should have struggled? There are more species that have become extinct, than are alive today, all due to natural processes. But this does not mean that the individuals in the species involved had to struggle. Nature does not normally discard the whole population of a species as useless. It takes some drastic climatic change or outside influence to do this instead. In nature, there is no sudden switch from one species to another. Evolution acts on the individual, or on the population, and gradually changes the relative frequency of its characters. The population gradually flows from one species category to the next. The individual at each point in time is not failed by nature and made extinct. Only the categories that we have invented, and that we call species change. There is continuity for the wild individual. The individuals or populations continue to flow through or back from those categories, as the relative frequencies of the characters in their population change very gradually. Some character frequencies flow into new species, while some gradually reduce in numbers until no more in that species category remain. But under natural conditions the individual would not feel the pressure being placed on the species' category.

Evolution must select for wildness, because it is the best and fastest way for any animal to read the information that is available in their ecosystem. The only animals that will be successful in nature are those that can read their information most wildly. They cannot grow up with the natures and attitudes that we have, or that we think should be given by evolution. They cannot stop wildness from entering their bodies, opening them up, and taking control, to the point where they can feel it all.

Because an animal must so heavily comply with the wildness, it must in fact consider all of its surrounding's first and not itself first. It must be open. It cannot become selfish in a way that makes it second guess to ensure that it is acting according to its own advantage rather than according to the wildness. If we only accept information that suits our selfishness, then wildness will not enter, the support it carries will fall away, and our world will become hard to read. Wild animals are selected because they are able to work within the ecosystem freely and naturally. The level of openness that each species has to the wildness seems complete. They do not even seem to think of themselves as individuals or as being separate components to the rest of the ecosystem, so open are they.

2.6 Self-selection or self-enhancement

The style that an animal has will grow to be very different under the two climates in which evolution could operate, struggle or wildness. Natural selection is currently thought of as being like some kind of self-selecting process. Such a process would be quite effective in a climate of struggle. However, I think the impact that evolution has on the nature of animals, is more in keeping with the style of self-enhancement. This would be the most efficient approach to take, if evolution worked in a climate of wildness.

Self-selection is the process of choosing yourself at the expense of others. An animal might do this in full knowledge and intention, or it might be an approach that becomes programmed into its genes so that they do it automatically and subconsciously. If evolution follows this type of course, it will teach animals to try to select themselves above the others in two ways. One way would be to try and promote yourself beyond your intrinsic worth. An animal could do this by cheating, deception, or false bravado. Another way would be to take any opportunity to reduce the fitness of another, thereby giving yourself more chance at survival. In either way, the process is destructive, as it wins through at the expense of others. Self-selection encourages natures that try to single oneself out above all others. It encourages natures such as aggression, competition, and selfishness. It lets its creatures find a position from which to survive, by taking the place of another within the available structure. Its creatures are less tolerant of others, because they are using up its resources and are competing for its place.

However, any system that self-selection produces will become unstable, erratic and stressful. Some of its creatures may be exceeding their true merit, due to their deceit or aggression. Each creature will be continually trying to undermine the other and take its place. Life becomes a struggle.

Self-enhancement on the other hand, is the process of getting chosen by making yourself more valuable and available. The more valuable you are to the system, the wilder you can be. You need to achieve a certain value before you can reach the functional level of wildness that all other species know.

Animals can enhance their own value in two ways. Firstly, they can look at their intrinsic worth and abilities, and ensure that these are being properly used to their full potential. This encourages efficiency and completeness. It makes them embody wisdom. Secondly, an animal can through evolution 'try' to find more value in themselves, as might occur when their line splits into two species. This change extends the bounds and structure of the ecosystem. If there is more structure or compartmentalisation within an ecosystem, then there are more positions available to fill. This approach encourages diversity and specialisation, as it creates more positions both within and at the edges of the developing ecosystem.

With either of these approaches to self-enhancement, the animal must become more wise and responsive. It must draw out more of its own value, while also staying on open terms with the rest of nature, so that nature will continue to support the animal's place in its system. Evolution becomes a creative process, as each component must grow in value within its allotted position. It produces a radiating pattern. Self-enhancement makes animals more tolerant, as rather than being in constant competition, beyond need, they each help to maintain in the ecosystem the specialised position of the other. An animal does not turn towards reducing the fitness of another, unless that opportunity improves its own value to the system, and helps to create or expand the limits of nature. Self-enhancement produces an environment serving rather than self-serving approach to life.

Each organism must become simpler and intrinsically more suited to a place in its ecosystem. This will strengthen the foundations of nature, and give it something solid from which to create and radiate. They do not become more complex and fidgety, in an effort to look for and exploit opportunity by undermining or struggling to take the place of another. They look for opportunity to enhance. The more enhanced or accomplished you are, the more naturally you fit the position, and the more free and wild you can be.

The approach of self-selection is to try and keep everything to one's self, and take a bigger piece of the pie. Self-enhancement tries to make the pie go further, and also make it grow larger. The natural progression of self-selection is that in the end, only a few species that succeeded in being most selfish and aggressive will survive. But this is not what happens in nature. There is such diversity and breadth of life that science has still to describe it all. Even now, our taxonomists know of perhaps only half of the species that really exist on Earth. Self-enhancement allows nature to put more species into each space.

Evolution might select for those individuals that seem to us selfish, but any animal that feels it must be selfish to win, will fail. There is a gap between trying to be something, and being intrinsically suited to the job. Wildness ensures that only those intrinsically suited and comfortable with themselves will survive. This shifts the purpose and efforts of an animal away from anything self-serving that we might imagine, towards trying to fit in beautifully. Animals must adapt in a way that will let them fit in with the developing wildness. They must adapt in a way that makes them valuable to it, rather than looking for ways to undermine that structure towards some individual purpose.

They must hold up their own end, rather than knock another down. Evolution selects by making things more beautiful, rather than taking note of self-promotion. A self-enhancing nature can be relaxed, natural, free and wild. It produces something that nature can build upon, rather than making nature look back on itself for its deceitful pretenders. Eventually, the process of self-enhancement spills over until it also enhances the ecosystem. The natural consequence of self-enhancement is to find that you have sufficient reserve to share. This spark in humans has lead to the development of ethics and altruism.

For every case of selfishness in nature that science has come up with, I think the view should turn towards seeing it as an attempt at self-enhancement. The underlying drive in nature is to create or enhance a position for life out of nothing. The purpose each animal assumes, is to feel valuable in relation to the other wild animals and components in nature, so that nature will 'agree' to put you into its balance.

To illustrate, let us look at two examples of supposed selfish behaviour provided by Dawkins (1976) in his book *The Selfish Gene*. One is that certain female praying mantises are selfish because they sometimes eat the smaller male that attempts to mate with them. In pure survival terms, the benefits to the female are obvious. She gets a free meal at the expense of the male. The male might even fail to spread its genes further, if it fails to inseminate the female before being eaten. The female selects for the survival of her own genes, as paramount over the genes of the male. This kind of selfish behaviour could become inbred through evolution, as the offspring continue the habit of cheating the needs of others to ensure self-survival. However, selfishness could only become inbred if that female could ensure that she only produced female mantises. Otherwise, half of its offspring as males must display the opposing altruistic behaviour of allowing themselves to be eaten. This shows the problem of thinking that animals can develop a nature answerable only to themselves, in the same way that humans think they can.

I would classify the mantis behaviour differently. This form of cannibalism might be necessary if the mantis species is to live comfortably in the niche that it occupies. If food for the mantis species were scarce, then it would make sense for males to be eaten. Perhaps the mantis species would fail if its female could not with fast enough reflex speed rely on just the one instinct, to attack anything small enough to eat when hungry. A conflicting instinct that forced her to distinguish between small males and small prey might slow her response and make it hard for the species to live comfortably. Under these conditions, the cannibalistic behaviour of females is not self-serving or self-selecting. Its style instead is to find a way to best gear a life to the resources and interactions available in the niche. This is self-enhancing, as it both ensures that a life can grow from the resources available, and the genes that show how to do this will be preserved. It fills a niche that would otherwise not be there; full with life that can then give further structure and support to the ecosystem as a whole. The mantis species can become a food source for some other species, or it can provide a means of population control for another. The ecosystem benefits. Only individuals that strengthen and enhance life in that niche turn out to be selected.

A further example of selfish behaviour was that the blackheaded seagull would attack and swallow its neighbours' chicks if the other parents were foolish enough to leave their nests unguarded. However, the raiding seagull is not trying to be selfish so that it can continue to be amongst the chosen fit that are to become selected by evolution. It eats the chick in response to hunger, and to the nature that it needs to live comfortably in that niche. The behaviour of chick eating is probably now little noticed by evolution. There have probably been as many chick-eating episodes for that species, for as long as that species has existed, as there are today. The bird that swallows the chick of another will survive at the expense of another, but it is not evolving to produce a more efficient and selfish chick eating species. The behaviour simply maintains the relative frequency of a behaviour that has been found to work and enhance the position of that species for many thousands of years already. That is sufficient reason for the behaviour to continue. Rather than being extra selfish, the individuals can simply follow the code of behaviour that has been handed down through the generations. The gulls are not abiding by the code of selfishness, but by the code of environmental necessity. It might make good sense for this species to eat some of its neighbour's chicks. If the nesting site is so crowded that another nest is within easy distance, then there are probably too many seagulls anyway. In the longer term, the species will be better off with fewer individuals that have to live within a niche of limited resources. The behaviour of chick eating helps keep the species in balance. The behaviour helps maintain the vigour of a species that evolution found through selection to be the most suited to that niche.

Of course, neither is the raiding bird eating the chick for the good of the species, nor to keep the species in balance. It is the niche that determines the relative frequency of the genotype that produces this behaviour. The niche that the bird occupies must call for some level of chick eating behaviour, if that species is to live efficiently and wildly. The chick eating behaviour would be part of a scavenging way of life, where food supply is short and must be scavenged, especially around nesting sites.

Even though the niche is of limited resources, behaviour such as chick eating will eventually become detrimental to the species. It would reduce the population drastically, if the species turned more and more on to itself for food. It would become harder for the individual to find a mate. Also, a smaller population would reduce the flock size, which often needs to be large enough to confuse predators, and so increase the survival opportunities for each bird. Therefore, the excess of chick eating genes would eventually die out, due to other factors that the niche would bring to bear on the species. In the long term, aiming to self select through chick eating, or in whatever other regard is proposed, would not work or last. The niche will have the final say on what behaviour is allowed. That is why the animal will always be better trying to self-enhance, by making itself more appealing to the niche. This is better than continuing in the vein of self-selection, as such an animal will eventually run out of support, and find itself alone and dead.

We might find the behaviour of chick eating repugnant, so to us the individual involved must be selfish or struggling. Similarly, we might find the behaviour of animals eating their own faeces repulsive and so call them ill mannered or insensitive. We might call a lion that eats its rival's cubs brutal. But if you can get over the initial block of repulsion that jumps to mind by such acts, what is really wrong with those behaviours, if they work for those species? They do not really have to be selfish or ill mannered, if for those creatures the behaviours work, and have helped them to live comfortably as a variety or species for thousands of years. The art of biology is to understand a species in terms of its niche and ecology. If you know what niche an animal lives in, then the behaviour that it comes up with should look sensible to a biologist, rather than shocking.

Of course, it would be a mistake for our species to take moral lessons from the behaviours just discussed. We should not be guided in our behaviour by what other animals do other than to learn how they access the wildness. Other animals are entitled to their behaviours because it is the wild thing for them to do within their own set of special circumstances. For them their natural checks and balances are right, unless the species or animal is capable of more, as is ours. We should grant that what other animals do is best on balance for all in the wildness. We should see that if they are at the limit of their potential, they are doing their best, which is more than we can claim for ourselves. The only natural law by which we need abide is to discover what the wildness would have us do. Our own special set of adaptations will ensure that whatever it is will be unique and appropriate for our kind.

Evolution is simply the process of favouring those forms of life most suited to the conditions of a given environment. The animal is environment serving rather than self-serving. The resources of the niche help decide what behaviours an animal will have if it is to fill that niche. Natural selection aims to make an animal more simply fill the niche requirements. The animal will become no more selfish, aggressive, altruistic, or opportunistic, than the niche and ecosystem call for. Therefore, an animal must 'unselfishly' look to what the niche or the ecosystem asks of it.

The best way for organisms to influence their own selection and pass on their genes is to make themselves more openly and intrinsically suited to the ecosystem. They should find out what the ecosystem needs by 'consulting' the wildness, and allowing the ecosystem to test them and mould them into place. Wildness is the basis of harmony in nature. It opens all animals up completely to each other. It allows each part of nature to try out with another, to see how well they can build into a lasting structure. If wild, then you will always be on what is like the ecosystem's selection panel, and have a hand at influencing the selection of the next generation of organisms. How far this counterbalance and influence between species goes is remarkable. Some species evolved so closely in parallel that they are now totally interdependent. For example, many species of fig can only be pollinated by one species of fig wasp (Agaonidae). Similarly, the fig wasp male is so dependent on the fig that it lacks wings, and spends its entire life within the fruit.

There are many parts to an ecosystem, with each part having its say. Animals can be viewed by some other part of the ecosystem, from almost every aspect, so that there is nothing in them where they can hide their deceit. If wild, an animal already has all the impact on the ecosystem that it could ever generate. They cannot look to manipulate or secretly self-serve, as that would take them one step away from participating in the wildness. They must work through self-enhancement instead. They must openly express and participate. During this process they or their offspring might mutate and find that they have a small variation in ability. Still however, their best approach to continued survival is to put the new ability to the wildness to see if it can fit. The chance of being selected will always be greater under self-enhancement than self-selection, due to the importance of being wild within a self-balancing and self-compiling ecosystem.

You may be wondering how animals can be open, when they use a large array of camouflage, mimicry, and entrapments to hide from other animals. They are open in that they let the wildness in to have its effects. Therefore, they let in reasons that in the majority of balance are best and fairest to all. Wildness is like a judge of fairness that all abide by to the point of life and death. They 'allow' the wildness to have its way, which is why I say they are open. This approach is different to ours, where we try to capture or remove wild reasons to our own supposed advantage. An analogy might help. You will not show me your bankbook, and I do not show you mine. We hide, in a sense. But still I know that you are a part of the economy as you work for a living or are entitled to some benefits. I don't really know your value as measured by the system. You might even buy something I want. But I accept the result, as we are both willing to be a part of the economy and its method of assessing value and distributing wealth. We are open to the influences of the economy. The wildness is like the economy of nature. But while some people might try to cheat the economy, there are no advantages outside the wildness.

Since Darwin, biologists have been preoccupied with trying to narrow the terms of nature to the evolutionary box. Thousands of papers have been dutifully written to illustrate animal deception and selfishness. But we still miss the point. The genes and instincts that seem to guide an animal's behaviour do not exist for their own sake. They exist as mechanisms for achieving something else. The genes and instincts do not call the shots, because they can be sent to extinction if they don't live up to certain standards. Animals are being motivated on a broader scale. They must fit in with their environment, because that is where the wildness is. The truer they can be to their environment, the more comfortably they will live. This openness turns what at first might look like deception into shared environmental necessity. They share the common spirit or bond of doing what they have to do to live, but only if they can do it to be wild. Therefore, on a broader perspective what they do must strengthen the environment. Their purpose is wildness.

Because of the wildness, evolution lends itself to cooperation and harmony, not to struggle and selfishness. It lets variety and possibility explore for itself. The ecology of any animal is an amazing interrelationship of life, where it depends and interacts with a whole web of other species. The law of the jungle is harmony and exploration, not struggle and fear. We are not climbing out of a primal slime of pain and suffering. That is a climate of our own creation. Fulfilment and contentment are the natural wild states. Depression and frustration are unusual states to be found in extreme form only in us. The aim of life is not to survive, but to be comfortable. Animals need more joy out of life than mere survival. We owe our existence to the cooperation of all other species on the planet that have given us the environment in which we could evolve. We did not get the adaptations that we have despite the other species, or to overcome them. We got them because the other species provided us with the infrastructure from which we could evolve. Evolution is not an excuse for changing our view of true natures from being gentle and noble, to ones of selfishness and struggle. Animals follow the code of wildness instead.

Animals in their natural environment seem to be having a great time of it, thoroughly enjoying themselves and free to pursue whatever they want. They can do all of this while still remaining in harmony with their system. The nature of nature is something to admire. It does work to decent reasoning, and not to the hidden agendas of spite and selfishness. Its creatures are open and honest, and they are so willing to teach and share their system, that they do not even try to hide their wildness from us. All you have to do is 'listen'.

These are some of the reasons I find the system that occurs in nature so much more appealing than our own. For me, it was enough to discard long ago, all belief in the morals and opinions that humans have compiled to produce their failed system. The alternative has so much more class. There is nothing like learning about wildness, than learning it directly from those that already have it mastered to a fine art. Becoming wild does not mean that we must give up our adaptations of intelligence and social cooperation. Wildness already suits a myriad of different species that have all manners of adaptations. Wildness can cope with the peculiarities of one more species.

2.7 The niche

To learn how to be wild, we need to look more closely at the world of the animal. This will help show why wildness is so effective for them. Wildness works in terms of the worlds they occupy. It is only since humankind's overwhelming influence on nature that wildness can no longer give its many creatures all the answers they need on how to survive comfortably. We give them too much pressure, such confused signals, and so little time. We are not a part of the wildness, so they cannot influence us directly, nor can most animals adapt to us in a natural and compatible way. We have changed the conditions of the ecosystems they once had. However, the principle that they use to reach optimal effectiveness remains, even if they become lost.

The world of an animal is its niche. The niche is like a home, where things are familiar and comfortable. It includes everything with which an animal normally or naturally comes into contact. A better definition of the niche is that it is any interacting position in which an animal finds comfortable to live. An ecosystem offers numerous positions or niches within its structure, and it is through the niche that the ecosystem affects its creatures. A species may find a niche for itself on leaves, in the air, under bark near the base of a tree, under bark high up in a tree, in the soil, on any of many different plants, by the banks of streams, and so on. Any habitat imaginable in an ecosystem usually becomes occupied by some species that evolves to become even more specialised to that place. The niche of an animal is any part in the ecosystem it must interact with. Each niche has its own location, prey, competitors, parasites, and microclimate. The larger and more complex the animal, then often the larger and more interactive the accompanying niche. A bacterium living under a leaf has a small and defined niche. A possum living in a tree would have many more species and conditions to meet. A niche is like a subset of the conditions found within the larger ecosystem. There can be many thousands of different niches within the one ecosystem.

It is within the niche that an animal can become wild. Animals cannot be wild to all things. They do not have the adaptations that will allow them to interact comfortably with everything in the ecosystem. There are some places and interactions that they should naturally avoid. They must specialise. They do not see the total picture of wildness, but gain access to part of it through their niche. An animal needs the support of a niche, for it to be wild. The niche allows an animal to become wild to a subset of the total wildness that is available. There it can be natural. A species adapted to a niche lives in a position where it can get all of its wants fulfilled. When it stays in that niche, its first instincts and responses will in most cases be the best responses that it could produce. The niche provides the optimal conditions for an animal's nature.

Niche living is a two-way affair between an animal and its niche. The niche provides an animal with all that it could want, so the animal evolves a strategy and commitment to stay in that niche. An animal that loses its niche and moves into some strange place where it is not suited lowers its chances of survival. An animal that stays in its niche is much more likely to live comfortably. Its adaptations are most effective there. If an animal leaves its niche, it will be less able to find food, and is more vulnerable to predators and disease. For example, an animal relying on camouflage for protection will survive on its food plant, but will soon be eaten if it falls to the ground or moves to another tree. Animals monitor their surroundings and usually try to quickly return to their more comfortable niche position, where they can be wild, because that is where their adaptations have optimal effectiveness. A tree dwelling koala fallen from a tree will quickly climb another tree, power pole or person's leg in search of its proper niche. A ground beetle will quickly scurry from the light to find its log. An animal's senses and instinctive responses automatically guide them away from things uncomfortable, back to their niche. Animals evolve an attachment and commitment to their niche, because that is where they feel their best. Wild animals placed in a cage or in foreign settings, will often fret and die. Most successful zoos make their animal enclosures look as similar to the species' natural habitat as possible. An animal needs its niche before it can feel right.

The commitment animals make to their niche is complete. The niche helps guide an animal throughout its life. The niche is the world the animal can sense and interact with. An animal's greatest chances for comfort arrive by making the niche their prime source of provision. That is where their adaptations make sense and have most impact. The niche gives its animal clear directions and stimuli to follow and to respond. It is where they will find food, mates, and most easily avoid predators. Animals focus on their niche, and become specialised to them. To them, their niche is the whole world. They probably do not realise that theirs is but one of the many different niches that go into making up the larger ecosystem. They do not need to realise this, because it is their own niche that holds all the answers for them. To a beetle living under the bark on a tree, the bark and trunk is the home, and the tree is the limit of the world. To a fish hiding between the sedges, the pond or river is the world. To an ape living in a tropical jungle, it is a patch of forest that is the world. Another way to define an animal's niche is to think of it as covering their view of the world. What they see as being their world, is in fact their niche. We know they do not really see the entire world, but only that part that lies comfortably within their own terms. Similarly for us, the world-view that each of us has, is what I think of as our own niche view.

Our species once had a niche in which it could be wild, before change gripped us and sped us away. We once knew wildness like any other species. Our species evolved within an open forest ecosystem. Before we learnt agriculture, our species used to occupy a niche where we roamed large areas that held numerous trees, birds and other animals. We had to be aware of those animals, of our own predators, of how to find medicines from plants, and of how to hunt as a group to find prey. Our species would make temporary shelters amongst the sticks and grasses. Our niche in the ecosystem was as a hunter-gatherer. During these times we were in harmony with the environment, and caused it little damage. Any change we did cause was at a slow rate that the environment could repair.

Some of the old pristine hunter-gather life styles that we know about had many of the characteristics that I see in other wild animals today. Members of our species that lived in this original niche-like state were generally healthy, happy, open with each other, and in harmony with nature.

However, something started to make us change, more rapidly than was needed just to keep pace with the slowly changing environment. Did we do what no other species has done before, and begin to evolve in the absence of a selecting niche? Today, the things that we interact with change each year, even daily. New things that we must become aware of and consider crop up constantly. Each new appliance or technology changes our 'niche', home or society. It can change the environment in which we live. The interacting positions that we find in society come under constant change or threat. We no longer live in a niche that is stable, or that is going to last. The set of conditions that our children live under will be different to ours. There is no common niche that all of our species can live in or agree to at any one time. We each have a different set of beliefs, and see the world differently, often very differently. The world-view that each of us has, is like a niche that only each of us can see. Other species usually have just one instinct or pattern of behaviour to follow, because all of their population lives within the same niche. Ours has numerous kinds of behaviours and opinions, because our niche views and niche thinking are now of such variety. We might find some temporary niche position for ourselves in society, or in business, but those 'niches' are brief, and highly individual and exclusive. The rest of our species does not enjoy those niches.

The comfortable positions in life that we find cannot set up the relationships that would normally develop between an animal and its niche. Our niches do not last long enough for us to fine-tune our behaviour to the point where we can develop highly reliable instincts for those conditions. Our niches are not strong enough to contain us wild. The achievement of wildness takes time to develop, and normally requires living in a strong niche that changes little over many thousands of years. Any temporary niche that some of us might find in society will be lucky to last a lifetime.

Some other species undergo niche shifts. They move rapidly from one niche to take up residence in another. For example, some Indian minors have flown from the forest to the city. The Monarch butterfly has island skipped to different niches throughout the Pacific. However, these changes occur because a new niche for them is already available. The animals still have a niche to be wild with, even if it is new. They are still undergoing selection by the new niche, and become whatever will suit that niche most. The creatures involved can still be wild. The household fly has shifted home from animal dung to our garbage heaps. In the process of adapting to its new niche, the fly continues to evolve slightly by developing genes that are resistant to our insect sprays. But what selection force guides us? What new niche have we moved into? How can we see its wildness? What nature will we need if we are to see that wildness? While the Indian minor will not change its niche unless we change the environment for it, we can continue to change our own niche apparently under our own steam. We cannot predict accurately what our niche will be like in the future. We can however predict where the Monarch butterfly might spread to next, or what niche the drywood termite would occupy if it got past quarantine precautions and landed in Australia. When these species change niches, they are still wild.

There are of course, many advantages in not being bound to one niche. It makes us more adaptable, being able to move from niche to niche, to change, as we need. This has made us the most successful species on earth, and for our size the most populous. We have inventions and knowledge. Our quality of pursuits extends into the fine arts and culture. The species has travelled into space and could reach the stars. But what interests me is how the animal inside us feels about this, and if it has been able to develop at the same pace? Once it was used to niche life. Once it knew wild fulfilment. This might have been bliss in ignorance, but what are the lasting effects of niche living on us now?

Even today with all of the change that we go through, there is sign of the underlying longing that our species has for something stable and permanent, like a niche. There are still some sets of conditions to which we become attached, and to which we would like to return. Rarely are things as good as they were in 'the good old days'. This feeling is a way of defining the niche that we became used to when we grew up. Each new generation has a different set of conditions to live under. What was dear to one generation may not be dear to another. When those attachments become questioned, or lost to the next generation, we find out just how dearly held those conditions really were. Back then, they seemed instinctive and natural. It is often not until we lose things that we realise how much we assumed that they were solid in our world. Things that we often took for granted, and that we thought were a part of the real world, do change.

Like any animal, we have some attachment and commitment to the home that we learnt most deeply. Bonding to a niche is a natural process. This bond can be very strong when first felt as a child. Young children usually get homesick when they leave their family and home for any length of time. Also, many of the beliefs we hold do not arise from reason. They occur because of the bonds we made to family, peers, or the traditional way of life. It is natural to bond to the surroundings for which we became familiar. Holding dearly to a past way of life, that makes sense to us, and perhaps only us, seems natural. We do not want to part with certain things, even though the reason for not wanting them to change might not be clear. What world and set of ideas do you believe in, despite what all the others say? This suggests to me that the animal in us all is still clinging to what it thinks is its right niche.

2.8 Receptivity

Anything that an animal normally interacts with is a part of its niche. The trees, food plant, soil, the other species it meets, are all a part of that niche. The niche provides a species with its most secure and successful position from which to operate. No other species can live amongst a colony of stinging anemones and survive, as can the anemone fish. No other animal can swim along under the mouth of a shark, be fed and not eaten, like the suckerfish. No other insect larva can feed on a milkweed plant in daylight like the caterpillar of the Monarch butterfly. No other animal can fly in the night to catch food and during the day cling to the roof of a cave safe from predators like a bat. But if any of these creatures leaves their niche, their chances of comfort plummet. An anemone fish with bright colours could be eaten when it leaves its anemone and coral hideaway. A suckerfish that loses its shark might starve, as it is a poor forager of food on its own. A Monarch caterpillar blown off its milkweed plant might not find a suitable replacement to feed on, or might not be able to produce the distasteful chemicals that would normally repel predators. A bat flying during the day would suffer from the sun's heat, or be eaten by birds of prey. Therefore, all animals have adaptations that will help them to locate and stay within their niche. They can become quite desperate in their actions to return to their niche. The animal may maintain contact with its niche by orienting according to an automatic taxis response. It may follow trails or gradients of light, temperature or chemicals. The tiny crustacean *Daphnia* religiously follows a trail of light of certain brightness, to whichever side of a water bowl it is shone. It uses light to help locate its correct niche or water depth in lakes (Harris and Wolfe, 1955). If an animal is to stay in a niche that is more complex, it may need to develop its senses more highly. An animal might follow the call through the forest by its parent, or develop a mental map of its surroundings to help it return home.

However, simply moving into the environment of a niche does not ensure that all of the advantages of niche living will result. A tame lion released back into its natural environment is quite likely to die, unless it can learn to read the wildness once more. Its mind must change. An animal must become attuned to its niche. It must be able to read the signs of its niche better and faster than any other species. It needs to gain access to the full range of information that is available to help formulate its optimal response. Other species could exploit any hesitation that it suffers between availability of information and response. The animal could die upon hesitation. Also, any delay could make an animal miss its mark when it finally did respond, due to the changing conditions that occur within a niche. The animal must absorb immediately and listen to whatever information the niche has to send. A rabbit cannot notice from the corner of its eye, a gliding shadow, and think to ignore the response to run for cover. Its response must be instant. It should not sit there and consider whether to ignore the information or not, and decide if it is really relevant. A leaf beetle that feels a sudden jolt on its branch should drop to the ground instantly. It should not wait to see if the jolt was really from a bird landing on the branch, or just a cow passing by.

For an animal to become attuned to its niche it must get to know that niche very well. Ideally, it must know and respond to the niche so well that reading it becomes like second nature. The state of mind that allows this relationship to develop I call receptivity. It is the mind that other animals use to open themselves up directly to their niche, so that the wildness can enter them completely and guide their way. It is a mind that allows fine-tuning to such a degree that the niche relationship becomes automatic and instinctive. It is the method animals use to see the wildness. Receptivity might seem a complicated word, but it describes the process most accurately. It is actually a very simple process. Even an insect or lizard can do it. We don't know about it, simply because we have lost contact with the niche that once kept the benefits of the wild relationship alive for us.

Receptivity is the open relationship sought by all wild species with their niche. It allows them to avoid hesitation and gain tight connection with their niche, so that they can read its information faster than any other species. It is a relationship that binds the animal and niche together. At its wildest level, receptivity allows the niche to both send information and initiate a response within the animal itself. It allows any possible delay in processing the event to be cut, because as soon as the information is available a response can be forthcoming. Such an animal could react and move swiftly through its niche. It could act instinctively.

In receptivity, the brain allows the stimulation of information sent by the niche to travel unimpeded through its neural network and directly to a response. The brain does not divert that information into some other region, where it must decide whether or not to accept the information on face value and in pure form. It does not try to analyse the information to look for what niche or whose world it really came from. It does not have to be wary of any false deception. It does not have to consider if the information is moral. An animal accepts that it is in its niche, the niche is its world, and so all information is therefore necessary and directly acceptable in pure form. Receptivity does not label the information to change the level of importance and subsequent impact of the stimuli that it receives. Without any blocks to stop it, niche information can travel through a receptive mind to penetrate and spread deeply into the organism to affect it and change its mind, before that information becomes questioned and changed, if at all.

Receptivity opens an animal up directly to all stimulation that it receives. The animal evolves to assume that all information will come from its niche, which to it, is the world. Life would become difficult if it were to delay or abstain from its niche information. Attunement to the point of wildness calls for full opening to the niche. This makes an animal responsive, open, and honest. You can go directly to its soul, and such an animal is wild. All of the animal's innermost desires and potentials are there in direct contact with the niche. It is there for the wildness that lives in its niche to see. The animal can behave naturally rather than artificially because it does not try to hide its nature. Receptivity allows an animal's 'self-identity' to merge with the environment. Perhaps that is why a wild animal does not seem to me to feel isolated, alone or individual. Animals become attuned to their niche to such a degree that they become an integral part of its structure and can see the wildness.

Allowing the niche to select at least initially what an animal's response will be, gives that niche partial control over the animal. Over millions of years of evolution, animals have learnt to trust this approach because it has been so successful. The degree of directness and openness of the relationship that can develop through receptivity can become so great, that the division between organism and niche is lost and the two almost merge and only make sense as one. The organism becomes a part of its niche. The identity of the organism becomes defined in terms of both its form and its niche. A brown knobbly insect viewed in a museum cabinet may look grotesque, but when seen on the bark of its food plant its form makes sense. An organism forced to live and behave out of its niche does not show its true value and beauty. We will best understand the species in terms of its niche. Similarly for our own species, such bonding was evident. In Australia, elderly aboriginals often say that if they leave their land, they will die. Their identity is bound to their niche or land. To leave it, would probably be like losing half of yourself or your self-identity. Modern society especially does not understand this bond, because of the distance it has now moved away from anything resembling a wild niche.

There is a difference between receptivity and simply having an open mind. An open mind may view all of the information at hand, but still not allow it to penetrate directly and completely. There is no requirement for an open mind to allow the stimulation from the niche to pass unchallenged through the brain. That information is not completely free to choose its own natural course through the brain. An open mind can still hold back the information and view it as unusual or distasteful. Then rather than agreeing with the niche that all that it sends is already completely acceptable, the open mind can vary the level of acceptability that it places on the information. The open mind can categorise the information, and resist complete incorporation. Then it will view the world as complex and divisive, and believe that we must make even more allowances and compromises in life. The open mind need not change with the information that it accepts, and allow the mind to become moulded. Instead, it may see a greater complexity in life, and place more steps between availability of information and response, because we must first place that information into its appropriate compartment. This reduces the ease and speed of response. Choosing the right response can become uncomfortable and stressful, rather than instinctive.

A receptive mind would behave differently. It would allow the information to both enter the senses and brain, and make changes in whatever way it saw fit. The stimulation would have free uninterrupted passage through the brain. It could produce its natural and direct response. We would be unable to reject information.

Examples of the type of mind that we need for receptivity can be found in our species still. Fascination is a form of receptivity, when applied to just one particular subject rather than to a whole niche or world. In fascination, all clues sent by the subject are quickly detected and absorbed. Fascination can gain a hold over a person, and change them. Generally, those scientists most fascinated in their work are the ones that make new and revealing discoveries. We can usually see information in its most pure and honest form through fascination. Receptivity is like one step further into fascination.

Children are also born with receptive minds, because it is our natural wild state. Children begin life geared to assume that they will be able to attune openly with their surroundings. They are almost gullible, and will absorb without question whatever they are taught. But sadly, children must learn that the adults are still trying to make their own little worlds work, and so there is no common and reliable niche from which to learn. For their own protection, we dampen their openness and high expectations. They must be taught about the bad.

A further example of how our species' spirit develops when it approaches receptivity can be seen in tribes that are closest to our ancestral way of life, the hunter-gatherers. Receptivity is especially evident in those tribes that were sheltered from outside interference and contact. Tribes with stable or slowly changing cultures can often develop their niche interactions to an extent approaching wild creatures. In general, hunter-gatherers are happy, chatty and honest, have few crimes, sexual freedom, and no words for war or deceit (Farb, 1978: 96). They are almost child-like in receptive mind. Early Europeans often exploited this condition. Much land was bought, for some few beads and sacks of flour. But these cultures give an idea of the level of openness, honesty and trust that people can feel for their world upon achieving receptivity.

2.9 Instincts

Receptivity is the most direct way for an animal to find contact with the wildness, and thereby put its full range of adaptations and senses to optimal use. However, there are some disadvantages to receptivity. Each day, an animal might have many thousands of interactions that could each impact upon a receptive brain. Receptivity can leave the brain subject to continuous change. Amongst the full range of receptive information available, some may prove trivial and distracting, while others may be the first sign of something major. Unless the brain is large enough to provide sufficient buffering against continuous change, its outlook could become quite different from one day to the next. Such change could lead to inconsistent behaviour. While the general principle of receptivity is useful, animals are usually better off finding ways to take greater notice of a smaller set of interactions that link more closely with the pivotal aspects of their niche.

Animals use instincts to inject structure into their receptivity, in a way that allows them to specialise even further. Instincts formalise and harness the main pathways, learnt or evolved through receptivity to be a part of their niche. These pathways become permanent niche connections that an animal can keep. During the life of the animal, those instincts essentially will not change. A set of instincts can stay in the animal for the rest of its life undisturbed. Normally, an animal's receptivity and access to the wildness in no way suffers by the development of instincts.

Instincts are like specialised conduits of receptivity within the maze and abundance of total information available. Instincts streamline the receptivity that an animal has towards certain areas of niche. Much receptivity can be crammed into each small bundle of instinct. Imagine that each stimulation available in a niche feeds a line of information into an animal's brain, and that there are many thousands of different lines of information available. An instinct pinches a group of those lines together, forever linking them. Then, the stimulation of any one line or small piece of information can set off a whole chain of events because of the impact it now carries within an instinct. An animal with good instincts can make fast decisions and feel its way through life. It can turn instantly and naturally towards the most reliable course of action, based upon what might seem like scant information. Animals can pick up and sense information in their niche, and obtain great meaning from it. They can read signs that we might miss.

If an animal has enough instincts, it may learn to take notice of just that information contained in their instincts. The animal may be able to ignore the less structured information that tries to enter through the remaining receptivity. In this way, instincts can act like a filter to the full range of information available through receptivity. Instincts can keep out much background and lower frequency noise that might be confusing in its detail and variety. Instincts help an animal to specialise and see just their niche, not the whole ecosystem.

Instincts are especially important for small-brained animals. An animal needs fewer brain cells to read instinctive information than it needs to read unfocused receptive information. Instincts also prevent the animal from being easily influenced by any receptive whim. They provide a balance between the large amount of information that receptivity can provide, and what an animal really needs to live comfortably within certain niches. Much evolution, trial and error, is needed to determine which instincts, or pathways of receptivity, an animal should keep. There is always the danger that important information that could have been picked up through raw receptivity will be missed under a more specialised set of instincts.

Normally however, an animal can rely on its instincts when it is in its right niche. Instincts enable important niche information to drive deeply into an animal, so that the information can produce immediate and highly interactive results. With a few good instincts, the animal can greatly improve its chances of survival. The animal can use its instincts to feel and sense rather than think and analyse its way through life. Instincts should turn receptivity into a specialised format that allows the species to become highly tuned to its own niche and piece of wildness.

Although instincts are a more structured and specific use of receptivity, they retain its essential ingredients. Like receptivity, instincts can take control of an animal. Any stimuli that the niche sends can pass uninhibited into the nervous system of the animal. Once inside, the stimuli can find its mark, and take control so that the animal gives a standard or instinctive response. Instincts can tie an animal tightly to its environment, allowing the self-identity and the trust of the animal to pass without inhibition between the two. Instincts are normally highly advantageous and reliable.

Animals that rely on instincts for the bulk of their receptivity will do well in an evolved wild niche. However, such reliance on instincts can lead to disastrous results if the animal one-day finds itself outside its evolved niche. Instincts that work so well under certain circumstances or niches can look silly or dangerous in others. When the niche changes, it would be better to discard the instincts, and get back to the underlying receptivity that they originally tried to represent. By converting instincts back into their basic receptivity, a lost animal could reach the point where it can feel the wildness once more. Then, it could start again, and perhaps find a new set of instincts that will reflect more accurately the value of its true nature within the new niche. That will be our path.

However, instincts are very difficult to change. Animals have such commitment to their instincts that they can seem programmed. Their commitment can be so great, that they are easy to delude and trick if we mimic their important niche stimuli. The stimuli or niche tells the animal what to do. A moth cannot avoid but fly to a light bulb during darkness and flutter about pointlessly, even to die against the hot glass. It has an instinct tuned into the stimulus of a bright moon appearing at night that for millions of years before was useful for navigation. Some animals now might seem foolish for their instincts, but they are highly adapted codes of behaviour that were effective for a long time within a given set of conditions. They would still be useful, if we had not changed the specific conditions of their niche.

The level of control that an instinct has over an animal usually goes so far that the animal has no awareness that it is acting on instinct. The forces that control it can be unknown to the animal, because they are simply obeying and assuming rather than thinking about their instincts. Instincts are valuable because they prevent an animal from having to think about the alternatives. There is no need for the delay and stress of decision. The action that an instinct produces can take place almost without direction or guidance by the animal. The guidance comes from the niche.

In *The Physiological Mechanisms of Motivation*, Epstein (1982) provides a good definition of an instinct. An instinct is behaviour that produces a result, for a reason to which the animal is blind. Instincts make you unaware of your own reason behind certain actions. Therefore, if we could ask any animal, do you have an instinct, then their answer must be no. They could give such an answer, without realising that some or all of their behaviour was in fact instinct directed. What seems natural behaviour, for which there is no alternative in the world, really might be instinctive behaviour that is only relevant within a certain niche. What instincts do we have, while thinking with all the power we can muster that we have none? We might think we already know all about our instincts or the lack of them, and are therefore intelligent enough to think beyond their bounds. We might think we know our instincts, and are capable of self-control. But an animal is blind to its instincts, so how could we be sure?

All animals have instincts, of which there are two main kinds. Some instincts are inherited, while others are learnt. Inherited instincts are more common in the smaller animals and invertebrates. An inherited instinct is usually well targeted, and requires fewer brain cells or neurones to perform. Therefore, a small brain can hold sufficient understanding or niche wisdom to make itself comfortable. Animals with strong inherited instincts tend to live in simple niches, where the stimulation they receive is of a constant and reliable kind. An animal can more quickly set up its wild relationship with its niche using inherited instincts than learnt instincts, because the species can simply hand down their set of instructions to the next generation. Newborn animals with inherited instincts can soon leave the care of their parent, because they can use their inherited instincts almost immediately.

The greatest limitation for inherited instincts is the problem of the changing niche. Change can make past instincts irrelevant. Inherited instincts can give an animal a head start in life, but they can also put an animal on a dead end pathway in evolution, if those instincts cannot change. If instincts are inherited, then each individual or new generation has little scope to change their instincts. The advantage of instincts is that they save some of the time and energy needed to become receptive to a niche. The problem with them is that they then resist change, so that if the niche alters even slightly, then the instinct might lose some or all of its relevance. It might lose sight of its original goal.

The alternative to the inherited instinct is the learnt instinct. These instincts work on the basis that given a certain niche, each animal species with a certain set of adaptations will develop its proper set of instincts through receptive learning and interaction. Through receptivity, the niche will mould the brain of the animal into most suitable niche format. Many animals, especially the larger vertebrates, are able to learn at least some of their instincts. These animals often also have a prolonged infancy, where they can be protected during the time they need to learn their instincts.

By leaving some or all instinct development to the learning process, an animal will be more able to cope with small variations that might appear in the niche from one generation to the next. It would allow a species to inhabit a more complex niche that might be somewhat variable. Small variations might occur in the niche, over short periods of time, that inherited instincts could not follow consistently. The landscape might change, or the population of another species might temporarily increase beyond the normal balance. It would be better to learn some instincts from experience. This would make instincts more adaptable.

The instincts that animals learn I call mindrules, and they have evolved most strikingly in our own species. I equate mindrules to instincts, rather than knowledge learnt, because they become so assumed and automatic to the brain that they act just like an instinct. We are blind to their existence. Once formed, we cannot delve into them more deeply, because in assumption they become untouchable. They become assumed like an instinct, rather than objective data that we can reassess consciously. Whenever we use our mindrules, they become more and more instinct-like. We forget their reasons, and become their slaves.

Mindrules allow animals to become tuned to their particular niche environment after they are born. However, the process must happen quickly. An animal without good instincts will not last long. Most instincts are learnt while young, and while the brain is impressionable. However, animals should not rely on a capacity to learn new things forever. Eventually, they will have to fend for themselves and use what they have learnt efficiently and wildly. Eventually, the passages learnt by receptivity must become of instinctive quality.

There are two main kinds of mindrules, which differ according to the rates at which they are learnt. Some mindrules are learnt very quickly through imprinting, as best demonstrated in birds. Mindrules can be imprinted in birds within the first few hours of life. Once learnt, they become instincts that they will follow unquestionably throughout life. Konrad Lorenz demonstrated this phenomenon, when he became imprinted as a parent to some gosling chicks. He did this by being present when they hatched. The goslings imprinted, and would follow him wherever he went, in the same way that other goslings follow their natural parents. Under natural conditions, an inherited instinct could not have told the goslings who the parent would be, even though this information is vital.

Sometimes, imprinting makes mistakes. Cuckoos have learnt to exploit the inflexibility of imprinted mindrules in other birds. They can lay their eggs in another species' nest, thereby passing to another the effort of raising their chicks. The surrogate parent cannot be objective about what it learns when fledglings hatch in its nest. Upon learning its instinct, it cannot see from a broader perspective the obvious species differences. However on balance, imprinting in birds is successful. It allows the brain to remain small, so that the bird is light enough to fly.

The other kind of mindrule is learnt more slowly. It also has the greatest potential to change or modify once formed. I call these instincts pliable mindrules. Again, most pliable mindrules develop when the animal is young or first born, and formation would be similar though slower to imprinting. Both processes occur most strongly during sensitive periods, when changes in the brain pattern and behaviour of an animal are most easy to induce (Rauschecker, 1987: 194). During sensitive periods, certain stimulation can have a profound effect on the organisation of the brain (Rauschecker and Marler, 1987). However, the imprinting process in mammals is usually more flexible than for birds. In mammals, this cortical plasticity has been studied most extensively in the visual regions of the brain, because it is easier to conduct experiments on vision, by blocking or adjusting the things that an animal can see. In one experiment, kittens were reared part-time inside a drum marked with vertical lines (Blakemore and Cooper, 1970). After this conditioning, the kittens were virtually blind to objects held perpendicular to the orientation they grew up with. They would only play with a rod that was shaken vertically, not horizontally. The instincts of the kittens gained an orientation bias, so that they could only see in a certain direction. Similarly, visually impaired animals and people can compensate for their loss of sight by improving their instincts for other senses such as hearing and touch (Rauschecker, 1987: 208).

Sensitive periods are when mindrules are learnt most strongly, and are the times when the brain is at its most receptive. The sensitive period gives an animal the opportunity to become attuned to its environmental stimulation. This compares to simple learning, which is a process of more ordinary modification and development of the cortex. Simple learning is typical in adult animals, and the animal is more conscious of the process and end result. What we learn during sensitive periods however, becomes more deeply entrenched and instinct-like. It is much more difficult, or impossible, to recall and modify with reason. It becomes assumed.

One of the main triggers for closing the sensitive period, and settling with the mindrules that we have, is competitive exclusion (Bateson, 1987). This is a process where existing mindrules begin to exert their influence on any future instinct learning. As the capacity of the brain for mindrules fills, further additions become harder to make or are even rejected. Competitive exclusion can close the sensitive period. However, the sensitive period may not close fully, as there often seems to remain some ability for future modification. Alternatively, new sensitive periods can arise during later stages in life, especially if a new desire appears. For example, the awakening desire for sex in teenagers can make them more receptive to their peers than before.

Attunement, especially during sensitive periods, is a natural process that is still with us today. Once, it would have made our instincts receptive to the wildness. It now fails in this task, because our niche is changing so rapidly. However, if the process continues in us without our knowing, what are the effects? Do we learn instincts tailor made for unstable and false niches that change and become lost? What instincts have we learnt as mindrules, that are now false due to our changed conditions? Would we still support them if we knew? Any instinct can influence all subsequent reasoning, so these are important questions to answer. The instinct is the starting point from where the animal then views its world. If we do not get our mindrule instincts right, how can we expect the reasoning that we then construct to be strong? Our species might become so deluded through its mindrules, that it can no longer contribute to the wildness. If our reasoning ever hopes to become well based, then it must first penetrate through the mindrule barrier to find out if there is good order in the ground rules of the mind.

Most of the instincts in humans we learn as mindrules. However, there is one more important instinct that we inherit instead, that strongly affects the way we behave. I call this instinct the cortex instinct. It is 'the instinct to produce mindrules'. The mindrules we grow are subject to learning, but our need to produce mindrules is inherited. That need is pressing and strong, and on its own, will produce characteristic behaviours in us that will drive us towards finding a set of mindrules as quickly as possible. In the past, that one inherited instinct was useful because it always drove us on to find a set of highly effective mindrules. However, in the changing niches of today the cortex instinct causes devastating results. It makes us accept second-rate mindrules.

The cortex instinct to produce mindrules has been operating in our species all this time, without our questioning. Many generations have come and gone. Our species has allowed itself to accumulate many fundamental mistakes within its mindrule structure. Through the pressing need of the cortex instinct, many false instincts have become established within our species that can only survive under unusual and artificial environments. They hide from the wildness, so their weaknesses have yet to be revealed. The mindrules we have contain many fundamental errors that we do not see simply because they are now our instincts. What problems do they give us, and what excuses do we find to protect them for the sake of having a 'complete' mindrule set? If we ever want to get a true reading of the value of our mindrules, we will have to find a way to delve behind our mindrules. We will need to contact the underlying receptivity and wildness where it all began. That is the only position from where we could find a clear view of our mindrules and their developing behaviours.

There are various mindrules. Some can become fixed and imprinted, while others can remain initially somewhat pliable or plastic and open to suggestion. Eventually however, both the imprinted mindrule and the pliable mindrule must move further into the realm of the immovable and blind instinct. Evolution selected for ways to harness and formalise the receptive process that binds animal and niche together. It selected for instincts that would allow the brain to assume its relationships, so that the brain could turn its energies towards the other tasks of life. At some stage, mindrules must become instincts that we can assume. Originally however, the main aim of instincts in whatever form they take, is to provide open conduits to whatever the niche can send. Instincts should allow an animal to become more efficiently wild.

The reason we have mindrules is not to allow those mindrules to become laws unto themselves. We evolved our capacity for mindrules so that we could become wild with our niche. This result of attunement to wildness shows the main difference between receptivity, and the period of sensitisation. Receptivity feels the wildness, so that any changes to the brain happen under wild direction. Sensitisation also moulds the brain, but this may happen without wild direction. It can go wrong. Receptivity is the basis of a live relationship with the wildness that continues throughout adult life, while sensitisation usually vanishes once its youthful time is spent. Sensitisation can lead to receptivity, but not always. It depends on whether during sensitisation the mindrules can tap into the fabric of wildness, and so feel the strength and openness that will take those mindrules to their most accomplished state. Then receptivity can continue, even when sensitisation finishes. Sensitisation is an adaptive way to try and find receptivity more easily. Receptivity is a relationship or state of mind that can be live and interactive with wildness for a whole lifetime. It does not need to reject anything that the environment sends. Sensitisation can lead to attunement also, but it does not have to lead to wildness, because it can attune to things false. It can therefore feel dead and empty. It will often reject the wild information that the environment sends, because that information may go against the foundations of the mindrules that it learnt. Receptivity is a relationship that recognises and seeks attunement to wildness, while sensitisation simply seeks any kind of imprinting.

An animal is blind to its instincts, but once we become aware of them, there is a chance that they can change. We could place the instinct at one end of a scale that measures the level of awareness that an animal has for the reasons behind its actions. The instinct would occupy one end of this scale, where the reasons for a particular behaviour are unknown. Alternatively, if we do become aware of one of our instincts, but cannot stop it from happening, then that behaviour moves from an instinct to a reflex action. Once we become aware of the cause, reason, and end result of an instinct, we move into a position where we can consider and perhaps control it as a reflex response. We could at least control the stimulus that it needs to run its program. We are no longer blind to its end. We know that when we move into a dark room, the iris in the eye expands to allow more of the available light into the eye. We know the cause, and what will happen, so could stop the behaviour if there was some great need, by choosing not to go into that dark place. The movement of the iris is a reflex action. However, if we did not know that our iris altered its shape under different light intensities, then to us that behaviour would be an instinct. Similarly, a baby grasping and sucking at birth displays what for it is an instinct, but to the adult is understood as a reflex action.

Still further along the scale in our ability to control and know our own behaviour, are the points where we have sufficient knowledge and control to consciously direct that behaviour. The degree to which we can direct our own behaviour, will depend upon how we are motivated and what we feel comfortable with. If we rely on others to make decisions for us, and to get us going, then we might not be fully aware of their reasons. Our personal control over our own actions will not be complete. We might know some of their reasons, better than if we were acting under instinct or reflex, but our knowledge will still not be complete. However, if we act only upon the reasons that we know, then we are responsible for our own behaviour and are self-motivated. Our control over our own behaviour will be complete. With such realisation, we will live at the other end of the scale to the instinct.

Most animals will never have sufficient brain capacity for objective consideration, sufficient to allow them to realise their instincts. But we have the adaptations that could allow us to become aware of all our instincts. This gives us the potential to move about on the scale of self-awareness, and so overcome the perpetuation of those dead-end mindrules that are preventing our species from attuning to the wild. We could find a position where we know and control all of our behaviour. We could repair our instincts, and thereby make better judgements in life. Our behaviour, or its various components, can move in status from instinct, to reflex action, to motivated and then self-motivated behaviour, or visa versa. However, if we are to have any chance of moving the drive for our actions from instincts to self-motivation, we must first become aware of our instincts, and of how to separate them from our true nature. Being self-motivated in some parts of our behaviour does not prove that we have exposed all of our other instincts. Our every action can arise from a different place along the scale of self-awareness. We may only be able to claim self-motivation in some areas. We might be blind to other parts of our behaviour, and so be under the control of a mindrule instinct.

2.10 Wit

Once more, we see the importance of the niche. It is within the niche that instincts and mindrules become relevant and receptive, to the point where an animal can see the wildness. However, our species no longer has any stable or proven niche with which to bond. Half of the relationship equation, that can deliver wildness to us, is missing. Without a true niche to tune into, receptivity can be a painful process. It opens you up too much, for all to see. If there is nothing strong and solid to accept such openness, we could be left alone and vulnerable. Receptivity is like feeding out a personal line of desire and potential, to leave it dangling in the wind, hoping that it will find a niche that will accept it under its wing. But in the absence of any clear direction, how can we expose all of our inner feelings to the environment? We must be wary instead and close off receptivity. We no longer openly take in everything that we see, as we do not believe that it all comes from our world, or a world that we would like to bond with openly and honestly.

The balanced and natural niche that our ancestors once had thousands of years ago has gone. It could not keep up with the changes we now go through. It is gone, and has been replaced with the little worlds of other individuals, who do not see things the way we do. If we are receptive, we can be touched deeply, and reveal the entire world that we feel. Others might ridicule our beliefs and what we feel, while rarely being able to replace it with anything better. Opening up, to the degree that receptivity requires, can be too much to bear. There are too many conflicting niche views surrounding us, to know who will make use of such openness, and to what purpose they might deliver us. Therefore, we cannot expose our true feelings and make ourselves vulnerable.

It is now deeply entrenched in human culture to automatically block out receptivity. Wild feelings and desires become buried automatically, so they do not bother our mind with their expectations. If we can block receptivity, at least partially, we can hide our true feelings and thoughts, eventually, even to ourselves. Dampening receptivity gives us more time and room in which to evaluate and respond. This might make us slower and less care free, but it might also make us safe. The different worlds that people see give us crossed purposes. It has all become relative and matter of opinion. There is no single or stable niche that we can all agree upon, that could allow honesty and trust between people to develop fully. Receptivity is a difficult process to use when there is no uniting niche in sight. But wildness in other species looks so good and inspiring, to me anyway.

While there are good reasons today for blocking and restricting receptivity, there might be a way of opening it up again to see the wildness, while keeping it all secret and safe inside. Who would know what you were up to? Is there a way of awakening our own receptivity? It is a process that can restore the wildness. Who is game enough to take this plunge, when there is no guarantee of success, and the course it takes is uncharted? Some today can keep a little wildness alive inside them, but it is a small part of what is really there. For people to be wild today, they usually have to lose control. But animals can be wild without needing to change themselves or lose any of their control. Wildness goes right through them, and is there all the time. It is not just a 'Saturday night wild'. Initially, receptivity will make mistakes, but if you can keep it alive throughout its infancy, wildness can go a long way. Eventually, it might make us as wise in our ratio of development as the most finely tuned of the wild species. It could iron out our brains into a format that was wild and accomplished. What would it tap into then?

Wildness develops by opening up receptivity, and receptivity really only works when it can link up with a niche. So the next step is to find a niche that we could link up to. At this point we reach a major obstacle in that there is no such reliable niche in sight. A niche is like the view of the world we have, and the things we see in it as important. But the view of the world that you see is different to mine, yet we all live in the same world. So one of us is wrong, and I think it is you. And visa versa of course. This must lead us to conclude that we are all probably wrong in our own world views or niche views in some way, though each of us is not objective enough to know how. We are each blind to certain things. Most people realise already that each of us is at least partly mistaken in the views of the world that we have. Therefore, we realise that we should not get carried away with our own views and commit to them completely. We must be wary.

Otherwise, we will probably only incorporate a lot of mistakes that we must have but are not aware of.

The natural receptivity in our animal brain cannot distinguish where it gets its information. It evolved to assume that we are in a stable wild niche that is harmonious and has been tested to perfection. However, if our niches are now scrambled and temporary, receptivity can just as easily transfer the mistakes and instabilities of those false niches into our mindrules as instincts. We could learn to rely too heavily on our own false and misleading information. We might become receptive to some false niche, and believe our mistakes seriously. Therefore, there is one more ingredient humans need to combine with their receptivity, in the absence of a niche that we can trust. The necessary ingredient is wit. Receptivity is used to being able to look in just one direction for its information, that is, the natural wild niche that the ecosystem provides each species. However, we cannot claim to be living in any natural and time tested niche. Wit lets us train receptivity to look elsewhere as well.

Wit encompasses a large area where people are different to animals, and I think it is the best characteristic for our species. Wit allows people to become courteous, gentle, disciplined, gracious, and much more. But all of these traits come from some level of realisation that our own little worlds are not right, and therefore we must make allowances and be prepared for alternatives. Such a wit must come from maturity, because we have to learn first that we can be wrong. We must learn not to take ourselves too seriously.

It is possible to tie wit to receptivity, so that receptivity becomes more adaptable in the absence of a true niche. We could combine the best features in both approaches to life. Wit requires us to be aware that we are not yet in a position where we can know all the right answers, so better alternatives might be elsewhere to find. Receptivity must then take in all of that information, including the alternatives, and sort out the most common and impressive patterns from them. With wit, receptivity becomes prepared to look in many different directions for its wildness.

If we use wit alone, without receptivity, then we can still see the alternatives, but we might not be able to see the most wild alternative. Instead, we might give all alternatives equal rights. We will not be able to see through them with sound animal senses. Our judgement will be poor. We will not look for the wildest answer, as demanded by receptivity. Wit and courtesy on their own can make the world seem more complicated, as we give more and more rights equal billing. Receptivity is like a divining rod for wildness. It makes us continually look for the optimal wild answer out of any collection of alternatives. It makes us select just one possibility, the one that seems most wild. With just one right wild outlet, the world becomes simpler.

Of course, receptivity can go too far in its own direction if left alone without wit, because eventually it will produce mindrules. It can make us think that we have found the one right world, which will turn us single minded. Then all of the errors and assumptions of our believed false niches can enter and become a part of us.

However, if we can keep receptivity alive by preventing it from turning into mindrules, it will continue in us to look for the wildness. Wit can keep receptivity alive by making us accept information from all directions, rather than settling into belief and instinct. Receptivity does not have to follow its mindrules into the assumption that they are modelling the one right path. Receptivity can remain live always, and not shed its power to mindrules. Then even during rapid niche change the wildness can take hold. If we force receptivity to take its information from all directions, or from all of the niche worlds that surround us today, then eventually by itself it will pick out the best wild patterns within that wealth of information. Receptivity naturally seeks out wildness, and wildness is a most powerful force that is hard to ignore. Wildness will eventually get through the maze of misleading information that is laid before it. Eventually through receptivity, we will recognise the paths that contribute best to the wild reality. We will find pathways that link us more directly to the true structures that exist throughout the universe.

Of course, we can never believe that we have reached such a perfect state of wildness. That scepticism is necessary to force receptivity to look continually in all directions, instead of just the one direction that mindrules and the cortex instinct want us to find. We will have to keep our receptivity stronger than our mindrules, if we want to keep the wildness that surrounds us live. To develop our true potential we will need to tap into the original motives and receptivity of the animal inside us, and not leave it to the mediation of a redundant mindrule process that we now outpace.

2.11 Confusion

It takes maturity to learn wit, whereas the brain's cortex is highly receptive during the first years of its development. Therefore, the cortex instinct to produce mindrules takes hold well before we can train our receptivity to look elsewhere for its information. The realisation that we should not believe everything that we are told or see comes too late. The single interest of the cortex instinct is to make mindrules quickly, and then to tie them together in a way that makes them seem complete. Mindrules are highly efficient in our species. They readily become our instincts, without our needing to know that they are being constructed. The thirst the cortex instinct has to learn mindrules allows much of our early and most impressive information to pass through our minds unquestioned. That information becomes our first mindrules, and the first mindrules are usually the strongest and most rigid that we can learn.

The mindrule forming process begins long before we have the maturity to attach wit to what we learn. So how can we expect our deepest mindrules to realise that they might be wrong? They must be there, assuming they are right, which is just what an instinct is supposed to do. There would be no problem with this process if all that we learnt came from an environment that was honest and stable. It would be fine if the ground rules for the niche in which we live did not change. But the environment from which we learn our mindrules is ambiguous and changeable. We cannot expect those early mindrules to be in tune with the environment as we find it now. Therefore, they cannot deliver the level of completeness and achievement that would allow us to become wild. This is a major failing of the cortex instinct, and it hurts us deeply. However, because these reactions occur within our instincts, it is a failure that our mind does not always realise. Instead, we live with their burden.

Never before has an animal had to consider that the information it was receiving might be jumbled, and coming from a niche that was neither proven nor a part of nature. Never before has a niche changed so much in so short a time as in our civilised history. The niche for animals was always so clear and strong that it could give them guidance to things substantial, and their opening to the wildness. But we have lost that source of reliable information. The information in our niche is now matter of opinion and changeable. If we had the opportunity again to learn those same early mindrules, but this time with wit, would we still let them through so easily? Would we let them reside inside us now as instinct? Were they really that good?

In today's world, it is hard to judge where to get the right information and influence. It is hard to keep out things that are false. For example, we can tell young children that much of the world that they see depicted on television is make-believe. However, no matter what we say, children are very poor at telling the difference between the reality and the pretence of what they view. They readily believe television shows, and mimic what they see during play. They absorb the information, often deeply. They may not be able to put that information in its right place until they mature and find greater control. An adult is much more able to tell which parts of television are real or not. However, we must first learn how to make such a distinction. The animal in us is not used to having to mistrust some of the information that it receives. It is not used to thinking that some of its information is wrong.

Similarly, the prejudices and opinions of our society easily influence us. Children especially are easily indoctrinated with the views of our schools or parents. For a while, children can seem like the walking mouth-pieces of their parent's opinions. We can pass much information that is wrong, through the generations of our species.

The ideas and mindrules that each of us learnt early in childhood might not seem that wrong to us now. Often, we learn our best lessons as children. But unfortunately, this often also applies to our worst lessons. Are the mistakes that we made through this early receptive process minor and inconsequential, or are they so fundamental that they penetrate our self-identity and distort us to the core?

The first mindrules that any of us learns cannot possibly be fully attuned to any niche, because our niches change so quickly. Those first mindrules in each of us, upon which all else builds, come under stress as we lose the old niche and a new one appears. Even if the potential for errors from this process seems small at first, such small errors have had a long time to compound. We are a sociable species that teaches and communicates intently. Most of the rules and morals that we learn and take to heart, we learnt from our family and society. Much of what we learn is second-hand information derived from our ancestors. Any mindrule error that might have developed thousands of years ago has had ample time to compound into the major misunderstandings that surround us today. All might not see this. On the surface, society looks to be solid and successful. Indeed, we have managed to plug up some of the dangerous consequences of our instinctive errors, to produce a life that is bearable for most and comfortable for many. We are a very industrious and cooperative species. However, that does not mean those errors are not there, giving us a rough time, more than we deserve. There is much room for improvement within the human.

The errors that we have are fundamental, because they live in our mindrules. If we have fundamental error that we can never see, then our judgement will always be flawed and biased. Our mindrules give us basic misunderstanding. We will always get it wrong. Our mindrules are our instincts, and so we will assume their errors. Such level of fundamental error causes confusion in our species. Usually, we think that our problems are a part of the natural order. But what if the cause of our troubles is more simple than that? Confused mindrules could cause nearly all our problems. We don't know where the errors in our world come from, and are blind to them, just because they come from our own instincts.

I think that we have allowed the errors given us by our out-of-tune mindrules, to compound and self-perpetuate through society so long, that today they confuse us enormously. The world views that we now have are very much out of touch with the universal structure that makes all else work together so beautifully. We confuse and complicate the simple and the obvious. We fail to see true nature. We are nothing like other animals, and lack their style. We will need to break through the mindrule barrier before we can see the wildness properly again. My reading of the wildness is that problem and struggle will only occur for a species that has become deluded.

We lost touch with the essentials of wildness as soon as our niches began to change rapidly. This change happened many thousands of years ago when our ancestors began the agricultural lifestyle of taming and controlling nature. During that time, the wildness left and the confusion began. Errors and fears began to creep into our minds. Since then, we have naively allowed those errors to grow and compound in a way that affects us deeply. I think that we are now aware of only half of the true forces at work on us, and the other half we confuse in our efforts to make what we do know seem complete. We find it difficult to make what we do last, because we cannot tap into the wild structure that permeates throughout nature and the universe. Instead, our species faces many problems, which arise because we try to impose the world that lives in our minds on a reality that we know very little about. So much that dominates and complicates our lives can be reduced to such a simple cause of fundamental mindrule confusion. We have allowed our mindrules to run rampant in their own blind worlds, because we no longer have the wildness to guide them. We allow our mindrules to self-perpetuate under their own steam.

It is very difficult to judge the level of confusion in ourselves and society. A confused mind cannot really judge itself. Confusion is not knowing how or when we are wrong, because we are blind to the origins of that confusion. We believe that we mostly see the world as it is, and that we know how it works. Yet the cortex instinct instils such belief and assumption in all its creatures. This assumption is part of the natural process of learning mindrules. I think that confusion now runs very deeply through our species. The only reason that we can keep ahead of the mistakes generated by that confusion is that we work so hard and change so quickly. We have so far kept one step ahead of the full impact of our mistakes. But time for our species is running out. We have begun to degrade the buffers of the earth that took nature so long to build. We are eating into the ozone layer, oil deposits, biodiversity, the forests, deserts and seas. Some think that the resources we plunder might run out within a few hundred years. Where will we get the artificial supports for our confused minds then?

It is quite natural to think that the world we occupy is real and of central importance. Mindrules that are blind to the wildness will make its animals self-centred. To some extent, focusing the mind until it sees itself as self-important can help an animal function confidently. But left unguided, this belief can become so intense that our worlds seem to take on almost universal proportion. Two centuries ago, native peoples mostly thought that their own niches were the world. Their first sight of Europeans shocked them. They would conclude that Europeans were out of this world, that they were gods or devils, or that they were ill. They thought that eventually the invading Europeans would simply disappear or sail back to their alien world. Similarly, the recorded history of Europeans shows that they also thought their own niche was the centre of the world. They thought that anyone who left Europe to travel far across the sea would fall over the world's edge. Only monsters lived beyond. Native peoples that they found during their travels were usually thought of as some lower sub-species. Until recently, we thought the earth was the centre of the solar system and the universe, and that the sun revolved around us. Society tormented anyone who suggested otherwise. Many still believe that we are of such prime importance in the scheme of things, that God created us in his own image. God of course, looks nothing like a crab or a duck.

The earth is full of animals living in niches, each believing that they occupy the world. Their senses are being used to the full, so they think they see the world. What they see is only their own niche of course. Other niches are naturally beyond their grasp.

The context they think in is niche, not world or universe. Similarly, we humans think we are not in any niche, but that we occupy the world, and can see it as it really is. However, perhaps we too can only see and think niche, and do not see the real world after all. Could this gap in what we perceive explain the hidden agendas that give us problems? We might commit to our own niche so much that we could see no alternative and become blind to the true picture. We could convince ourselves that our niche was the world. We could call what we see right, rather than niche. To us the niche seems right, just as it does to any other animal.

3. The nature of mindrules

3.1 Mindrules

In this section I will give more detail about the nature of mindrules. I claim they are our instincts. They are what humans grow to become instinctively attuned to their niche, and thereby become wild. They are what we now need to avoid in favour of the original receptivity. But what is the actual structure of our mindrules, and how do they develop?

The largest structure in the human brain is the cerebral cortex. This structure is found in other animals as well, but it is most strikingly developed in us. It is our major site of learning, and fills two hemispheres, making our head quite bulbous above the eyes. The cortex is where most of our mindrules grow. There are about ten billion neurones in the cerebral cortex. Each neurone begins its life bearing hundreds of threadlike extensions called dendrites, and one much longer thread called the axon. The branches from each cell enable them to link up with many other cells, to form a neural network. The brain is like a huge meshwork of cells. When the brain is first born, each cell may be joined to hundreds or thousands of other cells. However, when the brain starts to learn, the number of connections decreases. Only a select set of those branches possible remains. Learning is a process of sorting out and keeping just those connections that turn out to be true and workable. The cortex keeps only those branches that seem most useful and reflective of its niche world. The unwanted branches fade and become resorbed. The cortex begins with an abundance of possible connections, but as it grows, only about half of those connections will remain (Wortman *et al.*, 1992: 76).

The cortex has to rationalise and lose many of its initial branches, because it cannot function with a maze of undecided connections. It needs its mindrules, and it makes them through learning. With learning, the more a particular branch is used, the stronger its connections become. That branch becomes more entrenched, until it reaches such prime importance within the cortex that it assumes the status of a mindrule.

When a new brain is stimulated, the energy of that stimulation will impact on some part of the virgin neural network. The neural network needs to find a way to disperse that energy. With so many branches to take, the brain will at first be slow to offer a set of pathways that best suits and responds to the stimulation it receives. The response will hesitate. It will not flow smoothly or feel attuned. Eventually however, the stimulation will find a path to travel. The energy of that stimulation will flow, but as it does, it will not leave those branches unaffected. Instead, it makes them stronger and more stable by burning an impression into them. Next time, that branch will not be so difficult to find. It will become stronger and more entrenched than its unused neighbours. Those branches, upon which stimulation can flow, become like fast tracks through the neural network. This process of mindrule entrenchment would fit quite nicely into a process described by Changeux and Danchin (1976) and Llinas (1987). They describe how from the maze of connections that is available in the neural network, certain branches become dominant through a 'natural selection' or 'selective stabilisation'. Certain connections become reinforced through use. It is a matter of use it or lose it (Wortman *et al.*, 1992: 76). I think that the more reinforced and selected those neural pathways become, the more rule-like and assumed they will be. They become the instincts of the brain.

Mindrules are any habit forming set of neural pathways that we learn, and that eventually become instinctive. We might have some memory of what we learn at first, but usually the important pathways become so instinctive that their identity slips from the conscious into the subconscious. Once our memories move into the subconscious, we usually no longer think about them. They become assumed. Our mindrules become so efficient and entrenched, that we learn them and allow them to become our 'second nature'.

In his book *The Mechanism of Mind*, De Bono (1969) gives an excellent model of the mindrule forming process. In that model, a plate of gelatine represents the memory surface or neural network of a newly born brain. Spooned drops of hot water represent the stimulation received by the cortex. The niche and the body send the cortex its stimulation, from which it makes all memory and learning. The first drop of hot water flows and melts its natural course into the gelatine to record a memory as a scallop or groove. Different drops of stimulation fall from different spooning positions. However, some of those drops might fall near where a groove is already present. Then, rather than those drops being able to follow their own natural path on this gelatine plate, they are influenced by the groove (mindrule), and bent off course. They follow a different course, the mindrule course. The hot water follows the original groove, melting it more deeply seemingly to reinforce and justify that mindrule even more. Natural reality must change slightly to conform to the mindrule view. The larger the groove grows, the wider the area that it influences will become, and the more rule-like it will be in enforcing its own recognition.

The need to produce niche rules is surprisingly strong. We see this best in children. They are usually eager to obtain information about the structure of their world. They ask many questions, and readily believe whatever they are told. Charles Darwin (1871: 100) noted that "It is worthy of remark that a belief constantly inculcated during the early years of life, while the brain is impressionable, appears to acquire almost the nature of an instinct." All animals have instincts. They need them to give fast and well-tested responses to the variety of challenges thrown up by the niche. However, humankind had to lose most of its inherited instincts. Inherited instincts would only hinder the evolution of a cortex that needed to become more adaptable and adept in understanding and learning. Mindrules are humankind's way of obtaining the automatic speed of an instinct, without the burden of having to inherit them. Mindrules are experience learnt instincts.

Mindrules begin to grow as soon as the cortex is able to receive information. They probably start as early as when the embryo is several months old in the womb, because even then we are apparently able to sense and learn. Mindrules are constructed for us in the subconscious, by the process of selective stabilisation. There they continue to strengthen their beginnings and spread their influence through further selective stabilisation. This is a passive mechanism. We do not have to know that it happens, and we do not have to make any conscious effort to make it work. To do so would have been inefficient. Selective stabilisation is a process that lets mindrules fall into place on their own. That is why we are not conscious of how strongly we are becoming programmed with our own mindrules. Evolution found that selective stabilisation would automatically give us a good working model of the niche in which we grew. There was no need to question mindrules, because the niche was not going to change, so the groundrules would remain reliable. All that we had to do during our evolution to complete this prescription for survival was to follow our mindrules instinctively.

Even now, most of the information we receive we simply absorb. The brain receives thousands of bits of information every minute, but we usually only consciously consider a small fraction of that information. We are unaware of most of the stimulation that we receive from the niche and from our body. Our brain absorbs most of its stimulation without us having to think about it. For example, whenever we look at something, we might think about the object, but all the background information in that view can go into the cortex unnoticed. When we look at society, we might look at its actions, but absorb its mood and standards as normal. The subconscious tends simply to absorb the background ambience as fact, without our knowing. We usually only pick out for conscious consideration those unusual parts that we see, or that others react to, and let the rest pass without question. Also, those things that we do think about, we eventually forget. The information slips from the conscious into the subconscious. We do not lose that information. It works its way into the mindrule network. Once in the mindrule network, it might still have some long-term memory associated with it, in which case we might remember the reason for its existence. However for most mindrules, we lose the memory surrounding their construction. Then we can never again recall all of our reasons, or question them directly. The information our mindrules contain will influence us for the rest of our lives.

The mindrules that have most influence over us are the ones that have become most assumed and entrenched in our cortex. Usually, these are the mindrules that we learn first, because they are the backbone upon which all subsequent mindrules must build and conform. Most people have no memory of what they learnt during their first few years of life. The brain incorporates those first mindrules so deeply that we are unaware of their influence, and cannot imagine anything beyond their framework.

Training is a way of capitalising on the mindrule effect. Repetition of the one skill allows it to become like second nature. Speech accents are another example of what mindrules can do. People are generally unaware that they have an accent, until they move to another country. Although we do not inherit the accent, it is almost impossible to change in adults and teenagers. We learn our accents as children, and continuous usage makes them automatic and 'instinctive'. This is the power of mindrules, and they have the same level of control over the way we think and feel. Mindrules let us become instinctive in much of our behaviour. They learn to control most of what we do. However, they also make us instinctively think in their context. The niche in which they were learnt becomes the context in which we think.

Once the mindrules become settled, they begin to exert their influence strongly in our minds and behave as rules. It is within their natural function to demand compliance and expect to be right. If they are in their right niche, such a mindrule nature is of benefit to an animal. Mindrules give its animal speed and success. However, if mindrules are in their wrong niche, its animal will fail in wildness. Mindrule insistence will confuse the animal instead. An animal that cannot change its instincts during rapid niche change might find itself on the pathway to extinction.

For our species today, each mindrule adds to the confusion. When mindrules receive new stimulation, rather than allowing that stimulation to follow its own natural course, the mindrule makes the stimulation bend and conform to its own course. In the gelatine model described earlier, the second drop of hot water might have naturally flowed and melted a groove heading in a different direction to the one it actually took under mindrule influence. Because a mindrule groove was already present, the second drop had to go the way of the mindrule instead, and in the process seemingly reinforce and justify the first mindrule. That second stimulation bent from its natural course towards the mindrule. The degree to which stimulation must bend to conform to a mindrule is the degree to which it becomes pushed out of emphasis. It is misinterpreted. An animal receives thousands of stimulations each day. When all of these losses in correct emphases accumulate, they add up to produce a level of confusion.

As mindrules are instinctive, we fail to see the confusion they produce. We become acclimatised to their confusion and think it normal. Mindrules naturally make us assume that the errors they produce are minor. They are strict and demanding, and have no concept that they could be wrong. They rule our mind to see things in a way that will not allow us to question their position. They do not allow us to solve any of our problems by seeing their faults. Of course, some loss of accuracy in the fine detail of events is often acceptable, in favour of having a set of rules that allow us to live efficiently. However, there is a balance between the level of accuracy that we need, and how long we can safely rely on our second-hand collection of mindrules. When niches are stable, the balance is safe and easy to find. However, when niches change, we need to become aware that our mindrules cannot cope and are in need of repair.

Today, the cost of not knowing about our own species' mindrules is great. We have even lost touch with the wildness. The gap between accuracy and the ability for instinctive action has changed, so that the errors that mindrules create for us are no longer minor. Even so, we still we do not feel this confusion consciously or recognise the fault. Mindrules have gradually pushed us into the world of the artificial, where the loss of wildness seems of no consequence. Instinctively we assume that we are right. Our confusion seems comfortable. We instinctively incorporate mindrule confusion into our repertoire of fact. To do otherwise would break the rules. Mindrule errors become a part of our reality. This has the potential to make us see things that are not real, and blind to things that are real.

Mindrules develop a strong preference for certain neural pathways and ideas. Without proper niche guidance mindrules increase our reliance on their available approach. They turn idea preference into 'idea-cling'. We might find ourselves clinging to ideas even if they are wrong. This forces us to assume a stance that can no longer be interactive or receptive. We develop personal beliefs to avoid being wrong. The potential for mindrule errors of this kind increases enormously during rapid niche change. Mindrules become snowed under during rapid niche change with loads of information to which they are not suited. Yet they continue to do what they are driven to do, and assume their way is right. They might try selling their position to others, looking for greater relevance. The result is that they produce even more confusion in their efforts to make it all conform to their structure. This confusion is now so great that it can be misleading and dangerous. The confusion produced by mindrules under the stress of change has only one way to go. Confusion believed in strongly becomes illusion. Such potential faults in our reasoning powers are well recognised. De Bono (1969: 256) speaks of 'self-perpetuating patterns that seem uniquely true.' While Crook (1987: 390) notes that 'reality is essentially an attribution of the mind, which can become illusory'.

3.2 Memory

The process of learning instincts involves a transition through various layers in our memory. There are three main steps involved. Each piece of information goes through a progression where the more often we receive the information, the deeper it becomes stored and the more it becomes assumed. The more we assume our information, the harder it is to remember, but the easier it is for us to perform automatically.

When we first receive information, it goes into the mind as short-term memory. We can be very conscious of that memory, and know its circumstances. We can easily think about the information, and reorganise it for better fit. However with time, those short-term memories or elements of them, convert into long-term memory. In long-term memory, all of the circumstances of our information are harder to remember. However, long-term memories do leave us with a feeling or sense of their essential information. We can often recall the parts that are important, after an appropriate reminder or trigger. It will often take great effort or need to recall the reasons for that long-term memory, but their lessons can fill our mind quickly.

The third step in the assimilation of our information is to produce mindrules. Information in our long-term memories becomes further forgotten to mind but entrenched in our world as mindrules. Mindrules arise from long-term memories that have become woven so completely into the fabric of the cortex structure, that they become the main organising branches of our cortex. With such important position, they are forgotten because they can never be questioned. They become the branches of neurones upon which we attach our smaller and finer threads of memory. Our memories then take our mindrules for granted.

It is upon mindrules that the process of information retrieval continues to build. The bulk of the cortex has its memory tracks stored as both mindrules and long-term memories. The long-term memories position themselves according to the plan provided by mindrules, while both our mindrules and our long-term memories influence short-term memories. However, we are only aware of the long and short-term memories, not the mindrules. The many long-term memories that occupy our cortex are in various stages of conversion into mindrules. Any memory, short or long-term, can have a mindrule effect. However, the deepest and most important mindrules are those long-term memories that convert fully into mindrules so that we can no longer remember them. True instincts are those that we completely assume.

3.3 Logical Instincts

Every organ of the body has a specialised function to perform. The function of the cerebral cortex is to learn instincts. This is a very specialised task, that has required much evolution to bring it to the level of development and ability found in humans. In most other animals, the cerebral cortex is small, or no larger than several other regions of the brain. There is little point in filling such a specialised learning structure with crossed purposes, such as making it a storehouse for inherited instincts as well. After all, it would be easier to store inherited instincts in the other older parts of the brain that are more suited to the task.

Inherited instincts are mostly involuntary reflexes that give their responses before the impulse governing them enters the cortex. Many inherited instincts and reflexes are concerned with the internal running of the body, such as the signal to release digestive enzymes into our stomach, or the response to shiver. They send their response without needing conscious consideration by the cortex. Sometimes, the reflex will simply inform the cortex of what it has done.

Humans learn nearly all of their important behavioural instincts, and most of these occur in the cerebral cortex. This part of the brain has a central role in the organisation of our behaviour. The cerebral cortex is where most of our learning takes place. All of our inherited instincts probably occur outside the cortex, in the other ample regions of the brain. The cerebral cortex functions as an information absorbent sponge. It is like a tangle of wires that need to feel the flow of energy before it can sort itself out.

We often think that the instincts that appear in the cortex and flash into our mind are inherited, especially when we do not know the reason behind their drives and feelings. Some of our actions appear to be in-built, drawing upon emotions when needed, to give us strong feelings that are hard to resist. Some of our actions might seem unreasonable, and therefore not subject to the learning function of the cortex. Some of these basic and emotional drives are common throughout our species. These experiences suggest those urges and instincts in our cortex are so basic, that they must be inherited. However, mindrules can produce all of these effects as well. As initial demonstration, let us look at one such supposed inherited instinct, the parental instinct.

The parental instinct is widespread throughout our species. It can be very powerful, and will call upon strong emotions when crossed. It can cause a parent to give up their life for a child. However, we do not have to inherit such an instinct to have these same characteristics. Neither does learning the instinct reduce its value as a code of behaviour. Mindrules have fundamental effect on all aspects of our behaviour, in the same way as an inherited instinct. However, having to learn the parental instinct would also explain why the parental instinct fails to appear under certain circumstances.

The parental instinct is easy to learn in our species. Humans have always been a social species that live in tightly knit groups. We need to look at our adaptations under that influence. When our species was evolving, our normal community lifestyle would have provided us with the social setting that would make learning the parental instinct automatic. Prospective parents within a tribe would normally see that family life was pleasant and fulfilling. Kin were a source of lasting bonds. Such bonds are highly desired by our species. This vision would make prospective parents keen for similar relationships. With so much expectant desire and emotion behind the event, the bond that the parent feels for the baby can be very strong from the start. We also have many adaptations that encourage us to learn the bond. Human babies are unusually helpless and bare-skinned. These adaptations encourage bonding, attention and devotion. Childhood in our species is exceptionally long, which prolongs and entrenches family interest and parental bonding. Sexual desire is postponed for ten to fourteen years in our species, whereas most other animals can reproduce after just one or two years of life. The experiences that a parent has with a baby have a strong impact on our mindrules through selective stabilisation, and the parental instinct becomes very strong. However, it takes much longer for babies to learn and bond with their parents. Therefore, the baby could find new parents through adoption without being emotionally affected.

Signs that the parental instinct is learnt, not inherited, can be found when this normal learning cycle breaks down during rapid niche change. Our species does not always have the parental instinct, or it may not occur the instant the baby is born. The baby might be more of a curiosity object than a person that elicits deep feelings of love. This lack of feeling may be distressing to the parent, if they were expecting that an inherited instinct should suddenly appear and fill them with strong feeling. Sometimes the instinct may never develop strongly, especially if past experience has shown that family life is not fulfilling. The parent will have less expectant energy ready to entrench the neurones that make the bond. Further, some might feel anger or revulsion for the baby, especially if there is not likely to be much community or family support for the mother, or prospects for personal ambitions are disrupted.

A further example of the breakdown of the normal learning pattern for instincts such as the parental instinct is incest. During our species normal development we did not need an inherited instinct that steered us away from incestuous behaviour. Mindrules would ensure that the relationships built upon non-sexual interactions for ten to fourteen years during family life would continue in similar vein. We will normally not cross such a strong set of entrenched mindrules. When the child does become sexually receptive, the original mindrules would again be sufficient to prevent them from wanting to change the basis of the relationship within their family. Under more natural conditions, their sexual urges are more easily met by finding new bonds outside the entrenched family experience. However, incest is not that uncommon today.

In general, mindrules will learn the most direct and logical route they can find between our various adaptations and experiences. They learn the most direct route through the cortex that will tie each adaptation and body part together as one. Each species has its own consistent set of physical adaptations, and so the mindrules of each animal will learn a consistent pattern of instincts within each species. Many of the standard instincts we see in other animals, and ourselves, are learnt because they are the logical or natural consequence of a standard set of niche stimuli and a standard set of adaptations. The mindrules learnt can be so consistent, that we can easily mistake them as being prescribed by an inherited plan.

For example, we might be able to train an animal to behave very differently to its wild cousin. However, often these animals go against our training, and produce their own characteristic wild natures, because they are meant to use and explore their adaptations. Any bodily adaptation pulls on the cortex to be used, and included into the instinctive nature of the animal. A lion has sharp teeth and claws, which need to feel pressure and sensation. Perhaps providing a teething ring or carpeted pole that they can chew and scratch will be enough for a while. However, the ease with which they can stimulate those adaptations will tease the cortex to develop mindrules towards them, and find the behaviour they were meant to find.

Some mindrule instincts will probably always occur in us naturally, such as learning the parental instinct. But during rapid niche change, the context within which we learn our mindrules changes, and so those mindrules will fail to leave us feeling complete. This goes against the drive of our most basic behavioural instinct, the cortex instinct. In desperation to find answers, the cortex instinct causes great confusion in our species. Our cortex instinct's failure to make us feel complete leaves us with various empty feelings instead. However, these feelings do not express our true or strongest nature.

3.4 Labelling

When the cortex instinct cannot properly attune its animal to the environment, it will try to work its mindrule creations even harder. During rapid niche change, it is important for us to become aware of how mindrules will behave in their extreme. Otherwise, we will fail to realise beyond their barrier of assumption to reach the receptivity beneath.

An important part in the nature of a mindrule is to label. Finding ways to label and condense information is important to an animal. There is so much information and experience available in the world that without finding a way to divide it into groups; we will be left with an unordered maze. Without learning how to see patterns, the world can remain a blur that the brain cannot fathom. The brain must make sense of its world. Mindrules construct that sense of framework. It is therefore in the nature of mindrules to try and quickly categorise all incoming information. The function of mindrules is to find common laws amongst the maze of information that enters the brain. Mindrules are quite vigorous in their effort. They make us quickly label, symbolise and categorise.

Labelling helps us remember. If you glimpse a tray of various rocks and try to recall them later, you will probably remember far less detail than if you were a geologist. While you would have to remember a whole range of descriptive words, a geologist could simply remember their names.

Humans depend more than any other species on their mindrules. We learn so much of our behaviour. We are often anxious to know how to categorise objects, events and people. For example, am I religious or not? Do I vote democrat, liberal, or for the republic? Am I a greenie, astrologer or land developer? If you could categorise my persuasion early, it might save you the time of having to read this book to determine whether you will find it in favour. It is often useful to sum up quickly, and work out early where to categorise things so that everything that follows is easier to understand. Finding the right label often lets us draw some associated conclusions. It can save us the time of having to take everything at face value.

Children are also keen to learn the human world and its categories such as good and bad. It is important to know the best and worst of your world. Once a label gains hold, it can be difficult to change. A person who makes a bad first impression can be so categorised and tainted for the rest of their lives, even if they change into something better. A person of certain colour, creed or personality might have certain prejudices levelled against them no matter what they do, simply because of their label. During early settlement in Australia, many patches of beautiful rainforest were cleared to make way for the European concept of gardening and farming. The forest was cleared because it was labelled as 'scrub'.

Under the guidance of mindrules, people eventually learn to think and communicate almost solely by their labels, and ignore the lesser-processed information, including those parts that are hard to fit. Some people will even deny the existence of a problem or non-conforming event in preference to thinking with their labels and neat boxes. Abstract art often tries to break free of our labels, to find some unusual interpretations instead.

The ability of mindrules to label is well developed in humans. The number of labels we can apply, and the detail and concepts they can summarise, continue to expand. Our species developed this ability until it was capable of language, where words label so much. We no longer simply accept events as they are, but must label them with words. Each word is like a mindrule, which can automatically trigger whole images into mind. We can use our words instinctively, and do not have to think about what they mean. We simply know. People now mostly think by their words, because we are so reliant on mindrules. Lesser processed and wisp information is almost totally shut out in favour of the labels and words. Our minds become hardened, and no longer receptive to the full range of information available. Wild feelings, wild information, if unable to be described and named, are ignored and lost under the dominance of our words.

Mindrules will follow their nature to label even when their labels do not really fit. They will keep trying, even if they must assume more to do so. During rapid niche change they will keep to this nature, become overextended, place true natures and wild information out of emphasis, and produce confusion. They try even harder to sum things up quickly. The faster they can label, the less time we have for doubt, and the less likely we will question their conclusions. Politicians often rely heavily on this technique to give fast and forceful answers to many subjects. They might rather give the impression that they are in command of the right answer, than in struggle to find something balanced. The faster we can label, the more efficient our mindrules feel.

Being fast to label and sum up is a direct attempt by mindrules to fulfil their function as instincts. However, this nature only compounds the mistakes that mindrules can make. By labelling things quickly, we give ourselves the impression that any new information we receive can never be particularly new or surprising. We think we know it all, or at least the important parts. We assume that our mindrules have already allowed for the possibilities, and are able to cope. Their rules do not need to be broken or changed. They continue to act as rules.

One of the labels that mindrules produce for us early concerns ourselves. Mindrules are quick to give us a self-image or self-identity. With such a central label and standard, we can more easily divide and categorise our world. The self-identity gives us a stable pivotal point throughout life from which we can further compare and judge. It lets us divide events, and assess our role in them. However, categorising people or ourselves into types is fraught with mistake. It is often the biggest delusion we are under. Basing our self-identity on what mindrules select for us will make us incorporate their limitations into our own self-identity and standards.

The process of trying to label things quickly now retards our understanding. The categories are all wrong. Any form of labelling today is nearly always premature. To undo the damage, it would be better to consider things on their own merit. Start all over again. Group things together as little as possible. Our current labels and groupings exclude so much more. It is best to reassess all information again and again from scratch, in an attempt to overcome the labelling and assuming nature of our own mindrules.

3.5 Niche maps

Each mindrule that an animal learns is like an individual track or pathway. However, all mindrules must in the end combine to produce one coherent niche map for their animal. The mind needs a niche map upon which to navigate. Crook (1987: 387) describes how animals need to produce 'models of reality' in their brain, so that they have an image or plan to refer to throughout life. The laws that we learn about our niche become imprinted as mindrules in our cortex. The map or model is like a guide to all parts of the animal's niche. It is a ready reference that the animal can use to tell it how to function efficiently. In times of danger, the animal can refer to its niche map quickly, rather than having to think it all out again. The niche map is like the instinctive framework upon which conscious reasoning can then begin.

One niche map is useful at guiding an animal through life. Two or more niche maps would only cause confusion and hesitation, as the animal would have to decide which map to use. No map at all would leave the animal lost in a mire of detail and often unrelated information. The brain of large animals is like a library. It is full of memories. To make use of the myriad of stored information, the brain needs to be able to summarise it all into a more useful form. It needs to put fast tracks through that information, and come up with a coherent map and system of retrieval.

Unfortunately, the need for one niche map compounds the confusion that mindrules are willing to make in order to achieve that map. They are willing to tolerate even greater errors during stress, in their effort to keep the map coherent. If one mistaken mindrule was to change, it might affect the whole network structure to which it is linked. Such wholesale change might then call for the niche map to change. It might even call for us to tear up the niche map, and find a new one.

Animals will not make such wholesale change to their niche map, especially if there is no replacement map immediately available. An animal without a completed niche map is vulnerable. It is important to keep the niche map intact, confident and functioning. Therefore, if we suspect one of the tracks to be wrong, we will need to make a choice between getting that one mindrule right or keeping the niche map complete. The need to correct the faulty mindrule usually comes off second best. It is excused in the interests of the whole. We might try to hold to our delusion instead. For example, some people deny that an ozone problem exists in our atmosphere, saying it is a greenie trick. After all, isn't the way society functions right? A more extreme example is that some people deny the occurrence of Hitler's holocaust during world war two. They would rather keep their prejudices intact instead. Our mind can develop many delusions to keep the context of its niche map the safe.

Once we give our subconscious commitment to the niche map there is no point showing the faulty mindrule to the consciousness forever, as this would simply bother and distract. It becomes easier for the niche map if each mindrule adjusts slightly so that the faulty mindrule can become 'right' in terms of the remaining map. We develop belief in our ideas, to excuse and override some of their weaknesses. We can become incorrigible as we persevere with our beliefs. We have numerous methods for making our errors seem right. What might begin as a difficult decision to ignore the fault, with practice, will eventually seem justified. Innocent casualties of war can become justi-fied in the name of a cause.

Our need for a niche map in the absence of niche understanding drives our belief for delusions subconsciously, where the mindrules live. We don't have to know about this process, because that would be distracting and draw our attention away from actu-ally using the map. Rather than put the niche map and its world view in jeopardy, our mindrules join together to fill in the gaps, and gloss over the errors. We learn instinc-tively to accept some level of error and confusion. We learn to lower our expectations. We accept that our niche map cannot fit easily or harmoniously with everything else. We see nothing wrong in having to be defensive. It is amazing how far mindrules will go to protect themselves and their niche map from change. Some of the things that we believe to help make the niche map seem complete are astonishing. For example, some people believe in the supernatural to give meaning and completion to their life. In a survey of 1236 adult Americans, Gallup and Newport reported in the *Skeptical Inquirer* (1991) that one in four people believed in ghosts, with one in ten claiming to have seen or been in the presence of a ghost. One in four believed they had had a tele-pathic experience. One in ten said they had talked to the devil, while one in seven claimed to have personally seen a UFO. Delusion in our species is rife.

Our mindrules are keen to come together and give us their niche map. If we feel under stress, they will try even harder and faster to give us their map. They will suck in even more stimulation than they should. The more they can rule, the more whole they will feel, and the more guidance we will seem to have. However, any set of rules believed in strongly and beyond their worth will produce confusion. The belief we have in our own niche map and world view can become illusory. For example, some dicta-tors become evangelical about the cosmic support they have for their rule. God is on their side. They might even build monuments and statues of themselves. In modern times it is difficult to keep the niche map looking rosy. There is so much extraordinary information that mindrules must cope with. Keeping it all together can be difficult. At times, the strain placed on the niche map can seem overwhelming. Then symptoms such as 'Future Shock' (Toffler, 1970) might arise. Our species is very good at working out the best way to do things once it has a stable framework or context in which to work. However, when the ground rules constantly change we have problems. Like any ani-mal, we are not used to having to change our niche maps. It is more natural to try and build upon them, errors, delusion and all.

The cortex instinct relies on the premise that it can work out the basic outline and highways for its niche map early in life. Construction of the niche map begins early in life. Normally, any new information that comes along would be in similar vein to what the niche map already knows. It would all be able to fit on to the one niche map some-how. In a stable niche, all information comes from the same direction or context. It is all in the same format. New information would simply refine the understanding that is already developing. The main backbone of understanding could remain. Any insight we had would cause only minor adjustment to that backbone. It would not call for some wholesale change to the very core.

The brain can still only make its understandings as niche map understandings. We cannot really come up with anything completely new. It all has to relate back somehow to what we already know. Each change should augment and expand our one niche map. The brain does not like to leave things unresolved. It wants to wrap it all up tightly and fill in the gaps. The mind cannot stay open and undecided. It has an animal to look after. It must find whatever information is available, sort it out as best it can, and turn it into a mindruled niche map that seems complete. In the interests of efficiency, the brain learnt to do this automatically and passively in the subconscious. Even if whole chunks of truth are missing to the mind, the mindrules will still complete the picture for us, and fill the gaps in themselves. Mindrules make us assume.

Magicians use this natural tendency to assume with great effect. They can lead the mind on to think in its predictable natural way, while doing something completely different. Before our eyes they can make things suddenly appear, because we do not notice what is really happening, but assume instead. Similarly, there are many picture puzzles that can make us see three-dimensional shapes that are impossible, because the mind completes the outlines for us in certain learnt ways. Mindrules can take the glimpse of a few objects before us, and turn them into a complete picture. Usually the gaps mindrules fill in for us are small and harmless. A completed niche map is more important to an animal than a map that is incomplete and full of doubt. However, now that our niche contexts change so rapidly, mindrules can do us more harm than good. Mindrules lock us into their context. They try to organise our new information according to their earlier contexts. They do not maliciously alter our new information so that it will suit themselves. It is simply the nature of mindrules to assume that they can give us the best parameters in our life.

Humankind is rarely aware that it always thinks by its mindrules, so our search for the solutions to our problems naturally strikes outwardly from them. The simple remedy of returning to the receptivity from where we can change mindrules is naturally beyond the grasp of the animal. We look elsewhere for the cause of our problems. Mindrules even invent things for us to blame, and because our thoughts always keep on their tracks, those illusions to us become real.

Mindrules try to make all incoming information fit their completed niche map. They judge and disperse stimulation according to how well it fits on to that map. Not all stimulation fits well and some not at all. It would be better for the map if there was a way to reject outright the information that did not fit. Mindrules make us do this by feeding us the illusion that there is a scale in the natural order of things that ranges from good to bad. By inventing this scale, anything that fits and enhances the map can be called good, and anything that does not fit and is disruptive can be called bad. We can then spend our lives fighting the bad and searching for good. This will keep the niche map content, but it will never bring us any closer to the level of understanding we will need to make ourselves effective to the point where we can once more see the wildness. Any wins and losses over the illusions can have no lasting effect. The potential for them to happen again remains hidden behind a veil of confusion. The reason for the problems stays free from change and beyond our grasp. Our labels of good and bad inhibit understanding. We need to disregard the 'no' reaction as it is often applied prematurely (De Bono, 1969: 240). 'Anything that is fixed, accepted or taken for granted should be re-examined in an attempt to set free the information imprisoned within it or to remove the blocking effect' (De Bono, 1969: 241).

Because our niches change so rapidly, we can no longer assume that the way our mindrules learned to interpret things in the past will always work in the future. Our mindrule instincts have become aligned to niches that no longer exist, if they ever did. This sounds simple enough, but until we completely undercut and expose an assumption, we cannot know its size. I have tried to show that the assumptions that our mindrules make are so large, that it fills our society with an underlying confusion. Those dead-end instincts make our species so inefficient and obtuse that we can no longer be a part of the wildness. During the times of our ancestors, similar assumptions were small and useful to make. We even entrusted our spirits' desire to the care of our mindrules. However, we now need to make a distinction between the concepts produced by mindrules, and how we want to feel. We are currently confusing mindrule nature with human nature.

3.6 Individuality

The influence that mindrules have over our species is extensive; however, we do not know their influence because we are designed to assume them as our instincts. Our instincts are the basis from which we launch our thinking and much of our feeling. We do not know underneath them. However, now that we know the function and nature of mindrules, we should be able to work out their influence by imagining what their nature would do unimpeded and within the stress of modern change.

There are several natural consequences that will emerge out of the drive by mindrules to produce their completed niche map. If we do not take control of our instincts with our stronger will or desire they will make us believe in a number of programmes designed to keep themselves intact. The cortex instinct will make us believe in a wide variety of illusions, to keep its mindrules strong. One such illusion is that we are individuals, and that individuality can best serve our interests. However, while individuality suits mindrule nature, it can only retard and confine human nature.

Individuality is a belief that will arise out of mindrule nature when they start failing under the strain of rapid niche change. Mindrules that have not been able to attune to any real niche find little support throughout their life. Their solution to this problem is to create a world of their own where they do make sense. Then they will seem complete. However, if mindrules follow this solution to excess, their world can become so detached and alone that they will turn us into individuals. An individual is allowed to have its own little world. In that world, mindrules can remain safe. They can block out the information that would pour in if they attempted direct contact with the real universe and its nature. Mindrules need individuality to shun anything with which they do not feel compatible. They need to keep some things private and true only to themselves. An individual does not have to try and relate everything together within the wildness. They can give up, by looking for exceptions.

Society now spends much of its time looking to improve the freedom of the individual. We try to give their worlds even more artificial structure. We give them rights so that they can keep their own positions alive while amongst the many other competing views. Rarely do we challenge the sanctity of the individual. However, individuality is but one of the many illusions that mindrules create to keep their hold over us. If we are individuals, then we do not have to relate openly with all things, because we are too individual for such an attempt ever to succeed. There is no need to try and place everything within the one framework. An individual can consider to be important, just those things that fit in snugly within their view of the world. An individual's circle of relationship can be different to another person's circle of relationship. We do not all have to answer to the same wildness.

The level of commitment that each of us has to the idea that we are an individual is a measure of how strongly mindrules have us in their grip. We are taught to be individuals very early in life. With the pace of niche change today, mindrules help impress this delusion on us quite strongly. They make our individuality very easy to believe. Today we have a society that is full of people who strongly identify themselves as individuals. However, individuality actually holds back our own personal development. It is time to discard the illusion, and find something that more accurately describes and reveals our true nature.

To be able to live in a wild niche, people must feel completely open and free. We should be able to relate naturally to all things. There would be no need for boundaries that would try to keep us separate and aloof. In the end, we will have to come to full and equal terms with all things. Our self-identities will have to leave their individual containers and species category, and spread their contacts further into our surroundings. We are a part of the universe, and arose from its common structure of laws. We are but a variation of a common creation. We are but a variation of each other. When we can all see the same things, we will feel the same, and will be wild. We are beings that are naturally open and receptive. There is no need to place ourselves into individuality boxes.

All of this might sound a bit fanciful, but the true test will be in what works and lasts. Individuality is the fanciful illusion, not the idea of being a shared part in a common creation. At every level of organisation that affects us, the idea that we are individual fails, while the idea that we are relatable to all other things succeeds:

Atoms: The idea that we are individuals does not make sense at this level. As we grow, atoms that were once a part of another organism join with ours. At what stage should we consider a carbon atom in a cabbage that we eat to be a part of our own individuality, as it begins to assimilate into our muscle tissue? The atom does not change its structure or nature upon joining our individuality. When we exercise, we use up a part of our muscle. We lose some of its tissue as carbon dioxide. Are we losing a part of our individuality as that molecule floats away and disappears into the atmosphere, to later become part of a rock or a tree? Atoms fly in and out of us on a massive and continuous scale, in a completely relatable way. Our 'individuality' is not an obstacle to them.

Genes: Genes are simply lengths of DNA molecules made from atoms. Therefore, the same argument used above applies here. The atoms that make our genes come and go in a completely relatable way. They do not stop at some individuality barrier. As the outer layer of our skin sloughs off and breaks down, the precious DNA degrades and disperses beyond our individuality. That skin might become food for a mite or a fungus. When does it stop being a part of our individuality?

Was the first cell in our body, containing our first set of genes, the source of our individuality? All of us began life as a single cell soon after conception. However, that first cell was really a part of our parent's bodies. When does their individuality end, and ours begin?

Perhaps the actual building blocks of our genes are not the essence of our individuality. Each gene has the same code in all of our cells. Perhaps it is that code that is important. The building blocks that make our genes are strung together in a sequence that is specific to each person. Perhaps we should base our individuality on that sequence. If I were to write down some person's DNA sequence of molecules on a very large blackboard, would they exclaim, "That's me"? Each person shares 98% of their DNA sequence with a gorilla, and more than half with a fly (Blakemore and Greenfield, 1987: 107). We share 99.9% of our DNA with each other. Not very individual after all. Is the 0.1% difference really that important? Perhaps if I wrote down the sequence of just that portion, it would be our individuality. Personally, I would rather lose 0.1% of my genes than 99.9% of my genes. Otherwise, I might become an amorphous blob. The essence of individuality is starting to sound arbitrary and insubstantial. A person that felt completely relatable would appreciate the contribution that went into their genes, from the thousands of ancestral species. We share the bulk of our genes with all other species. They helped build what we are today.

Cells: All people have bacteria in their small intestine. We need them to help us digest food. They also give us certain vitamins and compounds that are essential to our health. Are they a part of our individuality?

All of our cells have structures inside them called mitochondria. Cells need them to help in their respiration and oxidative phosphorylation. Without them, a cell cannot survive. They are in every part of our bodies. Mitochondria are thought to have once been bacteria that invaded certain primitive cells millions of years ago (Margulis, 1981). These bacteria found life in those primitive cells favourable. They began a symbiotic relationship with the larger cells. There they stayed throughout the evolution that went on to make us. Should we consider the bacteria in each of our own cells that we call mitochondria, a part of our individuality, or are they alien creatures that now reside inside our bodies? This symbiotic relationship fits in simply with the idea that we are naturally linked to our surroundings. Individuality finds it difficult to categorise and accept.

Brain: Individuality makes its greatest impact at this level, because it is the area under most direct mindrule control. We often believe that the core of our individuality lies in the brain. However, it is a predictable illusion put there by mindrules.

The brain evolved to commit to its mindrules very early in life. It needs them as any animal needs its instincts. Certainly by the time a person is mature, the brain considers that it has already found most of its important mindrules. By this time, the backbone or format of our niche map should be virtually complete. However, with today's rapidly changing niches, the brain keeps getting information that does not fit in with its mindrules. However, it is not in our nature to question our mindrules. We never evolved a reason to do so before. Given these constraints, the conclusion the mind will naturally reach is that it is a bit different to whatever has been sending the strange information. Whatever sends the information must be living under a different term of reference to our own. Why should this difference to other things exist? The answer is invariably that there is a difference because we have individuality. There is an essence in the person that cannot spread completely and evenly to other things. There is an essence that is of its own. We are no longer a part of everything else. We are individuals. Our mindrules will close our receptivity towards those troublesome directions. However, mindrules are no more a part of us than the cutlery in our kitchen draws. We may use them every day, but they are not us. Our true desires naturally trust our mindrules. Therefore, whatever mindrules think, we are willing to support emotionally. Therefore emotionally, we can feel individual.

There are several factors that determine the growing shape of each person's mindrules. It depends upon what stimulation we receive during learning, and in what precise order. It also depends upon the minor variations of physical attributes that mindrules must learn to coordinate. Very small differences that our mindrules learn when young can carry through in life and compound to become major differences. There is any number of permutations and combinations of mindrules possible. Each set will give their own view on life, and their own individuality, personality and attitude. Mindrules have a branching network, so that even apparently minor differences between them can grow to become very large. Identical twins can turn out very different, or similar, depending upon what they experience through their lives.

Once the brain becomes individual, it must also develop its own physci or soul. Mindrules realise that they are not able to bond or relate to everything in their world. Therefore, they cannot remain fully open to reveal their weaknesses. They can only relate to a very individual set of terms and conditions. Mindrules are what we feel comfortable with instinctively, and because they are inadequate they constrict all of the things that we can relate to openly and wildly, into what we call our soul. Our most treasured part of the niche map, where we can still feel a world of attunement, is kept safe and hidden in the soul. That is where we feel strongest. Our best and most pleasurable mindrules are in that soul, and it is a part of us that we will try to defend. It is the part that makes us feel best. It is closest to what our human nature wants out of life. It is where we like to turn and find influence whenever possible. We are unwilling to change the soul part of our niche map, or its surrounding structure, for fear of losing our self-identity. With a soul to turn to, mindrules do not always have to relate openly with the outside world to feel complete. They can do what they like, because they can always feed into and support a confused and restricted soul whenever we feel the spiritual need.

The soul is where we feel most true to ourselves and unchanged from the quality of what we really want to feel. It is the only part of us that feels complete and capable of attunement. The desire for something complete is a force that acts on us strongly. Our entire niche map was always meant to feel complete. In our own little niche worlds however, the individualised soul is as far as this level of completeness and strength can go. The soul is where mindrules can find their harmony. The rest of the world that lives outside the soul can be a problem, and is divided up and dealt with by mindrules as they see fit.

The soul often feels as though it is alone. It feels as though bleak and powerful forces could swallow it up. This can make us hide it from view. Exposing it might make us vulnerable. It might reveal our true motives and desires. The sense of harmony and completeness that the soul yearns for can sometimes make us reach out innocently for more. The attempt can prove painful. This can make us shield and contain the soul even more. It is possible to hide and bury the soul so far that we can lose touch with it. Then we become even emptier. This process of restricting our range of attunement is the true essence of individuality. It is a bit like giving up.

It would be better to expand the number of things that we can relate to. We should expand the things that our soul can touch. We should spread the strength and completeness that the soul knows, to all other things. Individuality should not keep it trapped. The soul we now know is only a cage that mindrules use to keep our desire for wildness and openness in check. It is best to remove this soul cage, and release the energy it contains. Let receptivity set our true nature free. What we cherish in the soul is the standard of feeling that it contains, not the cage or the word itself. Wildness offers the same feeling, but that feeling is free. It is possible to feel and relate to all things in the same way that we now only can do in the individualised soul. If each person keeps the strength of their wildness in their soul, it will wither away. The sweet wildness felt by the soul exists throughout the universe as well. We are not the only ones to feel it. Our strength could link up to a 'common soul' as shared by all things. We could put ourselves directly into the fabric of the universe.

Our confused mindrules drive us to individualise and contain the things that we can openly relate with. It is the mindrule way of explaining why they are not attuned to the entire world with soul-like intensity. They claim that in this universe there are many different souls. But in wildness, there is only one. Once we feel that common soul, living will become easy because through it we will become a part of nature and the universe. We will see the forces of nature at work most truly. The strength behind those forces naturally seeks to spread itself, and would normally flow through us unchallenged. However, in modern times it has become unnaturally frustrated, without us realising, by our individuality.

Universe: Individuality can make less impression on our understanding of the universe, because with science the universe is partly beyond the control of our mindrules. We are less able to delude ourselves here. Science lets us conduct experiments to determine the truth at the world or universal level.

According to our science, the universe is not divided into unrelated and individualised worlds. No laws exist on their own or in isolation. We can link all laws together somehow. Theories are being developed in physics that recognise this universal relatedness. Physics is looking for the one basic law that will one day be able to explain everything. That law should reveal simplicity and beauty in the universe, not complexity and individuality. The variety and complexity that we do see in the universe are not based upon individuality. They are based upon the ability of everything to grow from the one common stem. This shows up clearly in biology, where millions of different species and behaviours have all grown from the one tree of evolution. Variety and complexity come from the extensive development of a single theme or common soul. It does not come from the development of a host of different competing themes.

Following the concept of individuality as a pathway of development will yield little strength or support. It can only plunge us further into the illusory world of the mindrule. However, individuality can sometimes give us minor and temporary relief from modern stresses. Individuality can encourage a person to develop themselves further by making them concentrate on what they really are, rather than trying to live up to or be constrained by the standards of others. It can help people stand up for themselves. It can help us accept that we are equal to others, and so let us throw off their shackles. But we should not replace other people's shackles with our own. Our further step into self-motivation will fail under individuality. It is a mistake to try and contain our nature within the individuality cage, because the real source of our suppression comes from within our own mindrules.

Individuality can transfer the control of our behaviour from others to our own self-motivation. However, individuality will not let us see the mindrules in ourselves, so it will not give us control or knowledge over everything major that affects us. Individuality can reject the constraints known by society and others, but in the process we will more completely assume the constraints of our own mindrules. Without wildness to guide them, mindrules can become so confused and individualised, that today, people strongly identify themselves as individuals. However, individuality lowers our standards, as it lets us accept that what we learn does not have to be of a standard that is also inspirational to others, because they are different. It lets us miss an important test for the rationality and wildness of our ideas. A test of a good idea is that it should find widespread acceptance, to the point of producing instinctive unison within the species.

The main source of suppression that individuals fight does not come from others. It lives within human mind instead. The real battle to be won is in our own minds. Relying on individuality to find equality and strength will not lead far. Illusions cannot last long. It would be better to see through the mindrules and into the wildness buried beneath. The reason we are different is that each of us is mistaken somehow. Our mistakes can vary, but the true nature of people does not. With wit, we should be able to recognise our mistakes more easily. Wit is a path that will lead us into far more strength and equality than individuality could ever hope to find.

3.7 Alienation

If we leave individuality on its own to develop fully, where will it lead? Individuality believed in strongly will turn into alienation. Alienation occurs when we take our mindrules very seriously. Such a mind lacks the wit to temper the excesses of mindrules, because it completely assumes them to the exclusion of all other guiding forces or comments.

Alienation is the separation of things into groups on the basis that they cannot be equally relatable or interactive. There is a difference that we cannot bridge, because there is no common ground. One group behaves alien to another. Alienation provides an excuse for each separate group to go its own way, and to treat the other group according to a different set of rules, and with a different level of courtesy. What impinges on or harms one alienated group has little impact or relevance to the other. This is the logical conclusion of individuality.

The lower relevance that alienation can assign to some other groups means that those groups can become mindrule targets. They become open to the various disrelatable methods that mindrules use to try to corner themselves into the world that makes them seem complete. There need be no common bond or pity extended to the alien group. The group may be treated in a very bad way, not because human nature needs to, but because mindrules see no reason not to. The reasoning that follows from such mindrule delusion is that it is best to get rid of all non-conforming alienated groups. They are not a part of our world. When they are gone, our world or society can find harmony once more. Some examples of groups that can become alienated, and then treated according to different codes of behaviour are cultures, races, animals, desires, and new ideas. Alienation can result in violence, dispassion and desensitisation.

If the process of alienation continues on its way unchallenged by wit, mindrules will willingly self-perpetuate the illusion even further, taking its captor with it, into increasingly alienated states. A person might become 'mentally ill,' obsessive, and isolated. Alienation will reduce the amount of contact that a person can have with society and the environment. It can make things seem strange, heady and intense, because natural energies become confined in the head and its individualised niche map. Through alienation, the energies will be unable to diffuse through natural connections into the environment or other people. In this state, it will seem as though things can be manipulated, without the need to extend any feeling or compassion to them.

In a wild and relatable universe there is no support for the development of alienation. Its manipulations can only fail in time. All things have a common basis, and can fit together into common ground. Therefore, any action taken against others in the belief that they are alienated will somehow find a way to come back to affect or haunt. Wildness will find its way through all things.

3.8 Rights

For its individuals, society has bestowed them rights. It has not always been easy to establish these rights. We must usually defend and fight for them. They can be hard work. Rights are not necessarily natural or proven, but they are rules that have been generally agreed upon by humans, to become a part of their world. Most of our rights are human made, rather than being established upon scientific or external grounds. Without a society to support them, many rights would dissipate. Fighting for rights is the natural consequence of a person who feels that they are an individual.

However, the process of trying to fulfil people by giving them rights will by itself fail in the end. True or wild rights should have the support of the universe and its structure. Compatibility will flow to a true and honest being. Rights should be simple and widely accepted and supported. They should be universal rather than individual, and able to flourish in the wildness.

Of course, we might feel something is right rather than having the hard facts to support such a stance. Currently, our science understands so little, that it is not yet a good source of morals for our behaviour. I expect that the struggle of biology known by our species today will fail to inspire any of you as source of 'natural' rights. Instead, we have to go by what feels right as well. But true rights carry their own strength, so we should not need to fight for them. They should be able to persist and reappear on their own account, if the universe supports them and keeps them alive.

The intent behind rights is of course admirable. The intent is to try and keep people equal amongst competing demands, and encourage people to develop themselves against the odds. If this method is the best that we have to meet those intentions, then we will continue to need those rights. But having a set of rights will not give us lasting or workable solutions to our problems. Pursuing this course will only produce more and more rights based on individuality. Eventually, there will be so many rights of which each must be aware, that we will be unable to say anything freely, and the demand for lawyers will sky-rocket. Pandering to mindrules will make rights become more complicated, numerous, and open to conflict and interpretation.

Of course, we need rights in today's society. Mindrules have such a strong hold over our species today, that their delusions make exploitation and aggression amongst us rife. Rights enshrined in laws can protect people under these conditions. Rights supported by a majority can help make others change their behaviour towards a more equitable system. Rights can act as a balance mechanism in the absence of more substantial and widespread understandings. We need them in the absence of a common soul.

3.9 Mindrule block

The niche map of most animals can connect to its niche freely and wildly through receptivity and attunement. However, if an animal moves into a wrong niche, then its niche map will be unprepared. The natural approach to life will often fail or cause pain. It will be blocked by a harsher reality, and our response will not fit in beautifully. While it would be better to adjust our mindrules to renew attunement to the changed niche, this approach is naturally forfeit because an animal is blind to its instincts. Mindrules do not let us think that they are at fault or that they lack attunement. They do not realise that they are confused and alienated. They are designed to allow us to live wildly under natural conditions. If they cannot do this, then they will conclude that something is impeding their use. They look outwardly for the cause of their delays and difficulties.

Mindrules learn to identify the directions in which they find the going most diffi-cult. Gradually, they learn to place warning signs on our niche map, so that we will avoid going that way again. These warnings become stronger and clearer, until eventually they become like blocks in the mind. As the illusory powers of mindrules perpetuate, those blocks to us become even greater realities. We become aware of the blocks in our world, blame them, and call them names such as bad. We learn to identify blocks as the rea-son for our lack of freedom. We do not identify that our own mindrules are at fault. We do not know of their existence. We blame instead the blocks that mindrules have impressed on to our niche map as the reasons for their failure. The blocks become the limits to our understanding. When we reach them we may as well give up. We cannot expect the harmony that we desire to pass through them.

The blocks that mindrules need to make their world right are often of standard type that become formalised within society. Societies' blocks have many names and guises, such as bad, evil, devil, criminal types, limited or unequal talents, opposites, aggres-sive or selfish human nature, various political parties or cultures, and so on. The need for block as excuse for our failure to be free and comfortable is a modern invention. The history of our art demonstrates the change. Stone-age humans were prolific artists, and yet they did not paint any monsters on their caves or rock walls. Instead, their art shows their links to the spirit of other animals and a 'mother earth.' They felt at home in the 'common soul' of the wildness, and knew no monsters. It was only when our niche began to change rapidly, that our art began to depict monsters. That is when the changing niches began to overwhelm our mindrules, forcing them to invent their blocks. That is when our receptivity waned, and the monsters entered our mind.

Mindrules under niche change want us to find blocks for them so that we will not accept information that they find conflicting. Blocks are an illusion that mindrules cre-ate to keep themselves safe from conscious mind. Blocks are what mindrules use to keep our human nature contained. While under mindrule restriction, we cannot help but feel isolated, individual even alienated.

Once mindrules establish their blocks in our world, we have two options for deal-ing with them. One approach is to accept the blocks as part of our life. If we cannot move the block, then we cannot deal with it, and therefore must accept some loss of freedom and equality. This can lead us into feelings of depression and frustration. Alter-natively, if we do not accept that the block is dominant, we can try to go around or through it. Those blocks can become the focus of our attention and energies. Against them we can put our rage, aggression, hate, fear, prejudice, and deceit.

3.10 Bad

Anyone can see that there is bad in the world. There is war, crime, animal suffering, selfishness, misery and racism to mention a few. Some people can be bad, as can some of our thoughts. Bad should be neither approached, nor considered favourably. It is deceitful and dangerous. It is the limit where good reason will fail, and harm will result if we give bad a chance. It blocks both progress and complete fulfilment. The appearance of bad can produce an emotional reaction in us, ranging from annoyance to revulsion and hate.

Because bads are so bad, and act to a different set of laws of their own, we should not accept even a little of their side. If a rule is broken, or a barrier lowered, what is to stop a host of further bad flooding in through the breach? If we give an inch, will a mile be taken?

However, what if bad is just another illusion invented for us by our mindrules? Mindrules could use bad as a powerful block to keep their own positions secure. Bad could be just an excuse to reject anything that disrupts the niche map. Mindrules could use bad to stop any conflicting information from getting inside our being to cause them change. Bad makes very convenient blocks for mindrules.

Bad exists to us because mindrules need them as powerful blocks to the spread of our understanding. The blocks form a perimeter within which understanding and behaviour are free to develop, but beyond which we should not investigate. Any behaviour or thought that tries to include the bad, or go beyond them, becomes bad in itself. The bad usually stirs our emotions, preventing our thoughts from moving towards or through them. We do this by placing a mindrule before the bad that runs directly to the emotional centres that develop in the brain. The closer to a bad our thoughts or experience strays, the stronger the emotion against that train of thought becomes. Our emotions guard against the bad, making a calm assessment of their positions difficult. Emotions force us to take the bad seriously.

Mindrules are able to place bads about their entrenched position, and use them as a barrier within which they can become self-contained. Then they can fulfil their evolved function of producing a completed niche map within their rightful and just niche world. Anything within the barrier will be a part of our niche, and anything outside the barrier will be beyond our niche, which we may ignore or treat differently. A flow of ideas and feelings through the barrier is not permitted, thus preventing disruption of the mindrules.

Mindrules are able to make the bad seem real for us because from their instinctive position they can make us assume many things to the point of illusion. The feeling of individuality and alienation that mindrules produce make it very easy for us to believe in the bad. If our mindrules can make us believe in bad, then we will willingly send forth our emotions to guard and block against the bad. The frustration that mindrules make us feel through their inadequacy can be strong. Outlets for our energies fail, that according to confused mindrules, should have been successful. Reality does not go according to the niche map. Mindrules suggest to us that the reason for our failure is that a bad stood in our way, or it was bad to try and go that way in the first place.

The tactic that mindrules use of creating bad is highly successful for them. If people begin to question their own position, the discovery of a bad can end all further exploration. Whenever mindrules become threatened directly by stress or doubt, they will respond by directing more of our emotion towards their bad. Someone finding things particularly hard going will often be quick to identify bad, and concentrate much anger on it. The more emotion that mindrules can make us send, the more bad the bad can seem, and the more entrenched the mindrule position becomes. For example, when two warring factions are considering peace, someone might commit an atrocity to try and get emotion to rise and reinforce to each side the badness of the other. Mindrules may warn us of bad to such excess that we will look for even more bad. We might look for scapegoats.

Another way mindrules promote their illusion of bad is to make bad seem important and convincing to us. The more 'real' the bad, the more willingly we will believe them. News can be informative, but it can also be used to graphic excess with the effect of impressing us with bad. Today's society has an underlying need for this kind of news. Such bad can make us feel justified about holding the mindrule line and not changing our view of life through greater understanding. Similarly, films and documentaries can depict their bad graphically and unmercifully, and claim realism. They become highly sought by mindrules. The relative frequency of the seemingly bad event might be rare, but the cameras will travel or search wide to find them and give them great emphasis in our world. Most people go through life without seeing another person killed. But the average television viewer will see tens of thousands die on screen. What is the real attraction?

The reasoning mindrules like to give to the study or depiction of bad is that unless we take that bad seriously we will fail to resolve our life's problems. If we accept the bad realities of life, then we can take the next step and find ways to work around them or with them. Our species is so accustomed to considering bad real, that we think it comes from the one powerful source, rather than independently from many minds. The English language does not consider bad to be capable of the plural (bads). Mistake is accepted as being able to come from many different minds, so the word mistakes is quite acceptable. But bad comes from outside our world, as a dominant evil force.

What we consider bad depends largely upon the mindrule set of the day. We mostly learn what is bad through experience, or from parents and peers. What is bad can go in and out of fashion. This is a hint that bad is not real, but a function of the established temporary niche thoughts of the time. Sex before marriage, homosexuality, Russians,

witches with magical powers, jungles, thinking there is no god, and marrying someone from another race, are all examples of outdated bad. In the past, people thought that
there would be social upheaval if such bad were permitted. However, history and
greater maturity of understanding have shown that life goes on, even when we ignore
the bad. Change often makes society go beyond what was accepted as bad, to find the
broader understanding beneath.

While bad is illusion, wrong, error and mistake are very real. However, the two per-
spectives to the same problem will offer very different methods and hopes for reme-
diation. We can solve problems if we can find the mistakes. However, we will not get
far if we find the problem is due to bad. We cannot change bad because it is permanent
and intentional, whereas mistakes are for a reason so we have the potential to find their
solution. Often, we need to view bad from 'a distance,' to see that it was really just mistake. We should remember that if mindrules can make our wrongs seem bad instead of
mistake, then the pressure comes off them to change. We will be unable to convert our
mindrules into their original receptivity. The alternative of admitting to a mistake
might allow us to develop wit, making our mindrules pliable once more.

We do not have to excuse all wrongs as mistakes, and allow them to occur again.
Viewing child molesters and rapists as bad inhibits solution of the problem, which is
itself wrong. Of course, such people are mistaken, and harsh punishment to control the
behaviour still needed. However, viewing them as bad does not reduce the factors that
generate such behaviour. Viewing their wrong as mistake should direct our attention
towards mental development within those people and society as well. This might turn
our attention towards asking questions about our way of life that will permanently heal
the breach that is producing such behaviour.

The use of bad as a means of justifying and maintaining our own comfortable position produces two longer term problems of their own. The block of bad will limit the
quality of the total understanding remaining within those areas of the niche that we see
as good. The parts that we do like and accept become the poorer, because of their loss
of interaction with the things that exist beyond the bad. We will fail to reach the highest level of richness available in life. The loss of understanding in any area will eventually spread to become a loss in other areas, including those we cherish. The more bad
that surrounds a niche, the less fulfilling and workable will become the good things that
are contained within that niche. A person might get bored, even though they are surrounded with life.

Another problem with using bad to maintain a comfortable niche position is that
some day those blocks could be broken or deceived. It requires great vigilance to uphold
the bad barrier. The enclosed good cannot stay comfortable and calm. The discipline
needed to keep things good might be excessive. Some might develop a cleaning fetish
that makes life unbearable and sterile. Bad will place ever-present pressure on the good.
People must continually raise their emotions to guard against the bad. But it is not nat-

ural to be in such a high state of anticipation. Our brains are naturally inquisitive and want to seek out all pathways to discover their true and wild interconnections. There will be lapses of will, when strange unexplored desires overpower our resolve. Our human nature naturally wants to extend its reign of good interaction. With such pure intention, human nature is easy to trick, overpower or coerce.

During sleep, the emotional energy sent to guard against bad subsides. Thought can then stray into areas beyond the bad. However, the tracks found beyond the bad are always poorly developed, because we have not been allowed to explore them properly. Thought that finds itself past the block of bad can become lost in a quagmire of poorly connected neural pathways. Some of those pathways can lead to even more bizarrely confused images. A dream can turn into a nightmare.

Bad can be useful as an indication of mindrule confusion. When we attempt greater understanding, we should see that the bad was not a bad after all, but a mistake that we did not fathom. It is ironic that while our most fundamental mistakes would be easy to fix by releasing our mindrules from their fortress of bad, we do not take the first step because people dislike bad so much. We can usually only penetrate this circle of self-defence through insight and revelation. Good is much better served by overcoming the emotions that block the bad, than by defeating the bad. We cannot deny or ignore the circumstances that produce what we perceive to be bad. We cannot leave them out of our understanding. The things that are bad must be included into the full picture of our world one day and somehow. They are a part of our world. We should allow under-standing to spread to find its true connections. This process will strengthen and brace the good, and provide it with alternative outlets that are also good. How understand-ing straightens out the bad can be surprising and delightful.

3.11 Restriction

Mindrules that fail to find complete attunement in their niche search for blocks as excuse. However, the existence of those blocks in our mind will strongly affect the way we feel. We now have to live within our mindrule's defensive perimeter of blocks. We must contain our once free and wild nature. We allow our second nature to impose its restrictions on our first nature. Our true desires must learn to work within the blocks that mindrules impose. They must learn the bars of their cage. When mindrules look for blocks to consider and blame, then at the same time they program us to robotically give up our more natural and receptive efforts to live freely in all directions. Recep-tivity cannot flow beyond the blocks, so it must turn back and become restricted. Restriction inhibits our realisation and awareness of what is possible.

If we accept block, we will feel self-imposed restriction at an instinctive or 'natu-ral' level. At this level, the feeling will be like a knawing sense of emptiness or inadequacy that will be hard to control and fathom. We will not know why it is there, because mindrules work at a level that is beneath our conscious knowledge. Restriction will make us feel we have missed out, even when we seem to 'have it all'. Because the mindrule combination we each have varies, each person becomes stamped with their own particular style of restriction. However, the same underlying feeling of restriction and emptiness will be the same for all in our species.

The feeling of restriction can become emotionally unsettling. However, mindrules thrive on our acceptance of failure, as they can turn our unsettled energies towards their own defences. Our minds will be drawn to their blocks, until we believe them. Some of the blocks that we invent for mindrule's sake are obvious illusions, yet we keep them because they help us complete the niche map. They give our emotions some outlet to fight or concentrate, in the absence of the more fulfilling and free alternatives. We often realise that the villains portrayed in theatre or on our murder and mayhem films are not real. But if they can fill the role of villain for us, they become an object of blame through which we can release our pent up energies. We might take the villains lightly, in which case they can be entertaining, or we might take the villains seriously. Mindrules use this simple procedure on us far more than we realise.

Anything that seems able to block or restrict us is a part of the mindrule illusion, rather than a part of the wildness. This idea might seem unimaginable and overdone, but humankind has had a long time now in which to self-perpetuate its illusions. Blocks and restrictions are much less real than we know. Their only real source is within our own minds. It is time to step out of the circle of block and see what lies beyond.

Usually, the blocks seem so real and natural that we do not realise that they exist simply because our mindrules want them for protection. We cannot consciously assess or remove our mindrules directly. They are mostly hidden in the subconscious. However, we can detect confused mindrules if we realise that for them to survive they must throw up their circle of block, to shield against the wild and probing forces of the wider universe. Mindrules live in the centre of their defences, and it is their defences that we can learn to detect. They have a characteristic nature about them. They have the nature of alienation and restriction. These are not the natural feelings of receptivity, which must be open and direct instead. To become receptive we will have to win the battle against our own feelings of alienation and restriction. Only then will we find a position from where we could see the wildness.

3.12 Confidence

Confidence is a major determinant of how we are going to behave. A confident person will often make something work, whereas the same person lacking confidence might fail. If we feel confident, we are more likely to try something new and explore.

Confidence can also make us more accomplished, appealing to others, and happy. It will determine how fluently we can use a particular skill. But what determines the degree of confidence that each of us has?

Confidence is something that can be won or lost. It is learnt and influenced by past experience. An animal living in its correct niche would on most occasions be able to interact properly. It would be able to fill its natural desires successfully. Anything it tried to do to fill its needs would usually work. Because it has a well-founded niche it would feel secure. It would gain an expectation for success, and be naturally confident. It would probably not need to know that it was confident, or need to try and be confident, because without a history of impressive failures to affect the animal, it would automatically become self-assured. Confidence is a natural feeling for a species living in the wilderness. From what I have seen, all wild animals are confident in their niche, though timid out of it. In their niche they feel comfortable and at home.

However, when an animal is not living in its proper niche, its interactions will not happen so easily. Experiencing fundamental difficulties has a strong effect on our confidence and instinctive fluency. Our species does not live in stable well-founded niches, so we cannot avoid making important life mistakes. The results will often be unexpected and painful. In the face of continued failure, confidence will fail to develop properly. Insecurity will grow, because a person would be unsure of what was going to happen next, or feel unable to prevent mistaken or painful results. The more disastrous and bad the mistakes, the worse the insecurity and the lower our confidence will become.

We could measure our average level of confidence, and determine whether on balance it gives us a positive or negative approach to life. How do we perform when thrown in the deep end, or when meeting something new? Is life exciting, or is it a series of obstacles? How many failures can we take before our positive attitude changes into the negative? How much resilience or reserve do we have, so we can bounce back from failure? Are we versatile and adaptive? These are all measures of confidence.

Today, each person varies in the areas in which they are confident. A person might be confident in their social skills, or in their ability to repair things around the house, or in their ability to teach. Some people can appear confident on the surface, but not be so self-assured beneath. Few people are confident about everything that they do. However, because our species is not in tune with any well-founded niche, we all must have less than the natural level of confidence normally due to a wild animal. We can never be fully confident of our instincts while we construct those instincts out of confused mindrules. Confused mindrules can never be completely at ease in their niche. They will never feel the natural success that a wild species can assume. A lack of confidence is the natural consequence of an artificial life that avoids facing up to the wildness.

Most people would like to have more confidence, but it is very difficult to step out of the rut of what we learn, without breaking through the mindrule barrier. The degree of confidence a person has will help determine to what degree they can live beyond the rules of their niche map. Any gain in confidence can help to give us the spirit to take the artificial world of mindrules less seriously. If confidence is low, then we will cling to the safety of the niche map and be unable to leave its concepts. We might get into a rut, wallow in mindrule grooves, and fail to see the world as it is beyond their horizons. We might feel alienated. If confidence is high, we are more likely to dare to rise above the rules and restrictions and peer beyond.

The best way for our species to regain its natural wild confidence is to reduce the seriousness that we give to our confused mindrules. When we can take our blocks less seriously, new possibilities appear. Wit harms confused mindrules, but has no damaging effect upon receptive mindrules. We can regain confidence by realising that major mistakes are normal, given our present stage of development. We should take mistakes less seriously, and treat them with humour and affection wherever possible. They are not the true limits of our abilities. They are only the limits of our current set of mindrules.

3.13 Play

Animals use play to introduce confidence and fluency into the instincts that they learn. Play allows us to practice and reinforce into our mindrules the skills that seem necessary for life, without the danger of failure (or this is how play should be). It lets us explore and create as much as we like. It is not bad to make mistakes in play, because in play we are more willing to learn from those mistakes and make them part of the fun. The game is not serious, so the mindrules in the arena of play can remain pliable and closer to their original state of receptivity. We can learn how to turn from one approach in the game to another. This improves our resilience, as we learn the ability to explore alternatives. The confidence and feeling of success learnt in one area of play could spread further afield to life in general.

Many animals use play to some degree. It is especially important to those animals that must learn their instincts. Insects do not seem to play, perhaps because they inherit almost all of their instincts. Being able to play means that mindrules are still able to change and improve. Play reflects the needs that animals have to service and tighten their niche maps. A bear or elephant might push at a tree. Cubs might play with each other or their surroundings. Play is particularly important in young animals, as they need to add relatively large numbers of mindrules to their instinctive repertoire. Under the arena of game, animals can explore a wider area on the niche map in safety, knowing that at the end everything will return back to normal. It is a way of testing and honing skills within the safe environment of a game. Play will help to create a successful animal that can apply its skills more widely and confidently when needed.

Humans are unusual in that they can play longer into their life span than most other species. We can play well into adulthood, although by then the play is usually more structured and confined as sport, hobby or game. The ability to play is an indication that in some areas at least, our mindrules are still pliable and willing to learn. When we cannot play or take a joke, then our mindrules are in danger of seizing up and becoming set in their ways. Failure to play is a sign that the mind has set and is no longer willing to expand and change. Play can help us remember and stay in touch with what we really enjoy. It can encourage us to transfer the spirit and fluency of play into our daily lives.

3.14 Comfort level

All animals try to become sufficiently attuned in their niche to be comfortable. It is the natural condition to seek. If an animal is not intrinsically suited or evolved to be comfortable within a niche, they might attempt acclimatisation. Humans can also acclimatise to certain conditions. Athletes might train on mountains so that they can acclimatise to lower oxygen levels and improve stamina. Similarly, people who have jobs requiring lifting and carrying will develop stronger muscles. The mindrules of the cortex can also acclimatise to their own specific niche conditions. It can take a long time to acclimatise, and it can take just as long to lose the acclimatisation when conditions change or return to normal.

While some of our attributes such as muscle tone, oxygen holding capacity of our blood, and mindrules can acclimatise, there are real limits on how quickly acclimatisation can occur. We might train until it hurts, in an effort to speed up the process. However, people mostly can only acclimatise to new conditions within certain tolerable limits. For mindrules, the rate at which we can acclimatise to new niche conditions is limited within the bounds of what I call the comfort level. Mindrules are designed to protect the life and well being of an animal, so they must move very surely. They can only change their style to a certain degree, as their prime concern is to find ways to maintain the comfort of their animal.

In the past, the changing of niches was a gradual process. There was never any real need for animals to evolve a mechanism where they would enjoy large and sudden changes to their niche format and outlook on life. Animals naturally prefer to remain comfortable within their niches. Evolution was always able to make the changes needed by the ecosystem happen at a rate that was imperceptible to the animal. Changing contexts and ecosystems do not disturb the comfort level and receptive state of most animals in nature.

However, our rate of niche change is now rapid and extensive. This places a need on us for mindrule change that we have never experienced before. While mindrules can change, they do so at a slow pace. To the remainder of change with which we cannot keep pace, our mindrules look for excuses to avoid the change. Mindrules can only change at a rate that keeps us within the vicinity of the comfort level. Expecting us to move greatly beyond this comfort level is unreasonable, and not possible without guidance or some real and comfortable alternative. Therefore, a level of change comfortable to one person may be unreasonable to another. Trying to go too far beyond our comfort levels can be stressful.

Each of us has our own peculiar mindrule combinations and formats. Each niche map that we learn will have its own attached level of confidence and wit. These determine how daring we can be in our change. It seems to me that we all try the same. What varies is how much success each peculiar niche map will allow us to have for the same effort. What varies is the starting point from which each of us must try.

Animals and people will mostly do what is comfortable for them. Everything about us will turn out to be a natural process in the end. Even the process that our species must go through to find receptivity with our final wild niche is natural, and does not require any great departure from the direction of change that we are currently taking. The comfort level in each animal maintains a balance between the changes we need to become right in our understanding of the wildness, and what we feel we can cope with now. These are natural constraints for any animal. Therefore, we should try to be patient with our rate of change.

3.15 Stress

Stress occurs when we find it difficult to maintain our comfortable position. Stress indicates that something is trying to pull us from where we are now, towards some new position with which our instincts are not fluently designed to cope. Stress often occurs when we believe that we must make a choice, and the way to interact is not clear. We have no instinctive feeling to guide. The harder the choice, the more distant we are from the comfort of the instincts of our secure niche, and the greater the stress. Stress is like trying to stretch ourselves to the limit to bridge the widening gap between what is comfortable and what we must do to accomplish.

Stress is symptomatic of an animal that is not living in its right niche. It is a condition found most severely in humans. Stress is common in our species, and some of its symptoms include increased allergic sensitivity, ulcers, headaches and constipation.

A wild animal in a cage can also suffer stress, because it is not in its right niche. In a cage, they have limited natural outlet for their energies. Contained energies overheat and damage the niche map. Those energies can even become self-destructive, searching or desperate. Caged animals often develop strange behaviours from stress. They might pull out their own hair or feathers. Stress is an agitated state, where our desiring energies are unsure where to go for relief.

While rapid niche change causes a certain background level of stress, people can further exacerbate the problem themselves. A heavy workload can place us under added stress, because we cannot achieve our goals simply. A politician or boss often must make many difficult decisions, so fall under more stress. We often consider such stresses to be a natural part of life. However, stress in nature is much rarer.

Stress has become a normal part of modern life. Our species has even reasoned that a certain amount of stress is good. It is said to increase motivation and activity. However, this might only increase our level of participation within the circus. All events are natural, even the modern ones. It is still possible today to rearrange our mindrules into a position where modern life is not stressful. All that we need is a better understanding, which can see the true forces at work on our modern species.

What is stressful to one person can be non-stressful even invigorating to another. The difference is simply due to the different niche maps that each of us has, and the ease with which each niche map allows us to be comfortable. The best solution to stress, and indeed to all of our mindrule problems, is to try and develop wit. We should take the stressful situations less seriously, and look for alternatives. Change will bring a new future, which can be hard to read while under stress.

3.16 Insecurity

Insecurity is an unpleasant feeling that arises when it is difficult for us to cope with life. It means that our basic approach to life is not comfortable. Insecurity develops when we make mistakes and find surprises, but cannot reason them out in a comfortable way. This makes us feel that we are not a natural part of the system. Excessive trauma, punishment or criticism will help instil this belief and increase our insecurity.

Animals can tolerate a certain proportion of mistake, before the mistakes disrupt their sense of well being. However, if mistakes are excessive and cannot be reasoned away, or if our reserve of self-assurance is poorly developed, then we will be more vulnerable to insecurity. The lines of contact between the niche and us will be insecure. The self-identity will be unable to flow untroubled along secure lines to merge with the environment to produce a common soul.

Insecurity is a natural consequence of trying to use confused mindrules as the basis of our understanding and behaviour. The individuality and restriction that mindrules make us feel will make us defensive, but will also hide the real reasons for our mistakes. Failure for reasons that we cannot see or change will make us insecure. We need to improve the quality of understanding within our instincts, if we want to feel less personally damaged by our mistakes. With a good understanding, mistakes become less worry. We need a certain level of confidence before we can accept change to our niche map. There comes a point in stressful situations where our confidence and wit are not strong enough to rebuild our niche map, because the chance of failure is too painful. This is when we reach an unhealthy level of insecurity, and begin to doubt the real ability of our own true nature. It can become difficult to expand the niche map after that point of insecurity, because the map becomes preoccupied with defending what little comfort in life it has already managed to acquire. It cannot afford the luxury of trying to fine tune or change the niche map. A niche map should be functional and live, but if it becomes insecure, it can become static, and may fail to mature.

3.17 Mental illness

A major difference between humans and wild animals is that many humans suffer from mental illness. For example, Andrews (1995) reported that a staggering five percent of the human population in Australia suffers from some kind of chronic mental illness, and twenty-five percent suffer these and other forms of mental illness and phobias. Mental illness is comparatively rare in hunter-gather tribes. It is also very rare in wild animals. Mental illness is essentially a modern symptom that has yet to be properly explained. Why should humans suffer so much mental illness? Is it really all inherited? Why would evolution produce such a phenomenon in such high proportion, when it has had so long to fine tune its species?

Part of the explanation for this modern condition might lay in our widespread use of chemicals. Some of the chemicals that permeate our world are unusual, and in high doses can have an important impact on our health. Yet another cause of our mental illness might be the stress and pace of modern living. However, I think that the largest single source of mental illness in our society arises from our reliance on confused mindrules. Our species has been unaware of mindrules and what they can do to our behaviour.

So many of the symptoms found in mental illnesses are just one step further into the mindrule's realm of confusion, alienation and restriction. How many mental illnesses have as their ingredients' confusion, alienation, insecurity, aggression, emotional swings, depression, voices, assumption, and single-mindedness? What we call mental illness is often just confusion taken to exaggeration.

A percentage of mental illness is of course inherited. Also, mindrules are very strong and their illusions very real, so we can assign no blame for being so trapped by ones own mindrules. I think that what mainly determines if one mindrule pattern of confusion is normal, while another is mentally ill, is an arbitrary line drawn up through consensus by society. What is the correct term for the mental state of a species that commits genocide to the tune of 10-30 species each day? Normal?

Most people temper the excesses of their mindrules by gaining feedback from other people, and from their day to day interactions. Normally, people would learn from experience to take the demands of their mindrules less seriously, in favour of advice and discussion with others about what is right. Wild animals do the same, but their source of information is the wildness. A functional level of wit, maturity, discipline and courtesy prevents most of us from taking our mindrules too seriously, at least beyond the level socially accepted as sane. Our wit and the tempering effects of social interaction control our own degree of confusion. People should maintain a certain level of responsiveness, to avoid settling further into the depths of mindrule nature. Social interaction and wit both help to keep the excesses of our confused instincts to a level that society finds comfortable.

However, what if a person begins to take their mindrules more seriously than social interaction would normally accept? This can easily happen when a person feels ostracised and unable to share their feelings and ideas. Individual mindrule illusions can then grow in stature. Those illusions can become real to the mind, and fears more difficult to overcome. Blocks will grow in size and breadth, and the mindrule cage will come down on the mind even more strongly. Much mental energy that would normally find outlet through social interaction or wildness must now rush to and throe while trapped in the brain. The confused tracks on the niche map must carry more energy in search of outlet, so those mindrules can become further entrenched. Those confused tracks will become stronger and louder in the mind until we begin to hear them like voices. The feeling of alienation grows.

If we do not temper mindrules through social interaction or the wildness, the self-perpetuation of mindrules will become even more bizarre and captivating. Many mental illnesses must begin when people fail to learn the confidence and security that we need to wrest control for our behaviour away from mindrule domination. Our true nature and spirit should regain control over our mindrules, and become more receptive.

Perhaps the best course open to cure some of our species' mental illnesses will arise when society realises the symptoms of confused mindrules. I am not qualified to go much further on this topic. However, for those mental illnesses that can be diagnosed in this way, the best way to repair them, again, will be through wit. If mindrules are less serious about themselves, then the consequences of their confused nature becomes less dramatic. Laughter generally is the best medicine.

4. Human nature

What have been described so far are the passive or subconscious consequences of the cortex instinct producing mindrules through selective stabilisation during rapid niche change. We grow our mindrules without having to think about them. That section described how our second nature is produced and imprinted into our subconscious to become the blueprint for our first nature. If we learn that blueprint during rapid niche change, the blueprint itself will try to create its own artificial world where it is safe from change. We create a monster, and unfortunately, the result for our species is problem and insecurity. But if we could return our mindrules to a more pliable and receptive state, we could learn once more how to see the wildness. Then we would experience the harmony and achievements due for our species. But to make this change, our species will first have to take control of its mindrules. We will have to find motivation stronger than mindrules. This brings us to desire.

4.1 Desire

The body is composed of many different cells that are organised into various tissues and organs. Each cell type evolved to perform a specific function that is essential to the survival of the organism. Those cells, tissues and organs send information, energy and hormones to describe their condition and progress. Their messages convey information about what they need if they are to reach optimal performance. There are different messages being sent from all parts of the body. The intensity of each message varies over time. Some cells become hungry, while others become satiated when their needs are filled.

The activity required to fill the needs of the various tissues can be involuntary and automatic, or voluntary and behaviour dependent. Some activities such as the heartbeat are automatic. We do not need to think about them to make them happen. The body can solve some of its needs through reflexive response. We do not have to think about adjusting the eye's iris to differing light intensities, withdrawing the hand instantly from a fire, or churning the stomach to mix our food.

Those messages that ask us for significant behavioural response are sent to the cortex of the brain for consideration. We could call these messages desires. They have a wish for the cortex to give them its attention when it is ready. They are not commands that can force the brain to act and give an immediate reflex action to fill their need. They are messages that we must turn our attention towards to fill. Their outcome or timing must wait upon our thoughts.

Some examples of the tissues and organs that are involved in producing desires are: The stomach helps produce hunger. The hypothalamus is involved in detecting a need for water, and it sends information to the cortex as thirst. If we become short of air, the lungs and brain will send the cortex a desire to breathe. The skin desires touch. The bowels and bladder desire excretion when full. The taste buds desire sweet or tasty food. The inner ear desires balance of the head when walking. Muscles desire rest or sleep when exhausted. The gonads produce hormones that develop our desire for sex.

Many different desires enter the cortex to try and have their needs met. However, the action that the brain tells the body to take must come from a consideration of all of these messages. The brain will try to fill those desires that are in most urgent need first. It may also try to fill several desires with the same action. However ultimately, there is still one more desire that must take charge of all other desires to give an animal consistency in its life. This desire can dominate all other desires, and is produced by the brain itself. It is a desire that occurs in all vertebrates, and perhaps some invertebrates. The brain is the most important organ in the body, and like any other organ, it produces a desire of its own.

I call our most dominant desire the interaction desire. It makes an animal want to interact actively and properly with its niche. It encourages an animal to live efficiently. It makes an animal want to develop an effective niche map of understanding. An animal could not have two different desires of equal importance. Otherwise, those desires might negate each other and achieve nothing. They could cause hesitation at a crucial stage in life. The interaction desire can control all other desires and make them fit in with its plans. For example, we can suppress the desire for food, and control when we eat. Some might even go on a hunger strike to the point of starvation, to make their point. The desire to excrete can be suppressed, for a while at least, by a desire to interact socially. The desire to interact in the right way can also dominate our desire for sex. Some priests can suppress their sexual desire all their life.

Conscious consideration and thought occur in the cortex. The cortex is the largest part of the brain in humans, and is where our understanding develops. But how does the body judge and influence the performance of its cortex? Most of the actions that the cortex decides to take are relayed to the rest of the brain and body through an adjacent part of the brain called the hypothalamus. It is the hypothalamus that determines how well the cortex is performing. As a general principle, it is best to leave the judgement of one organ in the body to another. The way the hypothalamus measures the performance of the cortex is through the interaction desire.

The hypothalamus is known to contain pleasure centres, which are interlinked into one unit (Routtenberg, 1980). I propose that it is the pleasure centre in the hypothalamus that produces the interaction desire. The desire from these centres can override all other desires. Routtenberg described how an electrode placed in the pleasure centre of a rat causes the rat to press a treadle to stimulate itself repeatedly. The rat will even prefer to do this and reject food, to the point of starvation. The pleasure centre gives the brain the basis for its interaction desire. It gives the brain control over the body, and what the cerebral cortex thinks. It gives the brain a means of assessing the quality of information coming from the cerebral cortex. Better arrangements give us greater pleasure.

In the natural environment there is no electrode to fool the interaction desire. It is located to see that all of the tracks in the cortex are being used to peak efficiency and in best combination. It seeks best pattern of niche understanding. The pleasure centre is linked to the cortex, and it feels pleasure when the neural pathways in the cortex are being stimulated. If they are stimulated then they have been used, so they must be relevant to the niche somehow. The more neural pathways that can be stimulated, the more likely the animal is in a position where it can live comfortably, and the more pleasure the interaction desire will feel. If the neural pathways in the cortex are not being stimulated, then the animal is probably not in its right niche.

The quantity of stimulation felt at a party or carnival will usually be greater than when sitting at home alone. The greater interaction experienced is a simple means of increasing pleasure and filling the interaction desire. However, there is more to the interaction desire than this. What is especially important to the desire is to have many tracks stimulated at once, from the same burst of energy. This gives us a measure of the brain's efficiency. It measures how well organised the neural pathways through the cortex are at coping with an interaction. If an animal finds a tree, then the sight of that tree will stimulate a few neural pathways to form a picture of it in the mind. However, if another animal knows that type of tree always bears fruit, then the sight of the tree will stimulate a few neural pathways to form a picture in the mind, but it will also stimulate some associated pathways that tell the animal to look up and seek food. The same vision stimulates more pathways in the second than first animal. The second animal will more likely be in its right niche. It will feel more comfort and pleasure from the interaction.

In humans, the interaction desire is very strong. We can interact with so many objects in our niche, and to such minute detail, that the interaction desire has much to control. Our brain is capable of understanding, and the interaction desire makes us want to organise our neural pathways into a pattern that has the best understanding. With understanding, all of the pathways in an area connect through a common stem. Understanding connects more branches together, along which the same stimulation can spread and travel, than if those branches were disjointed. Understanding makes it easier to send the same stimulation through a wider area. A good understanding will also be fast on the uptake, and improve our awareness and responsiveness. The better the connections, the easier it is to fill the interaction desire.

The more pathways that can be stimulated in unison from the same burst of energy, the happier we are. This is why we enjoy being right, humour, excitement, insight, heightened consciousness and awareness. It also explains why our species has such an appreciation for music. All of these can drive our input of energy through the cortex further.

This theory suggests that there is a way for the hypothalamus to measure the number of pathways being stimulated in the cortex at a given moment. The energy that we send the cortex and mind for consideration must enter and leave the cortex to carry its message. The start and finish of this loop are in the hypothalamus. The hypothalamus can therefore compare and measure what goes into the cortex with what comes out. If the hypothalamus finds that a burst of energy entering the cortex comes back from a wider area within the cortex, then the pleasure centre will feel good. If the energy comes back as a narrow tight stream, then we will not feel good. We might feel rejected. Routtenberg (1980) found that the pleasure reward system branches out to all major regions of the brain. It must also have its sensing network planted throughout the cerebral cortex. The wider the area in the cortex that a single interaction can stimulate, the more stimulating will be the feedback that the pleasure centre receives. This is why I call the desire an interaction desire. The more pathways that we can stimulate at once, and in the widest area of the cortex, then the better we must know the interaction, and the happier we are.

There are two halves in the interaction desire assessment loop. When energy first enters the cortex to find its way through the network, it does so as interaction desire. It wants to find the simplest and most wide reaching or beautifully connected pathways possible. After the desire has run its course, it comes back on the return part of the loop as feeling. The feedback that the pleasure centre receives is what we call our feelings. It is what we sense about the quality of the interaction that we had. The interaction desire launches into the cortex with highest expectation and desire, but it can come back feeling many things such as pleasure, fulfilment, sadness, hurt and so on. This feeling will influence the expectation contained in our next burst of desire.

The interaction desire makes animals want to use and tie together efficiently whatever pathways they learn in the cortex. For some animals, it will make them want to growl, hunt, hide or swim. In humans, the interaction desire has such an extensive network of pathways to work with, that its priority is to make us want to arrange our cortical network into its best understanding. The interaction desire will try to influence developments into a pleasurable arrangement. It wants us to organise our neural pathways efficiently, so that they let us interact well. Through understanding, or good and simple branching framework, many parts of the cortex can be stimulated at once. This is what our pleasure centre desires most. The interaction desire makes us want to seek the truth, because the truth will find broadest acceptance in the niche. The truth will widen the area that we can stimulate on our niche map. The interaction desire seeks a high standard, if only we could realise its potential. It makes us want to do the right thing.

While the thoughts and opinions found in our species varies widely, we all share the same interaction desire. It best defines the true motive behind each person. It describes our true nature. I think that everyone tries to do the right thing. What can make the universality of this desire difficult to see is that what we determine to be the right thing varies according to opinion and mindrule differences. Such differences arise only because we have lost touch with our true nature during niche change, and can no longer see its wild connections. There are many permutations and combinations of neural networks possible in the human brain, especially when learnt from so many different niches. For many, doing the right thing means doing something that is socially useful. For others, it can mean doing something socially disruptive, to try and shake up a smug and phoney society.

The interaction desire describes the essence of our species. Opinions do not describe our species well. They describe mindrules, and under confusion mindrules can find all manner of opinion. It is usual for a species to have something that unifies all of its specimens, and what unites us best is the interaction desire. It best defines the true motive behind each person. Everyone basically tries to do what they think is right. The differences arise only because mindrules confuse what each of us thinks of as being right.

The integrity of our desire to do the right thing has taken a battering in modern times. The simplicity of the interaction desire can be suppressed and confused. Society gives few leads on how to succeed and interact beautifully in today's world. Our attempts are often scoffed, dampened or hurt. Mindrules give us blocks, bad and alienation to deal with. Under these influences, the completeness of the interaction desire must fail. It cannot extend itself into the blocked areas and still feel right. We must modify its natural expectation. Our true desire must fragment. We learn to bury some of our desire's expectation in the subconscious, where we give it up to the mindrules.

There are many blocks in the cortex that stop the natural level of completeness and feelings of pleasure that we could obtain from each of our interactions. Mindrules give us complexity and individuality to work with. The interaction desire cannot penetrate through all of this. It does not know how to work in our phoney society. We must modify its natural expectation for receptivity. We give up, and mindrules modify the expectation of our interaction desire subconsciously. They do it for us without our realising. The interaction desire leaves the reality and practicality of how to meet its needs to the cortex, as this is the organ that should best know the workings of the niche. Our true desire must fragment as we learn to bury desire's expectation in the subconscious where it can be out of mind. But our mindrules have failed. Life can be miserable and full of wrong. Our mindrules keep the feelings of wildness away from our consciousness, so that we will not be bothered with its expectations. This is why the interaction desire is purest and strongest in children, at least until they learn from adults how to suppress their desires. They don't understand why everyone can't be 'good'.

It can be difficult to revive the interaction desire back to its purest form and highest level of natural expectation. Many of our desires fail when they try to find fulfilment within today's level of understanding. Something must be wrong. Rather than our feeble understanding being wrong, we are told that our desires are weak, childish, and dirty. What a perfect weapon to use against them. Even the highest ideals that humans strive for are not credited to our simple animal beginnings and the evolution of the interaction desire. Humans instead often think that they invented goodness themselves, by breaking away from the dirty and lowly animal mind. No wonder the interaction desire fails and becomes frustrated. We need to determine true wants, and get back to the basics of the desire itself.

During rapid niche change the interaction desire in our species is forced to divert and fragment from its original course. Where does it go? Our fragmented and buried interaction desire eventually returns to us as emotion, false desire, mood, attitude and displacement activity. Under these states, our minds are less demanding of truth. We can settle for less. However, we will not be able to contain our wild desires forever. Our interaction desire will continue to push us towards finding our correct niche interaction. The universe has great strength, beauty, and harmony, and it is no coincidence that these are the same things that we truly desire.

4.2 Pleasure

When we meet the needs of our desires, we feel pleasure. The return half of the energy loop that passes through the cortex shows the hypothalamus that the desire was fulfilled. Pleasure is our simplest measure of success. But mindrules can of course confuse our awareness of this subject as well.

There are many things that can give us pleasure. Some desires are easy to meet, while for others we have to work harder. There are many organs and tissues that can generate their own desire and give us pleasure. There is sneezing, scratching, excretion, releasing wind from either end, getting giddy, eating, drinking, sleeping, sucking, sex, and our use of the senses such as vision, hearing, touch and smell. For us to perform these actions we must involve both the cortex and some other part of the body. Another pleasure is music. However, music appears to be a luxury that arises directly from the cortex itself, rather than having a specific duty to perform. Accomplishment is a further pleasure that we can achieve through the efficient workings of our cortex. Accomplishment in its various forms can be our strongest and most lasting source of pleasure.

The intensity of the desire sent into the cortex influences the amount of pleasure that we will experience. The more energy or desire that builds in the hypothalamus, ready to go, the greater the pleasure could be. The longer we can hold off sneezing or scratching, eating or sleeping, the more desire that will build and the greater the pleasure we will feel upon completion of the action. Desire can build to such excess that it can reach almost painful amounts as tension, before its release into the cortex. Desire or tension can wait for a circuit to become available in the cortex, so that it can race through the cortex to find answer and outlet. The assessment feeling that returns to the hypothalamus will tell the pleasure centre how well organised the cortex was at dealing with the desire. If the tension was relieved we will feel pleasure.

What gives us pleasure will vary according to the information we sense, and how well we deal with it. If we obtain the information as sound, then we will find greater pleasure from that sound if we can assess it as music rather than bang and crash. If the information comes from sight, then a cortex that can sense art or a vast intricate landscape showing good arrangement will give us more pleasure than disjointed pictures. Words of poetry can be more pleasurable than a speech. It all depends on how well the cortex can organise and interact with the information it receives. For each burst of input energy, how well organised is the interpretation through the cortex? How accomplished are we at assembling the stimulation that we receive into a picture of beauty?

One example of physical pleasure is scratching. It takes a great deal of will power not to scratch an itch. Scratching is something babies at first cannot do, but when they learn to coordinate their arms, parents must cut their fingernails to prevent them from scratching themselves badly. The ability to scratch is learnt, yet such is the pleasure reward link that it is almost impossible to resist. Bacteria in mosquito saliva have exploited this link for millions of years. However, we may not always be able to respond to the itch immediately. You might be hunting, and need to remain perfectly still for some time. Then, the desire or tension builds but the cortex says 'no, don't scratch yet.' Finally, when you can scratch, the pleasure is the greater. What is pleasurable when you scratch is that a personal action solved or relieved an immediate need and discomfort. You relieved an itch. Therefore, there is a circuit in the cortex that is sufficiently well organised to allow you to resolve the problem fully. This task is a simple one, but it still reflects a level of accomplishment in the organisation of our brain. It shows that we can interact with the rest of our body and the environment to achieve a pleasurable end to one of our desires. It is one accomplished stage in the interactive ability of our niche map.

A sneeze can be even more pleasurable than a scratch, as the one convulsive action delivers a sudden burst of energy through the cortex. The sneeze is designed to efficiently send impulses through much of the body, to deliver the force needed to expel matter from the head. In a sneeze, nearly all of the bodies' muscles contract to give sudden tension. They send energy signals along the peripheral nervous system to the hypothalamus, and if the cortex allows the sneeze the release is correspondingly pleasurable. We get somewhat disappointed if we are about to sneeze and the bodies' muscles become tense and ready, but nothing happens. A sneeze is hard to hold back. We can stifle a sneeze somewhat, but then it does not feel as good.

Eating and drinking are other sources of pleasure that reflect a level of self-accomplishment. They are abilities that show we are sufficiently coordinated to fill some of the bodies' needs. The desires for food or drink build up as hunger or thirst, and if we have the power to relieve them, then as an animal we must be functioning well. Getting pleasure from being able to eat and drink makes adaptive sense. While some of our pleasure is from simple nourishment, the interaction desire is also involved. Much of the pleasure from eating is in terms of looking at the event as an accomplishment. Sometimes the need for a feeling of accomplishment and pleasure can make people eat more than the body actually needs. This happens especially if accomplishment is low in other areas. Then excessive eating might be a way of compensating to increase the overall feeling of accomplishment. An eating disorder or smoking must be as difficult to quit as it is to resist scratching.

Spinning around to get giddy can feel good, sometimes, especially to children. Getting giddy drives our balance receptor in the ear away from its comfortable or optimal position. It therefore sends a desire to right itself to the cortex. The longer you can spin, and put up with the associated nausea, the better the feeling can be when stopping. The pleasure is not so much from the resulting stagger, though if it makes others laugh this adds to the pleasure. The main source of pleasure is in being able to solve a problem or desire by stopping the spin. The mindrules know how to relieve the desire. This is the kind of information that a niche map must have. Getting giddy is a child's way of tricking or playing with the mechanics of the interaction desire.

The senses are tied to many neural pathways in the brain, so the more they are stimulated, the wider the area that can feed back to the interaction desire. If the senses are being well stimulated, then it is likely that we are in our right niche and are interacting well. Some pleasurable activities that give added stimulation to the senses include driving a car that lets us see many new sights at once, shopping and bustling (to a certain extent), seeing many different colours at once, or hearing many different sounds.

These pleasures can disappear however, if our senses become overloaded and we do not have the time or the real desire to handle all of the information being received. The cortex is therefore not accomplished at using all of that information for so long, and it no longer finds them a pleasure. Noise or bustle might be distracting to what could be our real desire at the time, such as a desire to accomplish in work, pursue a hobby, or enjoy a musical preference.

4.3 Sexual desire

The orgasm is among the greatest pleasures that the body can experience, for the brief time that it lasts. The orgasm is another example of the pleasure that we can gain from the successful relief of desire. During the basics of sex, there is a great deal of physical exertion and stimulation. This arouses many parts of the body, as well as those specially designed for sexual arousal. Those tissues and organs send energy and information to the hypothalamus ready for assessment and relief. But all of that information must wait until the mind's dominant interaction desire agrees to let it through. A great deal of sexual desire or tension can build before the cortex. When the interaction desire finally does allow a circuit in the cortex to appear for the relief of the sexual desire, the orgasm occurs as a rush in bursts of energy through the cortex. This rush of desiring energy highlights a wide arena of neural pathways in the cortex. The pleasure centre network feeds the feelings back to the hypothalamus to register that there was extensive cortex involvement and connection to an interaction. That finding is of great pleasure or orgasm. It is the rush and extent of returning energy over the pleasure centre that feels good.

There are various ways to enhance the sex and resulting orgasm. It may require some training or experience for the orgasm and the sex to work well, as the cortex needs to learn all of its sexual connections. Often, the longer the process or foreplay, then the greater the stimulation will be. Arousal and tension will build and convert into a greater desire awaiting resolution. The more rhythmic the sex, the more coordinated yet simple is likely to be the release. Similarly, the more senses that can be stimulated at once the better. This means that the more aware, understanding or romantic the event, the more intensely fulfilling is likely to be the orgasm. If we can include the interaction desire in the sex as well, the mind will be able to contribute more of its own energy to the event. The mind likes to feel its interaction desire in full swing.

Sex is a way of rapidly building desire. The tension can even make a face look pained. But we are willing to take our exertion to the limits for the pleasure that we learn is in store at the end, and perhaps for the meaning to the interaction desire that it can convey. Some might try to increase sexual pleasure by including the added tension of pain during sex. However, this action will be at the expense of stimulating the potentially wiser interaction desire. Pain or exploitation therefore will fail to produce the greatest pleasures available during sex.

In humans the interaction desire must be especially strong to cater to our large cortex. Therefore, sexual desire must wait especially upon the interaction desire, before it can pass through the cortex. The conditions in the mind usually have to become right for us to achieve orgasm. Distractions that make us think of other things may put us off. The mind needs to see that the interactions producing the sex are direct and honest, or romantic and loving. The interaction desire in humans is strong and must be met. Humans often need to have the setting right so they can focus more and more on the partner, until they feel they can share all their true desires.

Sometimes, if the orgasm happens without the mind being stimulated in the way it wanted or would normally expect, we can feel cheated and the sex might seem dirty. Also, if the mind does not see sex as natural or good then its interaction desire will not be so willing to give up its control to the lesser desires. The interaction desire might place many conditions on the sexual desire, before it is willing to let it pass and relieve itself through the cortex.

The orgasm is not meant to contradict the mind or the interaction desire. It is not meant to be a powerful desire that countermands the will of the mind, to drive us to fill basic sexual needs at the expense of other desires. Our desires did not evolve to make us 'reproduce or perish', or to make us feel dirty. The aims of the mind and the orgasm should be complementary and additive.

Sexual desire does not come from some hidden evolutionary knowledge that we should reproduce at any expense for our gene's sake. It is a part of what more simply drives us to look for a pleasurable position in life. If we are able to achieve orgasm, then in all likelihood we have found a good interactive position in life, at least at that time. We must be attractive to a mate, so we have organised our cortex sufficiently well to allow us to interact and bond with another. Interaction desire and sexual desire both drive us towards getting our interactions right. The cortex wants to be sweet enough to cope with its niche. Therefore the interaction desire also wants its sex to be direct and honest. The interaction desire likes its sex to contribute to the sense of attunement. The pleasure centre likes its sex wild.

4.4 Accomplishment

While the orgasm is usually the most intense source of pleasure that we can experience, the greatest quantity available over the life of an animal will be as accomplishment. Accomplishment feels good because it means that we have organised the cortex in a way that allows positive performance. It means we are capable and effective in the niche. It means we can do our things simply and beautifully. It is more important than any other pleasure such as the orgasm, and although not as intense (though some insights can be pretty good) its effects are much longer lasting.

Any means we can learn that finds a simple and effective way through a complicated task is an accomplishment. Some examples of accomplishment are insight, awards for mastering and understanding a course or subject, being proven right, winning a point in a game, and getting compliments (because we were right). Helping others is another expression of accomplishment. It means that we are so well organised and mastered in our own affairs that we can help others. If we are able to be altruistic then we must be accomplished. Perhaps we are a pillar of society or self-assured. Humans have a strongly developed pleasure centre because we must learn such a high proportion of our instincts. The natural progression in the development of a pleasure centre that judges its cortex by its achievements is altruism. Of all the animals, altruism is most strongly developed in humans (Mayr, 1988: 75). If we can help others, then the pleasure centre will judge that its animal is a master of its life, and has an excess of accomplishment that it can afford to share. That is why helping others can be a pleasure.

Our desire for accomplishment also drives our thinking. The interaction desire is interested most in the signs of our accomplishment. Accomplishment signals that the cortex contains simple backbones of behaviour that readily fan out to allow us to achieve in many areas. Thinking is essentially the process of trying to find a new circuit through the cortex maze that will give us greater pleasure than the current arrangement. We think to find better loops of understanding, that are simple yet wide reaching in application.

The interaction desire is our most basic drive. It makes us want to produce a niche map that is effective and artful in its ability to meet, interpret and handle day to day events. It gives us a measure of the quality of our niche map.

However, the interaction desire is also the cause of why we now tolerate the fundamental mistakes of our own mindrules. The keenness of our interaction desire drives us to find our niche maps quickly, so that it can begin to reap the pleasure rewards. The desire therefore drives us to accept and assume mindrules that during rapid niche change can only produce confusion. The interaction desire makes us go too early. It does not realise that if it waited and reassessed, the resulting changes to our niche map could let us fulfil a new level of desire not thought possible before.

We have a number of desires that need to develop before we can become natural. Most reading this book are probably able to fill their desires for food and water already. Some might also be wild sexually. However, we are all still unable to meet the needs of our interaction desire properly.

The highest state of accomplishment that any species can achieve for its interaction desire is wildness. Other species are wild not because they don't know any better, but because their evolution and experience have shown them what is better. In wildness, the cortex must be so well organised that it has the power to conduct its interactions at a receptive and instinctive level. In wildness, we will have to distribute our energy through our cortex in the most simple and beautiful arrangements possible.

4.5 Entertainment

The desire we have for easy interaction also gives our species its need for entertainment. This need is especially strong when blocks stand in the way of our other more direct and real attempts to fill the interaction desire. The hypothalamus likes to feel that the cortex has produced a complete and efficient map of the person's niche. It is a simple measuring device, that modern technology can trick. It enjoys feeling that our niche map can effectively accommodate any stimulation. It likes to feel stimulation racing along its neural pathways with comfortable ease. It does not like the notion that its map might be fundamentally flawed and in need of an entirely new context and backbone. Not much pleasure there. The simple measure the cortex has of the value of its mindrules is that the more pathways that can be triggered by the same stimulation, then the better must be those connections. Entertainment is a way of artificially accommodating the interaction desire.

Entertainment can package stimulation into a form that will find simple and guaranteed passage through the niche map. The value of entertainment is that it allows us to explore and test some of the limits to our niche map in comfort. Play and sport are other ways of improving the workability of the neural pathways, but they involve more exertion, excitement and possibly danger. Play and sport are methods of entertainment that require self-activity. The entertainment discussed here is that gained by simply observing its performance. Someone else has already done the work of its construction for us.

Our species' need for entertainment is especially prevalent today, because reality would otherwise find it so difficult to follow our confused niche maps. Our neural pathways need much more artificial stimulation, because we can gain such little pleasure from reality. Games are often not enough, because of the exertion needed to gain the same end result. It is usually easier to get the same feeling through entertainment. The popularity of television in our species is noteworthy, and says something about the current ability of our species to fill its own true desires through more direct and involving pursuits. Social activity has declined in preference for a night in front of the television.

During the current period of change, mindrules find it very difficult to make us feel good. Therefore, we might take our entertainment to the extremes, as a means of pampering to our mindrules so they can meet the pleasure centre's high expectations. In entertainment, mindrules can have their illusions and blocks portrayed as real. Their restricted and alienated pathways can at last be presented in 'real' form. In entertainment, mindrules see their own little worlds come alive. Entertainment can give pretend realism to the illusory blocks mindrules assume must exist.

For example, soaps can produce characters that are totally scheming and selfish. Some might even be good strugglers for survival. This comes as great relief to the niche map and its attentive and deceived pleasure centre, because it shows a world that mindrules know. In the soaps we find realism to our explanations of why mindrules cannot be wild and beautiful: people intrinsically cannot share or be trusted. It can become important to watch the soaps, to learn the full extent to which 'bad' people are willing to go. Perhaps they are behaviours that we should mimic to survive. For any animal it is important to learn the limits of their niche, so that we can be better prepared and accomplished. Westerns used to be popular, until a greater understanding of the plight of Indians made it more difficult to caste them into the role of the baddie. Entertainment can produce realism or phoney reality, through illusion and distortion, to appease the desire behind mindrules to make their world complete and accomplished. It is natural to look for the simplest solution to complete the niche map, and entertainment is an easy way out. We could become so hooked up to our TV screens and computer monitors, that we forget to take notice of what the real world is like.

Children generally seek a different kind of entertainment to that of adults. Their entertainment is simpler, meeting good and bad ends more directly, and they have greater hope for the end result. They are still learning, and so they have less need for realism and the proof that there is deviousness in the world. The desires of adults have been fashioned by mindrules longer, and so they view happy endings as naive, because mindrules tell them so. Children feel less comfortable with the twists and complications of our phoney realism, and therefore prefer entertainment that is obviously harmless or less impressive as block. Cartoons, slapstick, superheroes, funny monsters and fantasy obviously do not try to represent real people, and so they can entertain the developing mindrules without dampening hope too greatly. The entertainment is more purely for fun, than to give shape to excuses. In adults, science fiction might most closely fit this same requirement without the pretence of realism.

But children might also dwell too long on the bad in their superhero films or violent video games. They might learn the bad too well, to the point where it stunts their hopes and receptivity. While it might be better to do without even the pretend bad and violence, the cortex does need to be able to extend its tracks to find a certain level of completeness from time to time. It is good to remember how accomplished the pleasure centre would like to feel. Entertainment is one way to do this. It can encourage our drive.

Entertainment should maintain its true function of providing exploration and fun to mindrules as a temporary way of filling our interaction desire. Play and entertainment can both improve drive, by reminding us what is possible. Entertainment with an inspiring but not phoney end, is the best but perhaps hardest performance to achieve.

4.6 Spirit

The word spirit carries with it a great deal of mysticism, and yet it must also convey a special meaning or feeling to us that no other word is able. Therefore, it must have some real basis that needs addressing. The idea of a spirit seems common to most cultures and religions.

Each living thing can be thought of as having its own spirit. In some cultures, only higher animals, or perhaps only people, can have spirits. In other cultures, people believe that spirits reside in all animals, trees and plants, earth and rock.

I think of the spirit as being nothing mystical. It is simply the excess energy produced by the various bodily organs that is then free to travel and interact with the larger world. Any reaction produces entropy. This means that for any interaction there is some net loss of energy to the system. How that lost energy is collected and allowed to escape becomes the basis of the spirit in living things. The spirit is the energy left over from any interaction, which is then free to move towards another perhaps united purpose. Cells produce from their various metabolic activities energies or chemicals beyond which they need to survive. These excess energies then leave or diffuse from the cells. They are the makings of the spirit.

In simple or single-celled organisms, excess metabolic energy may simply dissipate from the cells. The excess energies that leave are poorly organised, and represent the basic level of what a spirit can entail. For higher organisms, the spirit of the cells and organs can be gathered for further processing towards a more unified purpose. The composition and amount of energy leaving cells could tell you something about the state and level of nourishment of those cells and organs. For example, can they afford to give off excess energies? For a multicelled animal, this information is very useful. Animals therefore gather up the excess energy as information, so that they can use it to alter their behaviour and perhaps improve the environment for their cells. The nervous system evolved to do this job in most multicelled organisms. It acts like a corridor or channel along which the energies of the body can give its information to the brain as a combined spirit. The brain will also produce its own excess energies that further add to the spirit. This spiritual energy can describe the essence of the organism.

In a similar way, a team spirit is where the enthusiasm and energies of each individual player channel into a larger entity or team. The team can then function as a whole unit, like a single minded and coordinated organism.

We could use the spirit collected from the body and brain to measure of the general health and wellbeing of an animal. It would be useful to be able read our own spirit. This would give us an overall picture of how well we were functioning. For example, if the spirit being sent to the mind is low, then the body is probably in a poor state.

The various organs can send their spirit information towards the brain in several ways. Cells in various glands evolved to become particularly adept at sending useful information as hormones. Other tissues became nerves, as they were better at gathering up and transmitting the spirit information from one cell to another. Some organ spirits are sent as desire. All of the spirit information sent by the various parts of the body merge into one, so we feel we have one spirit.

When cartoonists portray the spirit, they usually draw it as though a complete animal outline or shadow can step out of the body. When sick or upon death, the spirit can leave the body like a ghost. These examples show that our impression or feeling of the spirit is that it originates from every cell and organ that makes a body. When the animal is sick or dying, the spirit wanes or might leave the body. If the spirit is troubled, it might flicker or fade.

Channelling the spirit into the nervous system is like gathering up the communicating energies of the body. This spirit information can then move on into the brain to give life and communication to its neurones. In the brain, the spirit information might be easy to read and find fluent passage to the outside world. In higher animals, the spirit must go through some form of consideration in the cortex before it can so freely continue its journey. In higher animals the spirit loses direct control of the brain, and must become a desire instead. The spirit learnt to trust its cortex. In trust the spirit allows itself to be presented to the cortex simply as a desire. In this way, the spirit evolved to become our interaction desire. They are essentially the same thing. Through the interaction desire, we can best see our spirit or true nature.

As spirit, our energy does not have to know consciously why it is there, or what it is supposed to do. It can become mystical to us. All we might feel is that it wants to be free. For higher animals the spirit will mostly want to travel the cortex easily. But if we can know more about our spirit, by calling it the interaction desire, we will know better how to make it happy. It does not have to take on mystical qualities. We could send our spirit high if we experience accomplishment.

When spirits are high, a person is generally active and happy. Their activity and alertness will make the body generate even more excess energy that in turn can add to the spirit already being sent to the central nervous system. This extra energy heightens the feeling of our spirit. 'Keeping the spirits up' means the same as keeping the interaction desire active. A broken spirit is when there seems no chance of sending the spirit on the free and fulfilling course that it wants. The spirit can be broken by harsh experience and conditioning. Then, the interaction desire will have low expectation. The body will send less spirit or interaction desire to the brain, because the pleasure centre knows that the result will be hurt.

The spirit wants to flow smoothly and simply wherever it chooses. For humans, our spirit has become the essence of the interaction desire. Through the drive of the interaction desire, we try to learn pathways that are most free and natural.

The spirit feels most at home in the soul. The soul is the core of our niche map where everything relates together tightly and harmoniously. It is therefore the place where our spirit can move most freely. It is where everything for us feels perfect, and where the spirit likes most to spend its time. However, mindrules have a large hand in determining the shape of our niche map. They give us the tracks of our soul. Therefore in the soul, we can also experience all of the illusions that mindrules use to make their rules seem complete. Each person's soul has learnt to become different, and is stamped with its own individuality. Therefore, the things that thrill some souls might not stir another. Some souls might be thrilled and fulfilled by certain kinds of music or experiences. Some might be wrapped up with lizard natures. Some might seek spiritual guidance to help improve the outlet and feeling of their soul.

When mindrules become stressed and turn individual and restricted, the soul experience becomes limited. Mindrules under rapid niche change shrink the common soul of the wild species into an internalised form that can only exist within individual niche maps. The internalised soul gives the spirit a much smaller area in which to play. The spirit might even become lost. The restricted niche map may contain such little beauty and understanding, that it cannot provide a soul where the spirit could feel at home or maintain an interest.

The soul is the region on the niche map where life for us would flow most freely and simply. It is the region that has first and most direct linkage to the pleasure centre. If it is stimulated, we will feel our greatest pleasure. The soul is like a favourite set of wires in the cortex that we have learnt, like a record. The spirit comes from the whole body, and is our excess energy or what we call us. Therefore, we could 'sell our soul', but we cannot sell our spirit because that is the essence of what is us. There is nothing left.

While all animals have a spirit, not all of them would have a soul. The soul is where the spirit likes most to spend its time as it passes through the body. To have a soul, we need to have a region in the nervous system that can assemble our spirit and maintain its interest. The spirit flows continuously, so the nervous system must do this quickly. A single celled organism simply loses its excess energy. It cannot gather its energy into some internal sensing organ like the cortex. The spirit is probably less important to a single celled animal than to a higher organism, which attempts to read the condition of its own spirit by enticing it to the soul. For a worm, which does not have a cortex, the soul might be within the main trunk of its nervous system. The spirit would follow such a soul instinctively, so offer little awareness. Lower vertebrates have a cortex, but their inherited instincts would still predominate. Their soul may mostly or partly occupy other regions of the brain that are more primitive.

In humans, nearly all of our behavioural control has moved into the cortex. Our souls followed, and now reside on the niche map in the cortex. It is time to disentangle the spirit from the soul, and let the spirit go where it would most purely wish, rather than making it abide by what the soul knows. Confused mindrules now govern our souls, so they give us false information. If the spirit has higher expectations than what the soul can offer, then change the soul. Under a free and wild spirit, the soul can be made to open itself further to expand. If we could keep our spirit wild, the soul would eventually have to merge with the other souls. Then how our spirits would fly!

4.7 Music

Music provides a most useful and interesting model of how the interaction desire functions in the cerebral cortex. Our species' enjoyment of music is one of our more important and unique characteristics. Our species enjoys music because of the stage of evolution that our brain has now reached. Music reflects the reliance we now place on the interaction desire and its assessment of the quality of our mindrule understandings. Other animals generally have only limited awareness of music. The interaction desire can less influence the arrangement of their neural pathways, because their instincts are a combination of inherited instincts and/or less pliable mindrules.

Our enjoyment of music did not evolve for its own sake. It is not an adaptation that we need for survival. Rather, it is a side effect of our evolution in another area, the development of the interaction desire and it's learning organ the cerebral cortex.

But why should a series of noises that we call music be so memorable and catchy? Music can go beyond mere appreciation of the order in which notes are put together, to captivation. Music can fill us with a sense of beauty, and stir us to look for intrinsically simple but far reaching arrangements in other walks of life.

Music is not simply a progression of random noises. It involves a tune or melody. Good music is tightly played. It can explore side-tracks or variations with different verses, or with each beat, but it can also return to a central chorus or basic theme, which may itself slowly change during the piece. We can quickly memorise music and imprint its arrangement into our mind. It is the kind of arrangement that our pleasure centre likes us to remember most. But why should the repeated stimulation of a tightly bound set of tracks feel so pleasurable? Why do we enjoy music?

Music shows that there is a desire in the brain to have a neural network that can be regularly played, and that we can follow easily to explore the various parts of its theme. Also, that theme should be complete enough so that all explored paths will return at some time, to reinforce the value of the basic theme. Music is a way of creating a network in the brain that is easy to stimulate, and can lead simply or melodiously to its various parts.

Because music arranges its information so well, we may often only need to hear a few notes or bars of the song to recall suddenly a whole piece of music. Playing a few notes in the tune can go a long way because the rest of the song flows so easily. This ability to sense a great deal of information from so few notes is important in many other aspects of life as well, especially in the wild. Other animals have this skill in other areas of niche interaction that are important to them.

The simple melodious theme is the same kind of arrangement that the brain looks for in its understanding and arrangement of the niche map. The brain needs to measure the quality of understanding in its niche map. It evolved the interaction desire to see how widely its tracks can be stimulated and applied with minimal input and fuss. This gives some measure of tightness and relatability of the understanding. Music mimics most simply the general pattern desired by the brain.

There is rhythm to music, which is surprisingly constant between all pieces. The rhythm is generally simple and comfortable. Some songs have faster rhythm, and call for more rapid dancing or extra effort if we are to follow them. The fast music might not be as comfortable, but it can signify greater activity and stimulation, which is often what is wanted at a party. At a funeral the beat can be slow and meaningful or mournful and represents a slower rate of thinking and activity. It mimics a brain that wants more time to search deeply between each pulse of stimulation.

If music correctly models the working of our cortex, then its rhythm might suggest how the hypothalamus releases the energy of the interaction desire. It must release the energy in pulses that loop through the cortex before returning to the hypothalamus. This burst rate of energy release into the cortex also seems tied to the heart beat rate. A further intermediary may be the internal clock found in the substantia nigra of the brain (Meck, 1996). With each beat, a pulse of energy might try its circuit through the brain. Each beat would bring a fresh supply of energetic information from the body to the hypothalamus, ready to be measured upon its passage through the cortex. When the body increases activity, the amount of energy sent would increase and the periods between the pulses shorten. The rhythm would get faster, and the mind will race and heighten in consciousness. During sleep, there are long periods between the pulses, so each burst of energy will linger longer before being overridden by the next.

It would be nice to be able to take this further, and find the music to life that would give us a simple basic theme from which all things can be reached and explored. Thinking can produce a similar feeling of pleasure to music, when it pieces things together well. This is the level of understanding that the mind naturally seeks. Music can be soothing to the soul, and stir the spirit, because it simulates the state of organisation the brain wants to achieve. Music can invigorate, and encourage us to apply its methods elsewhere.

We find it easier to remember and accept messages if they can be put to music. Most successful advertising campaigns will include a simple jingle in its message. Many early stories and historical accounts were remembered as ballads. Music can also help bring people together, as it allows them all to feel and remember the same pleasure. It can be used to soothe, such as when planes take off or land. It helps give the impression that everything is complete and right. Music can penetrate us easily, and make things seem more convincing. It is often used to improve the impact of some associated message.

We can increase the impact that music has on people in several ways. Simply turning up the volume can increase enjoyment, especially if the mind is in the mood for something stirring or active. Also, if we can combine music with other bodily activities, we can increase the energy of the desire being sent to the cortex, thereby increasing the pleasure. We can do this by simple foot tapping, whistling, singing or dancing.

Music has been used throughout history to encourage various behaviours, because it is easy to remember and yet stirring and widely appreciated. Music can stir the desire and confidence of a group to work together. It can help the resolve to act bravely, remove doubt, and overcome perceived enemies as music makes things seem more achievable in the mind. Drums might be played when acts of bravery are required in war.

While music is stirring, the same track can become boring if we hear it repeatedly. A piece of recorded music does not change, so that eventually the music loses its freshness and ability to stir. Few songs last long in the top ten charts. If after a long absence we hear the tune again, it might rekindle the feeling of pleasure, though usually not for as long as when first heard. This suggests that while the brain seeks tight and beautiful arrangements, those arrangement must be able to grow if the pleasure is to last.

The understanding backbone of the cortex needs to be alive, with proof that it is amenable to new interactions. An understanding that does not grow into new things is probably false. The brain should turn away from such stagnant understandings.

We could speculate about the mechanism that would naturally turn the brain away from stagnant understandings. If we listen to a certain tune continually, then a certain set of neural pathways about the song becomes entrenched. But if there are no new variations to hear, fresh neural pathways will not form. The song will become deeply entrenched, but have no lighter pathways linking it to the rest of the cortex. There is backbone without ribs. It will become monotonous. Every aspect of the song becomes the part of a major highway in our cortex, but it has no associated side tracks that allows us to get off into other areas of the cortex as well. The backbone becomes an isolated blot in the subconscious. Energy cannot easily get on or off that highway, to spread out to where it can be detected by the pleasure centre's network of fibres.

This result in music suggests that if a neural network is to remain pleasurable, it will also need to contain a mixture of good backbone organisation and minor side-tracks. The major highway needs minor track connections to keep it live.

We need a cortex that has an understanding that can grow throughout life. We do not need a set of mindrules that once learnt do not grow further in their field of application. Normally in life, such a melody of understanding would be renewed continually from the days' interactions. Tunes, especially recorded tunes, do not grow but are exactly the same each time they are played. We might be able to rejuvenate tunes to some extent, by new recordings or live performance that offer some new dimension or variation. Desire will lose interest in travelling along old tracks or songs that do not expand and aid in the successful interaction of the new day's experiences. There is probably a general principle that if a track is not used regularly by desire and emotion, then it will begin to lose influence and merge back into a less active and noticeable state.

4.8 Dreaming

When we fall asleep we often dream. But why did dreaming evolve? Did it evolve simply to fill in time while we sleep, or is there a stronger reason behind the dream? Sleeping and dreaming seem to be especially important to those species that learn their instincts as mindrules.

Sleep is a time when our senses wane, the eyes close, and we can shut out most of our external influences and realities. It is also a time of rest. However, if the body just needed to rest, then why don't we simply remain still? Why go so far as to fall asleep? It seems that to rest we need to turn off the energy to the mind as well. Even maintaining a basic level of consciousness must be a significant drain upon our energy. Therefore, we cannot rest properly by simply going into a daze of vague awareness.

For us to rest properly, the consciousness needs to turn off completely. But this reason still does not seem enough to tip the edge into why we sleep. Sleep is such a vulnerable state to be in, yet for about one-third of our lives it is what we do. There must be strong evolutionary reason behind sleeping; otherwise, we surely could have evolved a better way to rest. We could have evolved improvements to our trance like abilities, which would allow us to be partially alert if danger approached. Dolphins are unusual in that they can send just half of their brain to sleep at a time, and thus maintain buoyancy and breathing. However for most animals, evolution chose a state of total sleep over basic consciousness as our way of rest, because the dream has an important function to fulfil as well.

The most important survival task facing any learning animal is that it should meet the essential demands of its interaction desire. The interaction desire is the animal's most basic drive, and is what keeps the animal functioning as a cohesive unit. It is the best measure that an animal has of how it is performing. Because of its link to the pleasure centre, the interaction desire also has the potential to adjust the behaviour of an animal into its most optimal and efficient state. It is therefore important to keep that desire as pure as possible, so that the desire can continue to ask the animal for its highest standards. Any animal that cannot meet its interaction desire is very likely to be ill equipped for its niche. It is far more likely to die through stress and failure in its niche, than from any danger that might occur while sleeping.

Dreaming is the method that animals use to try and keep in touch with their desires. Dreaming allows our true desires to ask what they want without interruption from outside influences or other people. It allows our desires to break free of the blocking impediments of life that seem so pressing and real during consciousness. Dreaming lets our desires bypass the niche map and its looming blocks, to search for other ways that might allow us to become more direct and wild. Dreaming is a way of refreshing our true desire and spirit. It is a means of repair.

During sleep, the need to rest and dream can vary. We might have a fitful night sleep, if our dreams are intense and pressing. Alternatively, we might be so tired that we remember nothing of the night's sleep. If we find it difficult to fill our desires in real life, we may prefer to sleep throughout the morning beyond what is really needed for rest. We might try to fill our desires through dreaming instead.

When we dream, our desires remain active even though the mind and consciousness turn off. Dreaming is a time for our desires to explore and sort the cortex in a way that returns them to centre stage. During consciousness, the mind can suppress desires because they are only requests to the mind. Many desires remain unresolved and unfilled when the day is over. Dreaming is a time when our desires can have their way, and drain away their tension. Desires have greater freedom during dream. Sleep turns off the niche map and its threatening blocks that tell us what we cannot have. In a dream, our desires look for ways to tell us what they really want.

Dreams are meant to remind us of our true desires. We often wake up in a better mood, if we had a good night's sleep and dream. If we remember the effect of those dreams, we might consciously try again to fill those desires more directly in our real life. We might try afresh. Dreams might give us courage, when we see from the dream how good it would feel if they came true. The blocks might have to answer to a conscious mind the next day that is more determined and carries its desire with higher expectation than before.

The pleasure centre wants its cortex network to be efficient and relaxed. When conscious, it does not want us wasting energy and time with complicated blocks and bad if there is no real need. The function of dreams is to unmask blocks and the complications of the day, explore beyond them, and perhaps find a new arrangement in the absence of outside interference. In dream, we can explore neural pathways that we would normally suppress. Sometimes, the dream can give us simple answers that would normally elude the mind. Aboriginals realised the importance of the dreaming. Dreams can give us great meaning and inspiration.

Unfortunately, we suppress our true desires far more than we were evolved to cope with. Our niche understandings lack wild and easy connections. There is much in-built confusion and alienation imprinted into the very fabric of our cortex. It is all under stress. Therefore, even when we shut out our external suppressions, restriction remains in us because it is built into the very fabric of our mindrules. These instinctive patterns might be so restrictive that even in dream, true desire cannot resolve itself sufficiently to feel good. The cortex may be so repressed, that anything desire asks of us during the dream will still be too much. The request will turn into a nightmare. This is a poor state to be in for any animal.

The blocks on our niche maps that affect our thoughts so strongly are neither simple nor natural. Maintaining illusions requires a lot of energy. However, during sleep we turn off most of our energy supply. The energy that the blocks need to exist, drains away, leaving an unprotected and confused mindrule dominated landscape. But if our blocks are internalised, they will not leave our cortical landscape completely. Our dreams will be unable to enjoy their desires, because the legacy of block remains. Today's human allows their blocks to have such serious and vivid impression on our minds, that even in dream our true desire cannot escape. Our desires will still see their blocks, and because during sleep we cannot guide them consciously, our desire will often fall into nightmare. The network cannot dream of a way to resolve or befriend the blocks. The spirit remains trapped. The in-built restriction pattern and its illusions are too strong for us to overcome.

Nightmares are not how dreams are meant to be. They are a symptom of dead-end mindrules. Nightmares are especially common today. Children have nightmares as soon as they learn about the bad. Restrictions and blocks in other animals are not normally strong or serious enough to give them lasting or regular nightmare. A niche understanding that is strong enough to overcome block during dreaming is the natural state.

If life is unfulfilling we might prefer dreaming to real life. The desire most in need, or conversely being most suppressed, will strongly influence the content of the dream. The dream might be sexual. We might dream about a hobby that is particularly pleasurable. If food is important, that might be the dream subject. If we desire simple resolution of all the world's problems, then superhero dreams might occur. Many dreams might be symbolic of what the desire really wants, but is unable to express because it does not have conscious knowledge.

The dreaming process can be so pleasurable that we might try to continue dreaming even when conscious. Day dreaming is another way to recall true desire. It can let us shut off the senses to outside influence and negative block. Day dreaming can also be time consuming, and prevent us from coming to terms with our immediate reality. However, day dreaming is also a sign that our desire is still higher than what we are currently meeting through reality. It shows that we are still searching.

During consciousness we can expand the general approach of dreaming and day dreaming to produce imagination. Imagination makes us want to create structure that can take us beyond the confines of the modern reality into more beauty and pleasure. Imagination is a refinement or more aware form of dreaming. Like dreaming, imagination gives desires greater say. It is an attempt to let our desires float freely towards what they really want. Then when we see what our imagination wants, we can try consciously to make it happen. The dream explores our possibilities in unstructured almost random ways, while imagination has more awareness behind it that can often produce more realistic creations. But of course, the novelty of what we can achieve through imagination might still be less than what we can see in a dream. Dreaming and imagination are more common in children than adults, as their mindrules are still young and not totally versed in the art of restriction and alienation. Dreaming and imagination are attributes that try to raise the importance of desires within our life.

4.9 Subconscious and conscious

Energy arrives in the cortex as information in two main ways. It can enter either through the senses or through desire. The senses are designed simply to inform or provide us with some points of observation. The senses can impress what it sees into the cortex. But it is then up to us to make use of that information and tie it all together. The energy that we send to try and make use of the cortex for behavioural guidance is desire. The desire enters the cortex as though in a dream. It does not know what to expect in its world as modelled by the cortex. It does not know reality. That is the job of the senses to observe, and mindrules to formulate into a niche map. All desire can do is to feel its way through the developing model to try and find out what is possible and allowed. It has to learn from its cortex what it can ask of its world. It has to learn from the cortex to what standard of pleasure it must adjust.

The amount of energy contained within each burst of desire that enters the cortex is limited. How can a desire with limited energy properly explore a cortex that contains billions of different pathways? Desire cannot trace all of the pathways in its cortex to find an answer. Instead, desire must trust the assumptions that the cortex makes, as a way of shortening the list of alternatives to search. At any one time we can use only a small number of the many pathways potentially available in the cortex. To find assumptions and address the limitations of our energy, the cortex divided into two main arenas, the large subconscious and the smaller conscious.

The subconscious contains the bulk of our neurones. We have to rationalise our information somehow, and to do that we place most of it in the subconscious. We send the subconscious just enough energy to awaken its niche map. In that way we can obtain a summary of the most important information in the subconscious. The rest of its information we assume to be adequately addressed by the niche map. If we sent more energy than is needed to find the niche map, the excess energy would soon become lost within the vast array of its possibilities. We might never get an answer back from the vastness of the subconscious.

While we do not have enough energy to explore in detail all of the subconscious beyond its niche map, we do have enough energy to explore the smaller conscious. The first stage in producing consciousness involves turning on sufficient energy to awaken the niche map. Our energy boots up the niche map, like a computer coming on line. The niche map lies just under the surface of our thoughts, giving consciousness the foundations from which it can then launch itself further into awareness. During consciousness we grease the niche map with a background level of energy, so that our thoughts have a structure upon which they can move about quite easily.

In consciousness, we are capable of various levels of awareness. Greater awareness generally allows desire to feel less bound by its niche map. It is more able to leave the confines of its cortex rules, and explore beyond to its heart's desire. Desire can use its cortex as a launching pad, from which it can become more interactive and wild in its dealings. But before we can use our consciousness in that way, we must first understand our mindrules and their limitations.

The minimal level of consciousness can provide a niche map that barely gives a sense of relationship to other things. A baby is born with consciousness but no awareness. Babies' neurones are poorly organised, and they have much to learn. No matter how much energy the baby sends into its conscious, it will fail to become aware. A baby is conscious without barely realising that its hands are a part of itself, while the cot is some external object. To become aware of that difference, it has to develop a more complete and accurate branching pattern to its neurones. We could not classify any branching connections that a baby has as understanding. Inherited reflexes such as sucking and clinging still largely guide their behaviour. They cannot yet rely on the neural pathways in their cortex, because they are still scrambled. The energy that they put into the conscious has little opportunity to spread and activate a coherent picture instantaneously. The neurones in their cortex are sufficient to produce consciousness, but not enough to produce awareness. Consciousness in its simplest form does not need to be aware. It can be a matter of simply getting enough energy to stimulate the niche map.

There are two ways we can raise our conscious awareness beyond what a baby might experience. One way is to increase the number of interactions that we have within a given time. This will increase the amount of energy contained in each burst of energy that we send into the consciousness. For example, during sport the activity and rapid interaction experienced can raise our consciousness to a new high. Also, a person can feel more conscious during parties, because of the added stimulation of conversation and interaction. Conversely, someone locked in a prison cell on their own would find it difficult to keep enough stimulation flowing through their brain to maintain a normal level of conscious awareness.

The other way to raise awareness is to increase the number of neural pathways that can be stimulated upon each interaction or release of energy. The greater the network of neurones that we can light up with our energy at any one time, the more knowledge and memory that contributes to a coherent picture in the consciousness. The larger and more detailed the picture we see, the more we will know about our world. The more aware we are, the more likely we are to survive and live comfortably.

The drive behind our consciousness is the interaction desire. Our interaction desire likes well connected branching patterns in its cortex, because then it will feel greater pleasure upon each interaction. Our desire therefore searches for better alternatives in its cortex. It tries to make the neural pathways in the consciousness more aware. It finds greatest pleasure in seeing as wide an area in the cortex light up with stimulation as possible. Under such a cortical arrangement, desire can explore and take in much more thrill with each ride.

The interaction desire makes us want to raise our awareness through understanding and learning. We try to improve the understanding behind a group of memories. Understanding increases the number of branches that can feed into one common stem. It ties our memories together more simply. Energy finds neural pathways easier to follow when we put them together well with understanding. Each thought and stimulation will spontaneously trigger a greater sense of consciousness through understanding. Our interactions will find more meaning. Each burst of energy that we send into consciousness can fan out along many branches at once to get its bearing. This will raise the level of awareness contained in each thought.

Evolution has advanced the level of neural branching and understanding capable in our species. Our species can raise its consciousness through several levels. We can grow from being simply conscious to becoming aware. We can gain a self-identity, conceive of language, and find sufficient understanding until we finally realise.

4.10 Variations in consciousness

Consciousness is not a permanently set structure within the cortex. It is composed of the most recently highlighted neural pathways. Therefore, the exact location of the consciousness in the cortex can move about slightly according to the day's experiences and thoughts. The most recently used neural pathways will usually include the niche map, and short-term memories or recent experience. We can therefore boot up consciousness from any part of the cortex. It draws itself up from whatever neural pathways were greased last, because they are the neural pathways that first attract our energies' involvement. Consciousness will come from the most recently stabilised neural pathways in the cortex.

Also, the energy that we send into the cortex does not travel as a tight stream. There is leakage along the way. Not all of the energy returns in the same burst. Some energy gets lost when it spreads into minor and less entrenched pathways. Therefore, the conscious does not have a sharp boundary with its subconscious. Its edges dissipate and merge back into the subconscious.

This leakage allows the mind to fleetingly explore the content of the subconscious. If that spare energy chances upon the beginnings of something interesting in the subconscious, we might consciously send more energy to that region. The mind can detect long-term memories buried in the subconscious if it concentrates on the edges of its conscious arena. With conscious energy, we can prize open long-term memories so that they gain greater stabilisation and impact within the niche map. They are more likely to become a part of the next round of consciousness. However, if we find that those memories were unimportant, they are unlikely to command much attention again. They will merge back gradually into the subconscious where they become forgotten once more.

Tiredness causes another variation in consciousness. A message that travels through the brain must go from one cell to another. A small gap or synapse separates each cell from the other. Messages travel from one to another, by way of a diffusing chemical. After a long day, we use up and lose much of that chemical. It takes energy and time to make more, and to get it into position where it can fire again. These steps make it harder for us to think when tired. It makes our consciousness, and especially the level of our awareness, less keen. It makes it harder for stimulation to flow smoothly through our network of neural pathways to produce large and instantaneous pictures. There is more delay at each synapse.

A further variation on consciousness is sleep. We receive very little stimulation while asleep. Finding a quiet place, closing the eyes, combined with tiredness, all reduce the amount and effects of external stimulation. The amount of internal stimulation coming from the body also drops during sleep, placing little demand on the brain. With less energy flowing through the cortex and its network, consciousness fades. Even the prominence of our niche map is hard to maintain under such reduced energy. The boundaries of the niche map become less defined. The position of the niche map can flex and move gently. The few stimulations that the cortex does receive have less stringent guidelines to follow, and longer time to explore. We cannot guide the energy to produce thought, so the energy wanders to produce dreams.

The few stimulations that do find their way into the brain during sleep can trigger dreams. Once our dreaming thoughts enter the cortex, they have much longer opportunity to travel before any fresh stimulation can quash their run. Also during sleep, we do not see the external references that remind us of the truth. We may not keep to the right track. Internal bodily stimulations can wander much further than usual. They can follow rarely used pathways beyond the niche map. We might find fears and doubts in our sleep that we would normally suppress. The forms the dream takes depend upon the level of external stimulation received while asleep, such as outside noises or the temperature of the room. Also, the physiological state and mood of a person will affect the dream, so can vary if we are tired, drunk, randy, or anxious.

During consciousness the internalised blocks on our niche maps draw much energy to maintain their illusory positions. However, when sleeping there is less energy available to keep our internal blocks in position. Blocks can fade away, leaving our dreams free to move about and past their normal limits without realising. The neural pathways beyond the block are always poorly explored. The consciousness has not been able to reason them out previously. Therefore, any dream that stumbles onto those pathways beyond the niche map can follow a strange course. Our dreams can more freely travel through the subconscious. Some pathways are so poorly explored and connected that they lead into nightmare. To escape the dream we must awaken. When we awaken from sleep, energy rushes through the brain to restore our blocks. The dream is overridden, and our thoughts will travel along their more conscious pathways.

The desire that flows through the brain could spread out further and further through the network if left alone. However, the stimulation that produces desire usually comes thick and fast. Any pulse of desire can in the next instant be overridden by a new stimulation. There is a time limit on how many neural pathways each stimulation can trigger before being overridden. Also, each stimulation might highlight a different set of pathways. However, there are some pathways that each burst of energy will regularly activate. These become our self-identity. If each stimulation that we receive were to trigger a completely different set of pathways in our consciousness, we would have little consistency of thought. For us to think, some of the picture gained in one instant of consciousness must flow into the next picture of consciousness. This overlap, on many occasions, lets us hold a constant subset of pathways in mind. This overlapping set of pathways becomes our self-identity.

The self-identity is never far from mind. It appears with many of our thoughts. When people are conscious, they generally think about their self-identity or their own relative position, as well as the task at hand. Not every thought triggers this self-awareness, but in a high proportion our attention will include amongst its pathways those that remember best who you are and how you fit. A person slips in and out of consciously being aware that they are in fact conscious. Even as you read this book, your attention might at one time be devoted to the words and nothing else, and in another instant to self-comparison where you also think about yourself and so become self-aware.

Humans have become the most aware species on earth. The networking available in our cortex has become so highly developed that the number of mindrules and memories that our energy can reach with each burst of energy is enormous. We are more aware than any other animal of the detail and breadth of our surroundings. We have a greater understanding of what makes the plants around our home grow, of where we live on this earth in relation to other land marks, and so on. In other words, our conscious flow can include more neural pathways over a wider area.

Our species' cortex grew to become very large. Therefore, our need to summarise data had to increase correspondingly. Mindrules label and categorise, and this ability developed in our species until we can now label whole bunches of neurones into single concepts and words. Saying any word triggers in our mind a whole succession of energy flows that instantly bring the dominant mindrule for that word to mind, along with its associated network of memories and pathways. Our words contain so much information that we can transmit great meaning with our language. If we try thinking about a word long enough, it can cause a whole succession of memories to flow into mind. Generally however, we cannot trace back for long the branches that each word summarises, before our attention must shift towards the next word. When we think, we often talk to ourselves in words, comparing different words more easily than recalling the whole bunch of neurones that each word represents.

The greater the branching pattern that each burst of energy can follow in consciousness, the more aware we are, and the greater the opportunity for us to develop self-identity. While our species is aware and self-conscious, we cannot be sure about the level of awareness in other animals. All other animals would be conscious, as that state simply needs the nervous system and niche map to switch on. The question is how aware are other animals?

Awareness would vary for each species. Those with less complex brain may not have sufficient networking to give them much awareness of their surroundings. They might behave entirely instinctively or robotically. Some creatures may have enough awareness to have self-identity. However, this would be difficult for us to judge because their self-identity would feel differently to ours. Self-identity is not the same as individuality. Individuality is probably a baffling concept to a wild species. Self-identity for a wild animal would flow freely from the self to other things, so that the self-identity blends freely with the environment. The self-identity of humans is now individuality-based and therefore restricted in what it can feel.

If we want our consciousness to become more aware, we will have to uncover our instincts. Awareness is knowing our limitations and assumptions. Awareness should not let us remain blind to our instincts. Awareness opens up more possibilities than our instincts let us see. A bird that can see food on the other side of glass might continually peck and jab at the glass, rather than think to go around the glass. Some moths will always fly to a light, even when thrown in the opposite direction. There is little deviation from a standard response. They do not consider the alternatives. If the energy moves along a single neural pathway for its entire passage through the brain, then it will fail to develop disparate points of reference for comparison, and there will be no awareness. The pathway will be an instinct, and there is little leakage of thought.

People vary in the amount of awareness they have and are realising. Following mindrules blindly and taking them seriously, will reduce the awareness of our consciousness. Mindrules live in the subconscious where we cannot look at them directly. Therefore we cannot become aware of mindrules unless we find the need or desire. We need to give greater attention to wit if we are to have any chance of turning our attention in directions our mindrules say are out of bounds. Following mindrules to the letter of the niche map will keep thought to a narrow set of tracks, like an instinct. This gives less opportunity to see the alternatives and insights that we need if we are to improve our understanding to a level that will break us free of our problems. We need to realise beyond the mindrule barrier.

4.11 Attention and mind

We need a minimal level of energy to boot up the niche map and make us conscious. Minimal energy in consciousness will follow those pathways most natural and instinctive, that is, those that are most entrenched. At this level of consciousness we are mostly at the mercy of external events, because we have only enough energy to travel the niche map according to the order in which we are stimulated. For us to alter the instinctive flow we must concentrate our energy so that it can break free of the entrenchments of the niche map.

We can use attention to try and work out the best way to fill our needs and desires. Attention is an intense source of energy that we can use to change the landscape of our consciousness. The more attention we can muster, the more change we can employ. Attention correctly directed can gain control of the consciousness and even make changes to the niche map. Attention contains the bulk of our desire, and it is quite able to change the structure of the thought patterns within the niche map.

Attention is the most active and energy consuming part of the brain. It is unlike the mostly passive process of memory storage and selective stabilisation, which requires little energy to perform. Attention can alter the selective stabilisation process to make us take different paths. Attention uses a lot of energy. The brain has 2% of our mass but uses 20% of our energy, mostly due to thinking, or where we put our attention. Attention allows humans to become more aware.

If attention is low it will be accepting, and unable to break the bounds of the niche map and its entrenched rules. Most information we receive we simply accept. It passes into the conscious where its impact eventually blends unquestionably into the subconscious. Most information goes through without attracting our attention. A person living in a desert would not think about a barren landscape devoid of trees, as it would be so usual. A person bought up in a forest and seeing that same landscape would think, even though the visual stimulation was the same. Any information that we allow through our conscious without offering some attention, will pass through unimpeded and contribute to the developing pattern of selective stabilisation. We can alter the natural process of selective stabilisation by paying greater attention to detail.

The passive mechanism of selective stabilisation produces most of the tracks in our niche map. Attention evolved to let us reassess small areas of the niche map and effect repairs where needed. Without attention our energy will be as a trickle that can only flow within the deepest valleys of the conscious landscape. But if we can send that energy over the landscape as a flood, then the valleys will fill allowing our energy to flow elsewhere. Attention can flood into other less used courses. If attention finds those previously forgotten or unrealised courses better or more interesting than expected, attention will focus and make us remember. The once unusual course will deepen under this flow of energy, and become the new course that is natural and most easily remembered in that niche map region. We could begin to change our instincts.

However, attention is essentially a repair mechanism that stimulates us into action when we see mistake or unfilled need. At times we are capable of great attention, but at other times we see little wrong and offer no questions. Our attention needs to work much harder and incisively than before, because our niche maps are now fundamentally flawed. Attention must chase up every detail, and assume nothing.

Attention makes us more aware. The greater energy that attention can send at any time will spread over a wider network in our consciousness. This gives us more points of comparison during our conscious flow, and so improves our awareness.

Concentration is a further step into attention that can focus our energy and change the instinctive flow of the neural network. Concentration can confine and hold energy over the same point for a longer time, to make further variations.

We can use attention and concentration to chase up wisp and background feelings and sensations that we might normally overlook. We can use them to wrest the control for our thoughts from instinctive flow towards more considered and aware flows in other areas. We can use attention to help us listen. The degree to which we can control our attention is a good measure of how aware we might become. It shows how well we can place attention on different areas, that we might not otherwise look upon instinctively. We can increase our attention through wit, as wit helps us recognise our fundamental mistakes. Wit is the process of putting more attention into different ways of looking at the same thing.

Attention works within the mind. The mind is like a work area on the niche map, within which attention can move about quite freely, concentrate, and at times defy the rules of the prevailing landscape. The mind can direct attention to different parts on its canvas, before those parts are forgotten or lost. The mind holds attention, and also other short-term memories and recent experiences. The mind is like a neural lake, already awash and easily tipped to look at itself from any point with attention. The mind is the closest we have to being able to create a new virgin landscape upon which we can imprint fresh pathways and ideas.

We can make our comparisons most easily in the mind. If attention can run through several points and memories quickly, they will all become highlighted and stored in the mind. The mind can then compare those different parts. In the mind, so full of energy, attention can most easily jump in novel ways from one pathway to the next. How aware our attention is, will determine how aware or how much varied information our mind can hold at once. Maintaining attention is like racing around trying to tweak various pathways here and there, keeping them all afloat long enough for the mind to grapple with them at once. The mind can then look for more combinations of comparisons and improve the arrangement of its information. Attention can change and expand our frame of mind. If the mind vaguely seems as though it might have found something interesting, then it is powerful enough to have attention race over to the area for a closer look. The mind is the arena that attention can create for itself by keeping a variety of thoughts highlighted at once.

But the mind can still only work on those parts of the niche map to which it becomes aware. There is a limit to how far back into the network of neurones the mind can penetrate. That limit is mindrules. The mind can only recall long-term memories and short-term memories, not mindrules. That is too deep a layer for attention to penetrate and know. It is the realm of the instinct. We must penetrate the mindrule barrier in another way. We can know they are there without actually seeing them. We must know our mindrules by their symptoms.

Attention usually takes the simpler pathways in the landscape, finding it easier to stay within the network of valleys. We must give attention more energy and a new twist, if it is to try and find some new direction, up and over the more difficult hills. Indeed, the mind requires inspiration and insight if it is to do the most difficult and defy the constraints of the niche map. Inspiration expands the niche map, while insight improves the understanding within the niche map. With inspiration we discover a wider realm or higher target that we did not realise possible. With insight we find simpler ways to find new meaning in what we have.

4.12 Feelings

Desire is the energy that we send into the cortex for consideration and instruction. Most of the energy goes into our consciousness and mind. It drives us to attempt interaction. After interaction, the energy returns to the pleasure centre as feeling. We usually pay attention to our feelings. Feeling enables us to register the level of success gained through the interaction. The feeling information feeds back into the pleasure centre via the pleasure centre's network that is distributed throughout the cortex. The pleasure centre judges the level of interactive success by feeling how many parts of the cortex were stimulated relative to the amount of desire or expectation sent. Feeling is sensory information that describes where the energy found itself after it travelled the cortex network, the model to our world. The progress of energy along the desire-feeling loop is what the brain uses to monitor and adjust our behavioural performance.

If the feeling we get back from an interaction is pleasurable, then that interaction filled or exceeded the expectations of our desire. That is what we want to feel. The more neural pathways that the same burst of desire can stimulate the more involved must be our various adaptations, and the more likely we are interacting successfully. We evolved to equate pleasure with success. Through pleasure, we see more possibility within each interaction. Being able to sense or read much information and possibility from small input puts us on the road to success. It is a way of making the best out of what we have. It is something that evolution can work with and finely tune.

When the feeling that comes back after interaction is pleasing, we will be happy to continue sending our drive for interaction through that same cortex as pure desire. It will mean that our interaction is going well, and that we are in tune with our niche. There will be no reason to change our approach. Indeed, we might increase our activity in that same direction so that we can send even more desire to its reward.

However, when we meet an obstacle upon attempting interaction, our energy will be blocked. Our desire will not travel very far through the cortex. The energy that returns to the pleasure centre will register a feeling less fulfilling and complete. If the quality or interactiveness of energy that comes back is below a certain comfort level, then the feeling we get will be below what we recognise as pleasure. The result will be an empty feeling. We may feel sad. The object targeted for interaction did not respond well or as openly as we would have desired. The link or bond did not get very far.

The function of feeling is to modify and direct our future expectations and attempts at interaction, so that pleasure is optimised and emptiness minimised. It is a process that allows the cortex to balance what we want with we can expect realistically. The cortex will build up a profile of those targets for interaction that produce emptiness. The cortex might teach pure desire that it should not always expect good interaction in that direction again. True desire always has an underlying need for quality of interaction in as broad a circle as possible. But how it goes about best achieving that state of perfection or comfort is a matter of trial and error with its cortex. It is up to the cortex, its organisation, and the feelings it returns, to tell our desire what it can and cannot do.

If interaction in certain areas is consistently empty, the cortex should warn desire much earlier, so that its expectation will not lead to sadness. The neural network should place some pathways carrying that warning information ever closer to the pleasure centre, so that desire can read the warning more quickly. Eventually, desire could read that information almost as soon as it enters the cortex. The warning sign might move from something that we suspect in our consciousness, to something that we assume in our subconscious. Those warning pathways eventually become blocks that instinctively divert our desire.

Desire does not know how good it should feel. We have to learn the upper limit of pleasure that we could expect from life. The instinctive mindrule blocks that we learn imprint us with their upper limits. How quickly mindrules can divert desire from its original course will determine our level of expectation. We learn our awareness of what desire could reach by making attempts and seeing the results. Those lessons can impress us deeply, even though the rules we learn might not maintain their relevance during rapid niche change.

By registering how an interaction feels, desire will decide if it is encouraged to take that route again. This combination of desire and feel gradually guides us towards our most comfortable interacting position. We will learn the set of pathways that can best cater to our needs. We will use that information more often, and entrench those pathways more deeply into our mindrules so that we carry them about with us instinctively. This comfortable position becomes our world. We learn to take it for granted.

The interaction desire produces the feelings of pleasure or emptiness in us through its measurements of interactive quality. Pain is a different kind of feeling that evolved to have a strong impact on the flow of our desire and behaviour. Pain can have a strong and urgent modifying effect on us. Pain makes us feel hurt, rather than emptiness. While the pleasure centre in the hypothalamus produces emptiness, pain can be sent from all other parts of the body. Pain has evolved to be a feeling that can more directly and decisively affect the pleasure centre in its pursuit of pleasure. We do not need to feel pain in the cortex, which is why doctors can operate on it without anaesthetic. Pain modifies the release of desire instead. The feeling of pain usually signals a more pressing request to the cortex that must be attended to immediately. Our feelings of emptiness and pleasure can usually wait, after the situation of pain is resolved. Pain can quickly end exploration in a certain direction. Pain has evolved mainly for physical protection, so that we know when to stop attempting some interaction that is physically damaging.

Surprise is another major category of feeling that impacts on the pleasure centre and cortex. Surprise arises through the senses, when they suddenly place a sense or feeling in the cortex for which we were not prepared. The surprise feeling did not arise from an assessment of our own desire. No desire on our part was sent towards the interaction. Therefore, we do not have a way to measure the impact or meaning of the surprise. It may take a few seconds for us to work out how to judge the surprise. To hasten our assessment, we evolved the reflex to jump upon surprise. This sudden action will help us quickly gather some spirit energy from the body that can pass into the cortex and provide us with the means of measurement. The desiring energy that we send after the surprise will either succeed or fail. Then we will discover if the surprise was pleasant, or something to fear.

There are many other feelings that we can have, but most of these build upon the four basic feelings of pleasure, emptiness, pain and surprise. There can be many degrees and mixtures of these four main ingredients. Other feelings are produced when these initial feelings are processed further to gain more information. For example, surprise might turn into a feeling of humour, fear, curiosity or excitement, depending upon our past experience with similar surprises, and depending upon how the rest of the interaction proceeds. Pain might turn into a feeling of anger or hate. Pleasure might turn into a feeling of ecstasy, fun or love. Emptiness might turn into feelings of sadness, loneliness or depression.

4.13 Expression

We cannot ignore the way we feel. It is a powerful force that can control our output of desire and drive. It shapes the development of our personality, and is a most powerful modifier of our behaviour. Our feelings have such control that they can also control the way we look. Each feeling can produce its own expression that is very hard to resist. Different feelings can make us cry, smile, frown, blush, laugh, grimace or snarl.

Expressions have become highly developed in humans, more so than in other animals. This reflects how strongly our behaviour is now influenced by the way the cortex feels. The cortex depends greatly on the guiding hand of the interaction desire and its associated feelings. It takes much feeling to guide the development of our cortex.

Expressions are natural and very revealing about how we feel. It takes much training to hide them. If the aim of an individual were to be selfish and self-selecting, then such revealing expressions would make life difficult. Whenever you were planning a selfish or deceptive act, a laugh, grimace or blush could uncover the plan. However, if the aim of an animal is to self-enhance and feel good, so that the cortex learns its best interactive arrangement, then there will be little concern about what the expression reveals. The feeling that we have upon interaction will be more important to us, as a measure of cortex quality, than trying to find a false position where we must hide our feelings.

Expression evolved as a way to show others how we feel about an interaction, so that they can add their view to what we feel, and perhaps improve our judgement or lot. Expression is especially useful to a gregarious species. Facial expression, gesturing, and vocal communication are all major human activities. The results of our communications will often help us decide whether to take our feelings seriously, or ignore them and try again. The awareness that others gain about how we feel can also change the situation for us, so that it will become more satisfying. A person crying will be soothed, or a person blushing will be forgiven. Laughing might calm a situation and keep everyone happy. An expression of anger might stop someone from being annoying or harmful.

In more simple times, just expressing a feeling was often enough to get that feeling resolved so that desire could find more pleasure. In a close knit tribe, there would be much concern and support revolving around how each tribal member felt. However today, there are many complications and differences between people that a simple expression cannot overcome. Simple expression now often does not work.

Sometimes, simply expressing a feeling can be fulfilling in its own right. It can become a means of releasing unaccomplished or tentative energy. Expression is a way of completing the accomplishment of an interaction. It is something we can do, to try and resolve the desire. It can be soothing to smile, and especially to laugh. Expressing grief can be an important step in repairing or finding a new lease of life after loss. Expressing anger or talking about a fear can also be helpful and soothing.

We only need to express when our feelings are not quite as fulfilling as we would like. They come when we do not feel comfortable or natural. They are a part of our attempt to make sense of our feelings, and find a way back to a more comfortable and pleasurable life. The aim of expression is to adjust our lot back to the condition where we do not have to express. Expression tries to adjust us back to where our desire can be wild.

The interaction desire that is naturally filled requires no expression. The wild expression would be relaxed and comfortable. The wild look is common to animals. It reveals a natural strength, beauty and tranquil receptiveness. The interaction desire can only be completely filled through wildness. In a state of perfect wildness, attunement develops to such a level that what we feel would be easy for others to read and understand. We would be completely open and direct, what we feel would be seen through the eyes of the 'common soul'. There would be no need to express or even smile. Everything would be instinctively understood.

We have some awareness of the wild look. Models try to mimic the face, and may not smile in their pose. However, I think it is too early for anyone to do the "I'm too beautiful to smile look" just yet.

Many of the expressions that people make can be found in other animals as well. Many animals can show anger, fear, sadness, pleasure, pain and surprise. However, there are two more expressions found only in humans. If we can find the reason for the evolution of these expressions, we should learn more about our own true nature.

4.14 Blushing

The uniqueness of blushing in humans is perhaps the most striking example of the extreme to which our species evolved in its quest to remain open about how we feel. It shows that we are meant to be a socially bonded and aware species.

Blushing is designed to signal embarrassment and personal mistake. For those who say that humans evolved to be naturally selfish and deceitful, the involuntary response of blushing must be very difficult to explain. A selfish and deceitful human should in times of embarrassment, withhold their surprise and play along, to pretend that they are not really mistaken or out of their depth. They should keep that information to themselves. Then perhaps they could find a way to get on top of the situation. If only the blush did not come.

We blush for several reasons. We can blush when there is a suggestion of sexual interest in someone who is supposed to be only an acquaintance. To our coy embarrassment, the blush can reveal that there is some truth to the suggestion. Skin reddening is often a sign of sexual arousal. Therefore the blush might have evolved as a signal to enhance sexual attractiveness. However, the blush can occur in many more situations as well.

A child can blush well before they develop sexual desire. A heterosexual man might blush when talking only to other men. A person who was once caught being naughty can blush with shame if that time is recounted. If we tell a lie, but realise at the same time that the other person already knows the truth, the blush can appear and we can have guilt written all over our face. If we recount a personal experience to a large group of people, we might be shy and blush.

The common factor in all of these examples is that we do not feel as natural and honest as we would like, and wish we could improve ourselves so that we will not be embarrassed again. The blush reveals that we do not know how to become more natural in the interaction, even though we have the desire. It shows a lack of experience or knowledge of how to be comfortable in an interaction where we would like to be comfortable. Blushing involves a reddening of the face when the surface capillaries dilate. It may include hiding or lowering the face, and averting the eyes. These are all a part of the signal that we cannot participate directly and honestly.

Blushing reveals that there is more feeling to a person than they can publicly demonstrate or explain. The desire that we send feels embarrassed or out on a limb. We are unsure how to continue in the same vein as others, and participate in the conversation, even though the desire to do so is aroused.

At times the blush might seem cute. The blushing bride holds the promise of a bond that will be tighter than she can publicly reveal. The blush can be mimicked by applying make-up, thereby suggesting that a heightened level of arousal is possible. The blush or make-up is effectively saying 'I have more to offer than I am able to reveal here under these circumstances'.

According to Darwin, blushing occurs only in humans, and then not until age 2-3 (Ekman, 1973). A 2-3 year old can stare at a stranger with no 'self-attention'. This young age reflects the natural state of humans, that is lost when mindrules begin to gain their control. Most 2-3 year olds do not strongly realise that they should be different to others, so they have nothing to hide and no differences to second guess and overcome. After this age, we begin to learn that there are limits to what we can interact with comfortably. There are limits to our desire. We begin to feel alienated and restricted. The blush is a sign that we are feeling difficulty or restriction in how we are allowed to behave.

The blushing person does not feel comfortable during the event, and dislikes it for what it reveals. But throughout our evolution it was more important to the survival of the tribe that people knew when we felt uneasy yet wanted to belong. The blush is a sign of discomfort that we share with others who might help us to amend. It shows that our mind is receptive and willing to change for what should be a more natural situation. The blush might cause others to make more allowances for us.

Blushing is a natural signal, so some sense of not belonging must have been natural during the later stages of our evolution. Blushing feels uncomfortable, and evolved to try and drive us back towards the state of wildness or social attunement where we feel no 'self-attention' or difference. Blushing evolved as a signal that greater honesty and naturalness is desired, but cannot be fluently expressed to the group. The blush does not elicit an aggressive response, unless conscious deceit was involved in hiding true feelings. The worst that a blush might do is to give the impression that we are naive and unpractised, or are harbouring unrealistic hopes. Blushing usually elicits a response of kindness from others, as they try to explain or bring the bond back to a level where it can feel comfortable.

4.15 Laughter

Laughter is the curious release of energy as noise. Most simply, it expresses happiness and joy. It is found in very few species, being confined mainly to humans and a few apes such as the chimpanzee. Laughter is produced when plans, thoughts, expectations or institutions are caught out as being less well founded than originally thought. It reveals a mistake that is fundamental. The line of thought being taken cannot be reasoned out because it needs repair at some earlier stage. The mistake reveals that our efforts are flawed or exaggerated.

Laughter is a signal that our expected loop of interaction has been caught out. Desire has nowhere to go because it suddenly realises that its course is fundamentally flawed. Laughter releases that caught energy, allowing us to recognise the mistake and not take it seriously. Laughter eases the pain or loss of having nowhere fulfilling to go, by offering our energy a pleasurable outlet in expression. Laughter is like a desire that follows its pathway but comes to the brink of a broken bridge. The desiring energy reaches a mistake that began earlier without it realising, so that desire now has no further connection to follow. Laughter lets this pent up desire disassociate from its track, and burst directly out of the mind as the raw energy that sounds like laughter.

The laugh allows us to complete the interaction loop by providing us with an activity that can release our trapped energy. The laugh rhythmically contracts various muscles, giving us an activity that is pleasurable because it allows us to become involved once more in the successful release of our energy. Desire does not need to convert itself into an emotion that must remove a block in anger to complete the loop. Desire does not have to become overwhelmed or depressed by the mistake. We enjoy laughing. It means that the mistake was not damaging. The most important concern of the interaction desire, above being right, is that we have a good set of responses that will let us live and interact well. Laughter signals that we are above the mistakes and blocks of life. We are sufficiently accomplished to feel comfortable even in mistake. Laughter is an expression that is fulfilling.

To be able to laugh means that we can see alternative views. It means that we are not trapped by instinctive thought that can only see one way. If our original course fails, we can change. Laughter signifies that our mind has raised its consciousness to a level that is aware of other options, sufficient to see that our own original option was wrong. It shows that we can think about possibilities, and attempt to follow one over another. Laughter evolved to let us see more easily that our assumptions can be flawed. Laughter recognises that our thinking cannot always be right. Laughter needed to become pleasurable, so that we do not become dissuaded from the risk of exploring new alternatives.

Laughter evolved at a time when our species lived in tightly bonded groups where minds were more able than now to share. The best laughter comes from a feeling of equality. Laughter can help to bond a group of people together, because it generates the feeling that mutual acceptance and equality is more important than our rules. Laughter is especially easy amongst children, because they still relate openly with each other, and do not take their differences seriously. Hunter-gatherers also spend much of their time talking and laughing, because the unit is cohesive and sharing. Laughter is a sign that we accept people as they are and are not too nervous about their differences. Those who we laugh with, we accept. Laughter extends friendship and warmth. It encourages the feeling that differences and disrelatabilities are minor and can be overcome by the equal application of wit. Our interaction desire remains stronger than our mindrules.

We often find it easier to laugh in a group. The group encourages the feeling that mistakes can be taken less seriously. A happy audience, or even its illusion through canned laughter, can make a joke work better. A group laughing together can help keep desire flowing in similar spirit. It is important in a group to remember that a common binding desire is more important than mindrule attitudes of difference. It is sociable to laugh.

While laughter grew up in societies where people felt equal, today's humour can sometimes hurt. The more individual people become, the greater will be the differences in our sense of humour. Similar minds tend to laugh at similar things. But today minds cannot share as well, and mindrules under stress raise the number of items that are off limits to laughter. There are certain blocks that mindrules do not let us cross, so we do not accept humour in those directions. Some mistakes do not seem funny. Some might see the mistake differently to another, so what is funny to us might not be funny to another. They do not see the fundamental error that made us laugh. Our own laughter emerges between a balance of what we have to accept, and what we can recognise as repairable mistake. This is a balance that can be different between people, and change through history. At different times people have been more or less able to laugh at the monarchy, races, religion, and natural afflictions.

If we have less concern about other people or races than ourselves then we might laugh at their mistakes more readily. This can give differences of humour in society, such as the racist joke. For laughter to repair and be well meaning, it should be applied from a position of equality. We should assume that we are as fundamentally wrong as our target. Therefore, an Irishman is better able to tell an Irish joke, because it is more likely that they are being equal in mind with their target. If the humour is attempted from a position of superiority, then we have no intention of sharing, and our joke will be racist and wrong.

The level and type of mistake that makes us see humour varies. We have to be more careful where we laugh today. There is much sensitivity in a world of individuals. If the mistake is simple and no one hurt, then laughter can be uninhibited and simple. If the mistake dashes hopes, the humour might be ironic. If we are unsure that the mistake is harmless to all, the laugh might be nervous. If the mistake by another should have been obvious to them, then we may employ sarcasm. If the mistake is dangerous it might be chilling and we will not laugh. Cartoons and comic movies extend the range of funny situations that we can laugh at, when they exaggerate or depict situations that are obviously not harmful. Then laughing at them is less dangerous.

Laughter does not know if it was right or wrong to take something less seriously. Therefore laughter can be cruel, justifiable, kind, crass, ignorant, revealing, helpful, repairing. Simple laughter innocently assumes that we are all equal. It is non-judgmental, but assumes that we are all sharing our laughter fluently within a like minded group. While we might like to laugh, we might not like to be the subject of laughter, as it can mean that there is supposed to be a mistake about us that we do not see. However, not being able to take a joke about ourselves also shows a lack of strength and wit. It shows that we are being dominated by our own mindrules, because we think we are above any real flaw. We might be too precious.

How deeply can our wit go? It should go all the way. We need to aim our laughter at ourselves most deeply before we can find the right way to laugh at others. If we can laugh at our own predicament, we will also begin to see the options that will allow us to get out of our own traps. Laughter increases the receptivity of the mind to new alternatives. It helps to keep mindrules pliable rather than serious and set.

Because humour evolved during relatively stable niches, it naturally expects to find mistakes that are small and unimportant. Laughter assumes that our true natures have the upper hand. Laughter itself does not determine right and wrong, as it can itself be mistakenly applied. It cannot detect all assumptions. We need to listen to others when we find that what we laugh at is not supported or causes pain. Today, perhaps curiously, laughter needs to be applied with wit. Humour that is also witty is best, as it takes into account the modern truth that large mistake and delusion occurs where we do not see.

Laughter should take itself less seriously. Humour and laughter were designed for stable niches. The addition of wit is needed during rapid niche change to enhance our laughter to the point where we realise that we should also laugh at ourselves.

To laugh at ourselves is an important sign of maturity, grace and wit. It is also a sign that we are able to consider alternatives, and reveals a higher awareness and understanding than if we did not laugh. Laughter encourages wisdom and receptivity, and it helps keep desire true. Mindrules can turn a laughing child into a serious adult, unless they develop wit. Indeed, desire likes to laugh, because it is a way of showing mindrules who has control over the mind. Desire laughs for the sake of producing good interaction, while mindrules are designed to take their work seriously.

5. Human nature lost

5.1 Emotion

The interaction desire seeks to travel through the niche map in the cortex in a way that feels pleasurable. The level of success that desire finds in its search for pleasure, we measure through our feelings. If our feeling of success is below expectation, then we judge the interaction to be painful or empty. Such a feeling will tell us that the natural flow of our desire was blocked. The interaction desire starts its journey through the cortex wild and natural. It does not like to find blocks and restrictions, whether self-imposed or externally imposed. These blocks narrow the breadth of stimulation within the cortex that the pleasure centre can measure. There is a limit to how often desire will turn away from its original course, and accept the less fulfilling outcome. This brings us to emotion.

If desire finds that its pathway is blocked, then it will have to try and resolve that block before it can expect to find pleasure in that direction again. The way desire first tries to resolve block is to turn itself into emotion. This conversion is an ancient reaction that is common to many other species as well. The more refined method of attempting to remove block by converting desire into thought and reason appeared later in our species.

Emotions have always been misinterpreted by our species. They are generally thought of as being inherited, and an essential part of our basic drives. They seem important for survival, especially against struggle, and occur in many other higher animals as well. In the past, emotions have been thought of as arising from some specific instinct that is an inherent part of the brain. However, emotions are a function of what an individual thinks and sees, rather than what a specific body organ needs. All instincts in the cortex are learnt, other than the cortex instinct. We have no other need for emotion, than to resolve the interaction desire. The interaction desire is the single most primal force in our cortex, and while it is wild it is happy and has no need to become an emotion. If the interaction desire lived in a niche where it could be totally wild, then we would never produce an emotion. Emotions only begin to develop when the interaction desire meets block. In the wild, block is rare. However, we feel emotions strongly because in our world block is common.

Of course, emotions often feel intense, and can appear before our conscious reason has a chance to know why they arise to overtake our thoughts. Therefore, emotions can feel primal as well. However, that feeling arises only because desire can bring emotions to bear as soon as it enters the cortex. Desire begins to construct its emotions within the subconscious, long before our consciousness becomes aware of what is happening.

The ways that emotion tries to resolve block are as many and varied as there are conscious and subconscious interpretations on how we live. At various times, some people have described some hundreds of emotions as residing in our species. However, such a complicated tangle of various emotional tissues would be difficult to inherit. Biologically, there is a far simpler way to produce emotions. The interaction desire can produce many changes to the pathways being learnt within the cortex. Three emotions or one hundred emotions are all within its power.

Emotions arise from each person's assessment of their own situation. Fear might arise in one person if they think that a snake is slimy and wicked, but not in another who sees the snake as beautiful. Something that turns one person to anger might not affect another in the same way. One person might never know the joy that another can experience. Emotions are highly personal, and depend upon the assessment that each person makes of their surroundings. It is dependent upon what we expect out of life, and the conditions under which we are used to living. It depends upon how our interaction desire has been taught its blocks.

Emotion can be a powerful tool when it perceives a block. It gathers its force from the interaction desire. The more convinced the interaction desire is of its block, the more powerful that emotion becomes. The interaction desire is usually free and diverse in the application of its energies, but under block, it can focus those energies into a powerful targeted stream. Emotion can wreck great changes in our surroundings and life. Emotion can shift us into a new interacting position. They can burn bridges or discover new bonds. They can put us into a position where our life becomes comfortable and pleasurable once more. A display of emotion may then allow us to simply be ourselves. However, emotions can also go wrong.

Emotion can strongly affect the blocks that appear in our life. If a block is imposed on us, we may have no time to find a way around the block through creativity and thought. The course to take may be unclear, or the block may suddenly appear and seem threatening. Emotion can hasten our response in the face of indecision, without us having to think. It can harness our energies in a way that can make us powerful enough to overcome the block. Emotion can move like a flood of energy through our cortex, and focus itself upon any small hesitation or block. Emotion can find new opportunities. With so much flooding energy, emotions can transverse our cortex network to explore less instinctive pathways that we might normally ignore. Emotion can magnify small differences between pathways, and plough new tracks for our future energies. Emotion can use off-the-road tracks that were dusty and overgrown.

In the gelatine model of the mindrule landscape, we normally find only the deepest grooves comfortable to follow. But under an emotional flood, we find it easier to see the shallower grooves that diverge from the main highways of our niche map. Some of the emotion might still follow the main highway, but some will also spill over into the side tracks. If that new track looks promising, the rest of the emotion will follow and support that path. It can overflow from an entrenched groove, and take a course we normally might not favour. When emotion decides to follow these new outlets, it floods along the track, deepening and entrenching as it goes. Because emotion carries with it such a concentration of energy, any minor track that it decides to take will become more entrenched as a result. This erodes the initial block or hesitation, making it easier to travel that way again. For example, once someone under anger finally decides to lash out and hurt another, and for them the result seems good, then that violent course might be easier for them to take again next time.

There is a ready ability to convert the energy of desire into emotion. No matter how attuned animals are with their wild niche, there will always be some amount of desire that cannot flow uninterrupted as original desire. An evolved niche is in balance with other niches in the ecosystem. It is not one sided. The needs in one niche must balance with the needs of those in another. Wildness offers optimal performance and efficiency, not guaranteed success on all occasions. There will be times of danger, competition, failure, when the ability to interact according to the highest level of interactive desire is blocked. Emotion evolved as the first back up response to desire. Thinking and attention to detail evolved in us much later

Some animals are capable of emotion, while others are not. Emotion is useful to those species that can learn and modify their instincts. Emotion allows an animal to take a course that for them is less natural or comfortable. It helps drive an animal to overcome blocks, if they are present. The more instincts that a species must learn and modify, the more need there is for emotion. Insects lack emotion. They have no cortex that needs to be measured and organised by an interaction desire. Their instincts are mostly inherited rather than learnt. Lizards also seem to need little emotion. They are highly tested and evolved creatures, and seem particularly wild. Perhaps only one percent of their desire need ever turn into emotion during the course of their normal life. Mammals seem to be the most emotional of the animals. Perhaps five percent of their desire is in regular need of conversion into emotion. Mammals depend much more on instinct learning, so emotional resolution of the interaction desire is more important to them. Our own species is capable of much learning, and therefore potentially many mistakes as well. Our own natural level of emotion may be around ten percent of desire. However, with so many blocks in our world today, our current rate of conversion from desire into emotion and its offshoots is probably around fifty percent even more.

Emotion allows us to explore alternative routes that might eventually but more indirectly meet the expectation of the underlying interaction desire. Emotion can help an animal adapt to a niche that is less natural or slightly stressful to the way it is designed to live. An animal can resolve or remove blocks with emotion, and then move back into its more wild and natural state where it no longer needs emotion. The main aim of emotion is not to reach emotional fulfilment, but to fulfil the interaction desire that lies beneath. When we find a way to meet desire more directly, the animal will discard its emotions.

There are two main approaches that desire can take towards our blocks, to try and make our future interactions more pleasurable. The approach we take depends upon how capable we feel about moving the block. If we think that the block can be moved, then we will give an active emotional response (Wortman and Loftus, 1992: 330). We will try to move the block by harming it, reducing its value, arguing with it, avoiding it or tricking it. This approach produces emotions such as anger, hate, jealousy, and deceit. We use these emotions when we know the identity of the block. Our knowledge gives our emotion a definite block to target and overcome. Because these emotions know what to do, the body becomes active and increases the amount of energy that it sends into the cortex to deliver that emotion.

However, if our active emotions are denied their targets, and do not know who to fight, their tension can build. The emotional energy can continue to rise, until some trigger unleashes the emotion and it tries to force the issue. Our emotion may lash out at some innocent bystander.

The other main approach that our desire can take emotionally is when our blocks seem immovable. A block may seem particularly strong and entrenched, or the cause of the blocking feeling may be unknown. Then desire feels unable to act and produce a result. This leads to emotions that have a low sense of activation (Wortman and Loftus, 1992: 330). Our feelings about the block do not show us a way out, so desire does not know what to do. It may just emotionally express the existence of its feeling. That expression may be poorly focused and not very active. The emotion may simply reflect the feeling. We may feel sad and act sad by crying, with little chance of resolution in our mind. In the face of uncertainty, desire may turn away from using its typical emotions, and plough most of its energies into expression and mood.

Emotion with low activation does not know how to overcome its blocks. This allows the wall of block to compound, and further contain our energy. The energy will continue to feel sad. The body can try to compensate by sending the cortex less energy, so that there will be less desire that must turn into sadness. With less energy trying to explore the cortex, we will feel less pain and emptiness. The mind and body will progressively try to turn itself off. We may sleep a lot. However, while we are conscious some desire must flow. If we cannot resolve the block, we will not be able to escape the empty feelings entirely. Therefore, the mind may think of further negative solutions to its failed interaction desire, such as suicide or escape.

Our own feeling about how we can resolve our blocks divides our emotions into those of high and low activation. Emotion can be further divided according to what effect they are likely to have on others. Our attempts at emotion may be harmful to others, or helpful to others. If our feeling is sad, we may use anger as our emotional attempt to resolve the block. This may result in harm and will be a negative emotion. Alternatively, we may try to use hope to overcome the block. The result will be more open and honest, and may have a broader positive effect.

While emotions can be called positive or negative, they are in fact all positive attempts to resolve the situation of block as best they can. What is positive or negative is the likely effect our emotions will have on the broader community. If we take our blocks seriously, then our emotions will focus more strongly and single mindedly on those blocks. We will become correspondingly less concerned about the effect that our emotions have on other people. Our emotions may become negative towards our environment. Our emotions will target the block in a negative way that relinquishes all bonds and connections. If however the blocks of life are taken less seriously, we may feel some connection or sympathy for the environment that produces those blocks. We may be less willing to destroy our blocks, so look instead for ways to simply turn them around. Our emotional attempts at resolution will be more positive, and try to change the block by improving the knowledge or outlook surrounding the block.

The energy that lives in the brain as emotion is keen to return to a state of organisation that lets us feel the ultimate completeness of our interactions. Emotion is keen to turn back into desire. When emotion finds a new outlet that appears able to transverse through the current set of blocks, our emotions will become more active, and they will also feel more positive at being able to surmount the blocks. The new outlet might be a new job, a new friend, or a new possession. Positive emotions can effloresce and bubble through that opening. The reservoir of pent up desire might decide to travel through that one outlet. More energy might flow through that outlet than it deserves. The positive emotion might overlook the errors and real worth of the outlet, ignore other areas and outlets on the niche map that are in need of repair, and concentrate on just the one outlet. The outlet might become our salvation. But with such enthusiasm, we can overemphasise the value of the outlet, and make it phoney. We can make it illusory, in our effort to fill our dreams. We can become single minded or fanatical about the outlet, to the detriment of other things. The emotional outlet might become a passion, religion, or love.

Positive emotions arise mostly from positive feelings, but the path that any emotion travels is still less stable than the path that a properly expressed interaction desire can take. Positive emotions do not always last, and do not always remain positive. They can readily convert into negative emotion. Love can turn to hate. While our niche map is poorly organised, we will have the potential to produce emotions of all kinds. An emotional person can have mood swings and emotional swings, from the positive to the negative. They swing from one side of the block to the other. So while positive emotions feel good, they can have a down side. They leave the gap open for negative emotions to appear. Our institutions help to keep our positive emotions positive. We have churches or marriages that give added structure to our positive emotions.

Because the pleasure centre is so important to us, what it feels will control most strongly what we do in our next attempt at interaction. Therefore emotions and feelings are often considered to be the same thing, even though they describe different sides of the interaction equation. We might feel angry, and produce an emotion of anger. Feel hate, and express the emotion of hate. It takes much training to intervene in this relationship, perhaps with reason or attitude. However, only when we can intervene between the automatic conversion of feeling into its closest emotion can we begin to explore greater possibility. Humans have this potential, when they see that the desire for accomplishment can often be better filled in ways other than emotional.

While most emotions express their feelings directly, some feelings cannot be fully expressed. The feeling of frustration does not have a strong emotion because it must hold itself back. When we relieve frustration, it is usually through borrowed emotional reactions such as anger or hate. The feeling of frustration is trapped, so cannot express itself directly. Trapped feelings are more likely to produce emotions different to their feeling. They tend to lie.

Emotions can have expression associated with them, but that is only because the same feeling is driving both expression and emotion. It is our feelings that trigger our expressions, not our emotions. Our feelings can do several things. They can make us turn desire into emotion, produce expression, and trigger other physiological changes to the body. Through our feelings we learn how to tie our emotions, expressions, and bodily actions together to make our emotional delivery more effective. The physiological changes can help us express the emotion, help the body ready itself for an emotional action, and produce changes in the brain that allow the emotion to take charge. For example, during anger, certain regions of the brain become activated. Various signals are sent from the learnt anger region of the brain. The expressions of the face reflect anger. The body prepares and the muscles tense ready for action. The brain becomes bathed in chemicals such as norepinephrine (similar to adrenaline) (Wortman and Loftus, 1992: 325), that makes it easier for the emotion to flood through the cortex, and perhaps look for ignored neural pathways that are of certain kind.

For each emotion that the feeling urges us to try, we learn all of the additional gear needed to express it properly. Each emotion needs to draw upon certain actions and regions of the body to make itself effective. Therefore not surprisingly, when an emotion is triggered, it is accompanied by the stimulation of a variety of other neural pathways that lead to these other bodily signals and processes. Each emotion will need to be associated with a core set of neural pathways. Each emotion will assemble itself and find its place within the cortex where it is most efficient at delivering all of the signals that it needs to make an impact. This forces each emotion into a certain position within the cortex. These are known as our emotional centres. They are usually found in the same place for each person, and might even be in similar places in other species. However, the existence of emotional centres is not evidence that emotions are inherited. Emotional centres signify that the best position from which to learn the coordination of each emotion is similar in all brains. Desires are inherited, while emotions are learnt.

A person that can keep receptivity open and wild at all times would not have any blocks to weave around. Receptivity is a state of mind that does not see block, because it accepts all information. Therefore to live, a receptive animal must grow or rise to a level above the block. A receptive animal can maintain a pleasurable feeling even during conditions that for others might seem adverse. As long as we can keep the niche map open to wildness and free of block, our interaction desire will continue to find pathways that are harmonious, strong, and positive under all conditions. Receptivity places a person in a far stronger position than any emotion can achieve. It allows our interaction desire to remain wild. A true desire properly expressed feels wild. It incorporates a much wider range of experiences and possibilities than the more specific emotions.

The cortex is very large in our species, and so there are many interventions possible between the pleasure centre's outlet and inlet points. We have sufficient cortex to allow thinking. With thinking, we can change the automatic response of our mindrules and find new ways to fill the interaction desire. If we could understand all the forces involved in our interactions, we could launch ourselves into a state of mind that knew one hundred percent wildness. We could fill our desires in a way better than even our stone-age ancestors could and other species knew.

5.2 Mood

When desire is blocked, our first attempt to resolve that block is as emotion. If emotion does not work and we are still trapped, then it might be time to change the condition of the neural pathways over which our energy must move. We can do this with mood. As mood, the energy in desire can alter the condition of the cortex by causing the release of certain mood chemicals. This changes the nature of the niche map. It will let future energy take a different course through the niche map due to the changed conditions that the mood produces. The energy can look for solutions on the niche map from a different perspective. Mood has evolved as a further method by which the mind can attempt to resolve block, when that block cannot be removed so simply with emotion.

Mood changes the conditions of the tracks in the cortex, so they become more slippery, rough, hard, or easier to traverse. Changing mood can be like changing the temperature of the wires in the neural network. Mood may act like a lubricant or a dampener. A different mood might change our mind from being set like granite, to one that is made of putty. Mood tries to wring out more information from its niche map, when the obvious does not work. A mood may last for a long time, quietly searching for an answer, before emotion or desire is prepared to try to drive against the block once more.

In mood, we secrete different chemicals, depending upon the kind of mood needed. Those chemicals can change the ease of passage for energy through the neural network. Those chemicals might affect the liquid surrounding the neurones, or the cells themselves. A chirpy mood might increase chemicals that make the neurones easier and faster to travel along, so that more energy can flow through them than usual. We might be drawn by the promise of more pleasure. The body will become activated to send more energy toward such an experience. This compares to a reflective mood that can slow the passage of an energy impulse through the brain, so that the energy must search around in the cortex for a longer time before it can come back as empty feeling. It will have longer time to look for alternatives. A depressed mood will further slow the passage of our desire through the cortex. Depression can also cause us to reduce bodily activity, to try and shut down the supply of energy being sent to the cortex and its fate of unpleasurable end. Some chemicals could also make passage through the synapses harder or slower, so that the loop from desire to empty feeling is slowed.

It takes time to produce the chemicals and changes needed to alter the normal condition of the brain into mood. Therefore moods can take a long time to develop, and they can take a long time to subside or diffuse. This compares to emotion, which blocked desire can produce in an instant. We can produce emotion within the pulse of a heartbeat.

Because moods are produced by the chemical alteration of the normal conditions of the niche map, it is possible to produce similar effects artificially. Various drugs and alcohol can alter our mood, by affecting the niche map or the cortex.

Wild animals are mostly not in mood. They are just natural. Similarly, if we feel comfortable and normal, then we are not in mood. Chemical secretion to alter mood is energy expensive, so the body will not produce mood if it can be avoided.

5.3 Caged emotion

The normal wild response to any block that causes us sadness or pain is to avoid it, and so find a niche where life is comfortable. This process of block avoidance helps to keep an animal in its true niche. Desire prefers its wild option, of not having to be an emotion. The wild reaction is to simply leave the block. That is why signals and bluff work so well in nature, and why most wild animals are timid. They instead seek their wild niche where blocks are few and surmountable. Similarly, hunter-gatherers often resolved their conflicts by simply parting company (Farb, 1978: 105).

However, if the animal cannot leave, or the unfilled desire is great, then the animal might have to stay and use emotion to try and resolve things more positively. When a wild animal attempts to resolve its blocks through emotion, those emotions are still of a free and natural kind. They are the primary emotions such as hope, love, anger and fear. They are the freest of the emotions, that try to remove the block totally from the niche so that they will not be encountered again. They try to return the animal to its wild state. The natural primary emotions have their equivalents throughout much of the animal kingdom.

What a wild animal does not do is incorporate permanently any of its blocks on to its niche map. It will always act so that blocks to the wild spirit are either avoided or resolved. However, humans take a more sociable approach to their emotions, and are willing to accept some block into their world. Indeed, by building settlements and agriculture, simply leaving became less option due to the investment and bonding at stake. Therefore, we do not always resolve our blocks with avoidance or by using the natural primary emotions.

By being able to incorporate some block into our niche map, our desires and emotions can no longer be as free and simple as they are for the wild animal. Humans differ from wild animals in that we have internalised much of our block, and so now correspondingly we have a large variety of caged emotions buried deep within our personalities. These emotions still carry the underlying needs of the interaction desire, but because the block is now a fixture on our niche map, desire cannot be as free or direct as it might normally be in a first natural attempt. Our methods must instead become hidden or indirect, even deceitful. Therefore humans display a large variety of less natural emotions such as belief, hate, deceit, worry, stubbornness, shame, guilt, excitement, jealousy, passion. Some emotions are more accepting or trapped by their block than others. However, all of these emotions look for some way to make do with a restricted situation that we cannot leave.

While this process is an understandable way to deal with permanent block, it marks the major turning point in difference between the wild animal and ourselves. This is the point that changes our view from one where we see block as something that we can overcome, to one where we assume that blocks are a natural part of life. It marks a point where we think it is natural to struggle. It is the defining point that separates the human category as it stands today from wild things. Moving the block on to the niche map makes us leave the wildness, because we learn to restrict instinctively our desire in certain directions. We learn the laws of our dead-end mindrules. We start to give up.

For an animal living naturally in its wild niche, the block does not have to become incorporated on to the niche map. The spirit can remain free. The wild animal is able to avoid or overcome its external blocks, because it is wholly adapted to its wild niche. It is able to handle all of the external niche blocks in its world, and keep them external. It is adapted to leave or overcome its restrictive blocks. Its blocks are minor and infrequent. Their minds can remain wild and receptive.

Humankind is unusual in that while desires can be found in both animals and humans, only humans are really considered to have the full range of emotions. In our society, emotions are usually cherished, considered highly personal, well meaning and noble. Emotions are a part of what makes people strive to break free for better things. They may be personal and erratic, but they are a part of what makes us human, and raise us to a level above primitive desires. Desires are generally considered debasing, primitive, and common. They are worthy of suppression.

This view is the legacy of our species allowing mindrules to determine the outcome of our desire. Mindrules drive our desires towards conclusions that are confused. Mindrules try to protect our feelings. The interaction desire, with its high ideals, must conform to the niche map that the mindrules make for us. It cannot be allowed to expect so much from the niche map. Otherwise, trying to realise our desires will hurt our feelings.

Most primary emotions are associated with an expression. However, many of the more caged emotions cannot be expressed adequately, because they are modern inventions of the way we live. They are not natural, so did not evolve an expression. Many animals can express the primary emotions of hope, love, anger and fear. For example, hope is like a wish, and its expressions are of pleading kind. Dogs can whimper or beg for food. Signals of love or bonding are common in other animals. Anger is another emotion that many animals can express. But what other animals cannot do under natural conditions is display belief, hate or passion. Such caged emotions must usually borrow their expressions from the primary emotions.

If we can automatically quash desire before it reaches our mind, then it will not trouble us so purely. We could smother desire, block it out, so that it starts out on its interactive attempt already full of doubt, and expecting that it can only achieve a lower set of standards. If desire starts out with low objectives, it will not feel as much loss upon failure. The earlier the desire is quashed, the less painful it will feel. For the sake of our feelings, we learn to put the blocks that affect us more deeply into our cortex. The blocks that we face in life eventually leave the mind, to move into the subconscious to become a part of our mindrules. There, we will see the blocks instinctively, before they can do us much emotional damage. This is a way of protecting our feelings. When desire enters the cortex, it is shown its blocks very early indeed. Our blocks become instinctive and seemingly unavoidable.

Eventually, our blocks become so internalised that they become a part of our subconscious. We do not need to think about them, and their existence is no longer a surprise. To us they become instinctive. We no longer become conscious of them as block. They become assumed and seemingly natural. Struggle is a natural part of life. This process has a major effect on our emotions.

Because internalised block can deflect our desire so early, we no longer recognise the true spirit of our desire. The caged emotion is all that we notice, and emotion seems to be our driving force. We lose sight of the desire behind it. We can feel our emotions very strongly. They can take control of our reasoning, and make us behave irrationally. Emotion can burst into our mind without our reasoned control. Therefore, we have often thought of them as being inherited instincts. The emotion of anger particularly, is often thought to be an important instinct necessary for survival. However, emotions are simply distorted forms of the interaction desire, and so have no necessity to occur if desire can find its more direct pathway to fulfilment.

The source of an emotion has always been more difficult to trace than the source of a desire. A desire can relate back to a specific organ or tissue, and so its motives are easy to understand and measure. The desire to feed is driven by hunger in the stomach, the desire to mate is driven by sexual organs and certain hormones, and the desire to produce a good niche map is driven by the interaction desire. But what drives emotions such as hate, anger, jealousy, revenge, fear, and despair? Where are the specialised organs that produce the energies for these? There are none, because they are the invented soldiers of the interaction desire.

The power of emotions is really just an indication of the strength of our interaction desire. The step that converts desire into emotion is usually not known to the mind, because that step occurs well before the mind becomes conscious of the deflecting block. Mindrules do the conversion for us in the subconscious. The confused mindrules, which dominate the subconscious during rapid niche change, are very indirect, and so produce a great deal and variety of emotion in our species.

All of our emotions are now caged to some extent, even our primary emotions. Desire is diverted and frustrated, feeling alienated and restricted, even before it enters the mind. The diverted energy in desire cannot disappear. It cannot evaporate. It must follow the more indirect pathways on the niche map, and search for another point of release. Diverted desire may have to search so deeply that it can become lost to mind and forgotten. But it will still be there in the brain somewhere. It might linger as a mood or irritability. It might displace and escape as a nervous twitch, or as laughter. It might linger deep in the brain out of mind, until it reappears unexpectedly and perhaps irrationally as a caged emotion.

Unfortunately, emotions provide little capacity for finding entirely novel pathways. They instead are a way of working within the niche map, and of looking for answers within its existing boundaries. Emotions just try out old and existing tracks that have been previously little used or unexplored. They try to resolve issues, by entrenching a different set of mindrules within the current niche map. Therefore in our species the emotional process usually only entrenches our mindrules further, to increase our level of confusion and foolishness.

Most of what we feel today assumes some kind of block, and cannot feel entirely natural. The problems caused by the level of confusion found in our species today places excessive use and emphasis on the various emotional mechanisms. This is partly why our species seems so much more emotional than the other species. But we have also evolved a capacity for wit, so have much more capacity to vary the response that we deliver out of our feelings, if we so desire. There are often far better ways than emotion to make the interaction desire direct and pleasurable. Emotions will not serve our desire for wildness well. They are not resolving the problems for us in the way they were designed. They retain our trap of restriction, because they do not know what can happen to mindrules during rapid niche change. We would be better off using receptivity as a way of trying to receive beyond the bounds of the niche map.

5.4 Attitude

When we cannot remove our blocks through primary emotion, caged emotion or mood, we must look for some other method of resolution. This brings us to attitude. If we cannot escape or overcome an external block, then it is a natural conclusion to learn that the block is a permanent part of our niche. If the block is permanent, then we will have to come to terms with it somehow. Otherwise, we will continually waste our energy trying to remove or modify a block that is permanent, through our emotions or mood. In the interests of efficiency and piece of mind, we learn to hide the block from our emotional and moody mechanisms. Rather than putting ourselves through the pain of consciously seeing the block and having to elicit the emotional response, we learn to move the block into the subconscious. We make the block a permanent fixture on our internal niche map. We can go from seeing and thinking about the block, to accepting the block.

The advantage of placing the block on our niche map is that desire will see it much earlier in its passage through the cortex. Desire will know about the block, even before it moves into consciousness. Desire will see more quickly that it should not build up its expectations unrealistically in the blocked direction. We can warn desire earlier about the permanent block if it is on the niche map. We can learn to accommodate the block without getting emotional about it. The existence of the block will not be a surprise. We will take the block for granted. The block moves internally to become a fixture on our niche map.

Wild animals do not have attitudes. However, humans live in temporary niches. Therefore, as we begin to learn our instincts, there comes a time when those mindrules start failing. They cannot keep up with the demands of change. At some point, mindrules want to harden and set. But after that time, we continue to receive a steady stream of new information that our mindrules cannot understand to a wild level. The new information begins to clog and block our mindrules. The only way left for our mind to resolve our blocks is to accept them on to the niche map, and forget trying to relate to them openly and directly. Those blocks become an automatic part of our life, and begin our attitude.

Emotional responses and moods are energy consuming, and if used excessively they become inefficient and stressful. The feelings they produce are not always pleasant. Our emotions often fail. Attitude is a way of making our responses less stressful. Attitude makes our automatic responses more comfortable. It reduces the demand on our emotional and mood responses. It makes us less confused about what to do. Attitude occurs when the block seems to be beyond emotional control. It also occurs when the mood cannot in reasonable time complete its task of finding a new answer under changed niche map conditions. Desire does not actually like having to become emotional or moody, so it tries to come to terms with its niche by whatever means needed. If it finds it needs attitude to do that, then it will learn its attitude, even if it is a bitter pill.

Attitude can turn what might normally be an emotional response, into our standard response. Then we can produce the same response without having to expend emotional energy. Such a response becomes standard rather than emotional or moody. Attitude lets us become non-emotional in the face of consistent pressure. A stock attitude helps us overcome our problems more easily.

A person might develop an attitude that is pleasant, aggressive, tearful, or tense. Rather than producing these responses emotionally or moodily, we make them our natural or instinctive response. Therefore, a person may develop an attitude or personality that is aggressive, and not need to generate much energy to display this approach. It can become quite natural for us to be aggressive in attitude even when we feel comfortable. This compares to other people who may require emotion before they can become aggressive. It is harder or more energy intensive for them to produce such a stance. Alternatively, a person may develop a confident attitude, so naturally attempt things of which another can only dream. What is a natural wild approach to one might seem unstructured to another. These approaches to life can be an attitude for some, while for others they will need to more actively or emotionally send their energy to produce the same approach.

It is often difficult to classify everything that we do as emotion, mood or attitude. At different times in our life, our same response can move through the three states. The source of our response largely depends upon how we perceive the block that we have to tackle. Do we accept it, or can it be overcome? At any time, that answer can depend upon what we have made as our natural mindrule format, the level of block that we have come to accept, the expectation that we let our interaction desire contain, and how comfortable we feel at the time. The various courses of behaviour open to us, hate, love, confidence, religious belief, are all capable of alternating between an attitudinal state to an emotional or moody state.

People are mostly able to find a comfortable or bearable position in which to live, so most of the feelings they send through their cortex are fairly relaxed and passive. It is not too emotional or moody. Their attitude will be fairly well adjusted or suited to the society in which they live. Normally, most people find a comfortable level of attitude that is positive, and do not settle for an attitude or personality that is negative. They mostly do not become mean spirited.

Even when we find our attitude, we might still continue to try to resolve our blocks further on the positive side, to find a more pleasurable existence. Therefore, an aggressive person might one day try to be pleasant, or a suspicious person might again attempt trust. Our attempt to others might seem positive or negative, relative to what they know. However for us, our attempt will always be positive within our learnt constraints. Everyone tries to do the right thing, or the more accomplished thing. That is a constant drive given to us by the interaction desire. Therefore, if another tells us that we are being negative, we might be surprised because to us we are being positive, relative to the blocks that we have learnt to accept.

A person may try to be positive, but fail drastically, and so become emotionally scarred. The failure may be so vividly hurtful, that they will not try with emotion again, to explore and repair the niche map beyond their attitude. We will form our attitude more strongly instead. We will be more prepared at the instinctive level next time to fend off the unwanted interaction or block. The restriction and block of attitude will become even more entrenched and accepted as part of our personality. New attempts will not be made, and dreams will be ignored.

The neural pathways in the cortex are like uncommitted wires that can connect into whatever arrangement they are moulded into by the trial and error of interaction within a niche. We are all born with essentially the same desire and virgin cortex. As we grow, the way we personalise the niche map is to send our interaction desire through it, to test it out, and see how pleasurable and interactive it feels. It is largely what we sense, and the flow of desire and emotional energy, which determines how the niche map will become structured and directed. It will determine what attitude or approach to life we will take. The way our cortex will set is not inherited. It does not have to become selfish, or emotional, or anything. The only measure our cortex takes notice of during its construction is the measure of the pleasure centre. The only way we want our cortex to feel is good, in the broadest and most interactive sense possible.

Attitude is totally convinced of its internal block, and cannot work around it. Attitude can run its programme like a record. Some people simply cannot consider certain possibilities because of their attitude. However, we should view all blocks, including our internal blocks, less seriously. If we can do this, then at least we might be able to turn our attitude into style. Style is a stronger and more pleasant kind of attitude. It is more flexible, aware, and fun. Style is less in awe of its own blocks. It makes us feel less constrained by the seriousness and universality of the block. It is an attitude that still has enough wit in it to enable us to look graciously for the alternatives. Converting attitude into style will take us one step closer to the original receptivity where it all began.

While we develop some of our own attitude, we often learn its majority from others. The main source of block on our niche map is not the block that we develop through our own emotional experiences. We learn to assume most of our blocks passively. We learn them from the accumulated history and mindset of our species. Many of the attitudinal stunts that our species learns throughout its history, we communicate and teach to future generations. Society develops a certain tone or average attitude. It develops a standard and accepted set of blocks that the species for a while at least will learn to assume.

5.5 Hierarchy of emotions

When desire meets block, and converts itself into emotion, the emotion that it becomes will depend upon the block faced, and our previous experience or attitude. It will depend upon how deeply internalised we have let our blocks become. All of our emotions, moods and attitudes appear only when the interaction desire begins to experience some difficulty in obtaining passage in a fulfilling way through the cortex. Emotions and their various developments appear when blocks appear, first externally and then internally on the niche map. It should be possible to assess our emotions taxonomically, and produce a tree-like diagram showing how each emotion arises from the ancestral stock of desire.

A new branch leading to a new emotion will appear each time desire strikes upon a new block. The kind of emotion produced will depend on the form and size of the block, and the previous experience had with or before the block. I will not here attempt the full construction of this tree. It could be a mammoth task. But it is worth having some concept of the tree. The tree-like structure will begin with one desire, but as our dead-end mindrules develop, the number of emotions possible compounds. More and more branches appear on the tree. In theory, there could be an infinite number of emotions and feelings produced, as more and more blocks and resulting experiences add to the tree. If we follow the emotional path, then eventually there could be at least six billion different personalities and attitudinal branches on the tree.

At first, emotions are of most pure kind, and most similar in meaning to the interaction desire. Emotions actively try to resolve the external block to make it all good. The emotions of children are mostly innocent and positive, and include emotions such as love and hope. Laughter is common. Also, when the negative emotions are expressed, they are also the negative emotions and expressions that are most simple and open, such as sadness and crying. But as failure and diversion continue to drive block internally, the emotions become more shunted from the natural course of their original desire. They become more indirect and accepting of the illusory blocks that are needed to give good feeling to confused mindrules. There are many paths that desire can take as emotion. When persistent failure happens, our desiring energy can become more spiteful, aggressive, fearful, guilty, and hidden.

In more simple times, an expression of sadness would have been enough to have things rectified. In many primitive tribes, sadness is as far as a negative emotion has to go. The problem is recognised, openly expressed, and there is community or tribal support to its resolution. A person would not feel alone with their block. But in a fast changing and individualised society, fewer people can relate to and help us, and understanding is very poor. Our blocks must quickly internalise and the negative emotions learn to take charge more quickly. Children learn how serious and permanent failure and block can be in today's world. As hope wanes, and we learn that things do not improve, emotions become more hateful, deceitful or sullen. Emotions can become extreme, as failure and the chance of positive resolution and opportunity seem to slip further away. The more difficult the niche map, the more extreme the emotions have to be to try and return a bearable feeling. Adults can become extremely complex creatures.

The interaction desire will only turn into emotion when we meet a block. Therefore, the first emotion must feel negative. It would also probably be hard to define, because it is the first restriction ever felt by the desire, and the emotional response needed to help resolve it would be very poorly learnt and expressed. Perhaps it could be defined simply as emptiness. This might first occur in babies. Their neural pathways are poorly developed to harness energies' desire into a coordinated and targeted emotion that can combine the expression and physiological changes needed to effectively deliver its message. A baby does not love, it simply desires or cries. The crying simply expresses a sadness or emptiness, or a desire not met. They cannot really tell us what is wrong, or name a block, or give an emotional expression that is more descriptive and sophisticated. It is quite natural for a baby to cry, so some emotion is normal. But under natural conditions where the family unit extends into a whole community, simple baby desires are easier to meet. There is time to hold a baby, or feed the right milk formula at any time of the night. Babies can simply express their emptiness, long before they learn to include the more advanced and displaced emotions of aggression and hate.

5.6 Hope

When the interaction desire fails, and it feels empty or sad, the first emotion that we attempt is usually hope. The sad feeling lets desire know that it might fail again, because a block of some kind is standing in the way. However, when we are young we do not know our niche well. The block might not be real or strong. It might be a block that is easy to overcome, or that might still be friends. Therefore, we are hopeful that things will turn out right through innocent attempt. Hope is a way for desire to try harder again. If hope succeeds, we will feel happy and confident about using hope again. Perhaps we will try our hope in other areas as well. We might even be sufficiently encouraged to turn hope back into its original desire, and express our true feelings once more.

We have a natural liking for the openness and desire of hope, because it is so close to the spirit of the interaction desire. Parents will encourage the emotion, over the less pleasurable and more restricted emotions that will invariably follow. We give children things that might prolong their hope, such as Father Christmas, magical powers, and tooth fairies. These beings can dance magically around our earthly and mundane blocks.

Hope is a positive emotion that tries to overcome a block, not by acting against it, but by thinking that there are other forces at work in the niche that know its right more powerfully. Our hope lets us think that our niche should not contain any permanent block, so we hope to see the greater strength of our niche come through. The block might not be as strong as it first seems. In hope, the blocking forces cannot completely restrict the spirit of our desire, and we will still make positive attempts to link with those higher things in the niche that exist beyond the block. We still trust our niche or world to come through.

However, there is a cost in using any emotion. If we use hope, we must also admit that we cannot directly affect the outcome of our important interactions. Instead, we must appeal to some outside force that we hope will bring things back into our favour. There is a difference between hoping, and making things work for ourselves. Hope reflects a lack of confidence in our ability to improve things through our own actions. We leave it more to luck.

It is good to keep hopes alive. It is a better emotion than most. It helps keep live a greater awareness of what we really want. Rather than letting our true desires become completely buried in the subconscious with mindrule excuses, hope can keep the feeling alive. If hope works, and finds that it is able to reach the powerful outside forces, then our hopes will remain high. We will try to bond more strongly with those more powerful forces by sending them our wishes.

Hope is the most basic emotion. It is strongest in children. It sees all of its blocks as external, and is a sign that we still do not fully accept that powerful blocks have a rightful place in our world. Hope tends to fade in adults, as our greater experience of failure takes its toll. We learn to internalise our blocks more deeply. Adults do not believe that hope can fulfil our desires, because we are more convinced with the reality of our blocks.

The problem with hope is that it does not make us try to understand the reasons behind the block, to improve our instinctive position. We simply hope that our blocks will go away. Therefore, hopes can be ineffective and naive. It is fairly easy to dash hopes.

5.7 Love

If our first emotion of hope fails then the block that stands in our way must be stronger than we thought. Our niche might not be as free as we would like. Alternatively, we did not appeal properly to the forces that we hoped would put the block back into its rightful place. We did not find the agreement that we were seeking. We may need to make a greater commitment to those stronger forces before they are willing to help. Perhaps we should spread our hope less broadly into the ether, and target our emotion more directly towards something or someone who will understand our true desires better. With their more tangible help, life might become more pleasurable. Therefore, the next emotional attempt that we usually make to resolve block is love.

Love is a powerful emotion that can be single minded in its efforts to bond with whatever we identify as the aid to the release of our desires. Love is more targeted than hope, and is generally more restrictive in its realm of application. We usually apply love just to the family unit, or to one or few partners. Hope seeks greater comfort for its niche, so casts its wishes more broadly than love. Hope can send its energies and wishes to the world. However, we cannot spread our love as far, even though it sounds nice to try. We can however turn the general approach of love into friendship, which gives it greater chance to act on a broader scale.

Love is an emotion that is thought to be strongest and most highly developed in humans. We have a large cortex, and to sort it out need a strong interaction desire. When failing mindrules restrict and block desire, our emotions will also run strongly. Love is one of our more natural emotions. It appears early near the base of the tree of emotions. Along with hope, it is a strong emotion in children and appears very early in their development. However, while hope follows a wishful approach, love can produce more direct results through its targeted approach. Also, others might find reward in the emotion, so return it in kind. Love is an emotion that would have been common even in the wild. Full wildness is not always possible in a wild niche. Some desiring energy will at times have to convert into emotion. Therefore, evolution was able to incorporate the prospects for love into our package of human adaptations. Our species has a prolonged childhood, and many sexual adaptations, that all promote the duration of our bonds, and the intensity of our desire for those bonds.

When we fall in love, the blocks and worries that once seemed so troubling can lose importance. They are less able to contain our desire. Love becomes a new pathway through which we can channel much of our desire. Blocks seem to be more easily forgotten and overcome. People can rise and accomplish new feats in the name of love. Our emotion can become bravest and most committed under love. It will overcome and overlook many faults, in favour of the bond.

Love is a desire to share and bond totally with another. It is a way of finding a new outlet in our niche world. The desire in our species is so great, that the promise of a new and pleasurable outlet can strongly draw our attention. The mind can become preoccupied with love. We will try to bond as directly as possible to the niche map of the loved one, so that the outlet remains tightly in place. In love, we usually seek a commitment that helps ensure that the bond will last. Once formed, we can discuss with the loved one all feelings and hopes normally kept intimate and secret.

A problem with love is that it can be blind. It can control so much of our attention and desire, that we ignore all other outlets and possibilities. A person may suddenly drop all of their friends, or ignore their work. A person may drastically change their opinions and habits, to better match and bond with the nature of the person being loved. When in love, we might take in whatever the loved one tells us as fact. But also, we will view very badly any deception that might occur if this trust is broken. Love does not necessarily improve our reasoning. It can have an opposite effect. Alternatively, a person who grew up with a suspicious attitude might suddenly loosen up when they find love. They might become more pleasant and helpful.

Love shows us how direct the interaction desire would like to be in its actions. It is our closest emotional window to true desire. Both love and the interaction desire seek honesty and directness in their interactions. They seek understandings that are strong enough to bond both sides of the interaction together as one. They can make us want to crawl along the bond and into the soul of the other. When this degree of bonding is targeted we call it love. When this degree of bonding is free and wild I call it receptivity. Love is a form of receptivity, but more focused in application. The two ends of the bond almost merge into the one being. Love makes us accept the insights of another. Sometimes, partners that are in love can approach a level of wildness with each other, where they can be honest and free, and know what the other is thinking.

Love might be strongest at the start of a relationship, but then wane upon familiarity and routine if left to its own devices. Love may create less personal growth between adults than between a child and parent, because of the differing stages of niche map development. Love in a family involves sharing a full range of developments in learning and play, whereas in adults the love might be based upon sex alone. Love between adults might be enhanced by sharing experiences over a wider range of issues important to each partner. It can move beyond sex by discussing plans and hopes. The relationship comes more live, rather than being a favourite record that may become boring. Changing partners regularly would be another way of gaining a new lease of love. But with each change, there might be a reduced confidence in what love can do, and in the level of intimacy that it can generate.

The function of any emotion is to find a more comfortable and pleasurable position from which to interact. Love was designed to bring the mind more in tune with another, and in the process find greater understanding. It is a way of swapping good niche maps, and combining the best of each into a shared niche map. The normal process of love is to bring people together so that they bond and attune until they can be wild with each other. Today especially, this process of attunement is cut short. All of our niche maps are such hard cases, so individualised, that we cannot take the next step through love to complete wildness. The end result of love cannot be delivered, and love on its own might not be sustainable. The prolonged use of any emotion will turn it into an attitude, so that it becomes more routine and energy efficient. This can be disappointing, as the vigour and desire behind love fades. The desire or energy in love was never meant to remain the strongest feeling between two bonded people. It was meant to be a tool that moves us on to the greater array of feelings that enter upon attunement to the wild.

5.8 Passion

Passion is a more considered or caged form of love. It develops when the outlet for our desire must be hidden or circumspect. It is hesitant desire or love that is trained to be more wary before we allow it to flow freely. It may be a secret delight or cause that only you seem to understand. Alternatively, it may target a person secretly. Passion is a form of emotion because it does not feel free. It arises after our true desires experience block, so is more common in adults than children. It is positive about its ability to overcome block, but must bide its time. It must learn the right conditions under which to release its stronger desires.

We have no evolved expression for passion, because it is learnt late as an adult, and is the product of having to internalise block. The expression of passion occurs when it finds a chance to release more obviously into some simpler emotion such as love. Passion requires an awareness that we cannot do whatever we want, which is a conclusion not normally reached in a natural wild state. Even so, once hopes are dashed and love fails, passion is perhaps the next best emotion that an adult can develop. It is a way of combining the spirit of the two, and keeping it safe inside through our wits and enhanced awareness. It is a way of keeping desire strong, even though it must be more secretive and selective about where it is applied and revealed. Passion is more patient than desire would normally like to be.

Because passion is desire controlled by wit and awareness, passion can be quite good at turning our desire towards more creative outlets. It keeps our spirit for high ideals alive, and makes us look for new ways to enable that spirit to be accepted. Passion can become inspiring and determined, and is the driving force behind many creative people. Someone might be passionate about their work, or about something that needs to be expressed. A person passionate about their work is more likely to succeed and find novel outlet.

However, passion can become damaging even spooky if it is left secret too long. Without expression and outside input, it may become serious and isolated in its objectives. It may become a false hope. We may become overly dependent on our passions for fulfilment, to the exclusion of other more simply expressed emotional releases. Our wit may leave passion, so that it becomes an obsession.

5.9 Belief

When our hopes and love fail to please the expectations of our interaction desire, we may either give up, or try belief as the next positive step available on the tree of emotions. To reach this point, the blocks in our life must have been too intractable to affect directly with our own hope and love. We cannot accomplish the good interaction with all things that we desire. Something stands in our way that we cannot overcome. Bad people or evil might exist that we can never hope to conquer. Alternatively, we may be at fault internally ourselves, so that we can never hope to become a source of the good that we seek. We might be sinners instead. With these constraints, the interaction desire has little alternative than to look for its paradise elsewhere. Complete fulfilment may not be possible in our world. Instead, we may have to believe that such interaction can only occur in another world, or in someone else's niche. We have to postpone the fulfilment of our true desires. If our interaction desire is to remain strong and honest, it may have to become spiritual to reach its highest dreams. It may have to transfer itself to another plane of being, to find the conditions where it can remain positive and whole.

Belief evolves when we become constrained in our world. Our interaction desire learns to accept that it should not attempt hope or love because of the dreaded realities of life. We must instead accept the 'facts'. If we are to keep our hopes alive, we must displace them into a new world where they can become spiritual or untouchable. Our hopes cannot expect to find their dreams in this world. Belief is different to hope in that it transfers our ultimate desires to somewhere imagined, instead of trying to keep them active and live in our current niche world. Hopes are naive if they think they can make bad dissolve, or turn around to our side. Hope will be quashed in this cruel world. In belief we accept our blocks of constraint, and seek to work around them. Therefore, we must escape those blocks, rather than hope for their removal.

The problem with belief is that it marks a definite change in the way we use our emotions to combat block. It is usually our first caged emotion. Believing shows that we now accept our blocks, because we must defer our hopes to another context or heaven. We now believe in two sets of rules. One rule world contains the blocks, while the other is reserved for what we wish. Belief is a sign that we have allowed our blocks to become internalised and a part of our niche map. This is something that a wild animal will not allow. They do not let themselves remain trapped for long. They do not allow their true natures to become restricted. Belief is a modern human caged emotion. No expression has evolved for its use.

Belief is an emotion that is willing to make assumptions. Therefore, it is the emotion most similar in nature and function to mindrules. With belief, mindrules can more easily perpetuate their illusions of bad and block as the cause of their failure. Belief gives their illusions extra drive. With belief, mindrules can gloss over their own inconsistencies. Belief allows mindrules to introduce new and unproven tracks onto the niche map to complete their neural circuitry.

Flawed mindrules need us to believe certain illusions if they are to remain intact. Through belief, dead-end mindrules can become a part of our niche map without needing to earn their place through direct interaction. Our beliefs can be taught to us, or we may work them out for ourselves. However, whatever form they take, our beliefs do not require proof to exist in our minds. Indeed, we have beliefs to try and raise ourselves above such mundane requirements. We do not believe to try and make ourselves more reasonable. We believe to find completeness for the interaction desire. The need for belief in our species can be so strong, that people can condition themselves with the emotion until they see their illusions as real. Some people will swear that they have seen sea monsters, miracles, demons, ghosts, apparitions, or that they have been beamed up into spaceships for examination by aliens. While our interaction desire remains trapped, the potential for the illusions that can grow out of our beliefs will remain correspondingly strong.

On the surface, belief might seem to be a quick way to complete our life's understanding. Individuals can hold their beliefs with much power of conviction. Our society sees beliefs as something to cherish. We give them rights or status of their own. We should not challenge beliefs because they fill a communal need. For most, beliefs are strong and can never be disproved. They are supported too strongly by our emotions. We romanticise our use of beliefs with institutions such as the church, or we give them pretend justification through our entertainment. Some beliefs can unite a group of people, as they help all to self indulge in the same illusions of just cause and glory.

However, there are other ways to improve the strength of our niche understandings. The things that belief desires, completeness and goodness, can be found by more direct means once the forces that contribute to the production of our niche map are known. Receptivity is still possible. We should not limit ourselves to our beliefs. They will only perpetuate dead-end instincts. While beliefs may seem to fill an immediate and important need, they will in the end become our own worst enemy. We are going to have to get it right some day.

At its barest level, a belief might closely follow the truth. Beliefs start out as predictions that are based upon what we know or sense. If our basis is right, then the prediction should come true. Conversely, if our prediction is wrong, then our basis must be flawed. However, mindrules do not like the admission that they could be wrong. Rather than accept defeat, they turn our mistaken predictions into personal beliefs that are above question.

Some level of prediction or belief can be useful. A belief might give greater efficiency to life. The fact that evolution produces instincts and mindrules shows in itself that some belief or ability to predict beyond what we experience is needed to make us efficient. If we can assume or believe some things, we do not have to continually reassess each new interaction. We can make predictions. In science, beliefs are closely applied to the facts. They can be objectively re-evaluated and are called hypotheses and theorems. They are 'beliefs', but they are not supposed to be emotionally supported. Before those beliefs can go too far, the evidence must support them. This is as far as I think all of our beliefs should go.

I predict that when I sit in a chair, I will be supported and not fall to the ground. That is a form of belief, but it is based upon observation, experience, and the senses. It is a prediction that can be examined from many angles and observed to be true. It can be experimented upon. So it is more of a prediction based upon observation than it is a belief. I use observations that I find to work, and will believe them sufficient to use them once more, or perhaps twice more, but if that observation then does not continue to work, I will change the belief. I prefer to stick to what I can sense and feel at the time, than get carried away with what I think I know. Receptive interactions need to be more live and responsive than a belief will allow.

I think it is best to remain sceptical at all times. Otherwise, it will be difficult for us to tell when we are seeing fact, and when we are in fact simply believing. The best way to reduce our delusions of belief is to realise that everything we think and believe is probably wrong. At the very least, we should only believe what we can see or touch ourselves. Anything second-hand will only contain the compounded errors of other people and human generations. For similar reasons, we should not fully believe our own reasons either. Otherwise, we will become bound by the limitations of what our mindrules learn.

Does a person without belief have no soul? Have they lost the desire for a complete worldview where everything comes together as one? If we do not have a belief, will we be empty? The spirit of our interaction desire needs to keep in touch with something that is complete, because that is how it will find most pleasure. It needs a return loop for all of its energies. However, what if the soul of our niche map is surrounded and fed by deluded mindrules? How can we trust our own beliefs when simple analysis shows that they are the agents of mindrules? I observe that beliefs work very badly in society. They are prone to mindrule exploitation. In their name, many ills can be done, and many mistakes and losses ignored.

I want no beliefs. That might mean I have to look further to find the same result, but it is worth it. No one knows anything well enough for me to believe. I got far more insight from a lizard, than I got from what any human believes. Observation should never have to stray that far away from the reality of what we can sense. You could say that I believe in wildness, and in the ways of nature. That is close, and certainly I believe it more than in ways human. But I still keep this 'belief' as an observation, and try not to let it envelop me completely. While some might use wildness spiritually, I see it as a practical tool. I learnt about wildness from animals, not people. Animals are not wild to be spiritual. They use wildness because it works and lets them self-enhance. Of course, wildness can fill all needs at every level, from the spiritual to the practical. However, a spiritual need only arises when we cannot fill our true desires on a more practical or direct level.

I will use wildness for a while further at least, because I find it works so well. It has given me this book. But even so, as I have expressed often, I hope I can continue not to believe it fully, but keep some level of wit about me. In the value of wit, I believe even more. It has never failed me. I have always found myself to be wrong in some way. All I have to do to see that I was wrong is to apply more wit. So perhaps it is wit that I believe in most, or the need to be sceptical about myself. It always works, and the forces that it opens up are always more live and fun. They seem to want to get in.

5.10 Supernatural

The need that our species has to believe can be traced throughout our history. In our efforts to keep our true desires safe in something that is untouchable by the supposed realities of life, our species has become drawn into believing some very strange things.

The supernatural has long been used to try and explain why things do not work naturally in the way that we would expect. The supernatural is composed of those forces that do not abide by natural laws, and are outside the normal structures of the universe. In the past, the supernatural held far greater sway than today, for most, because so many natural phenomena were either not understood, or could not be examined properly.

Today, we have a well equipped and developed science that can study supernatural phenomena. From its studies, science has revealed that what was thought to be supernatural in the past, were in fact occurrences that were due to interesting but previously unknown natural forces, or to tricksters. No supernatural force has yet been proven. All events and things can so far be placed somewhere into a framework that is both natural and universal. In ancient times, supernatural forces were thought to control such things as the weather, the growth rate of crops, pregnancy, sanity, and health. Food going off was thought to be due to spontaneous generation, until the existence of bacteria and fungal spores was discovered.

The main driving force behind our belief in the supernatural is not ignorance but desire. Ignorance only allows the illusions to flourish uncontested. However, restricted desire makes us seek out those illusions. Desire believes mindrules, and so we believe the alienation and bads that mindrules need to make their niche map complete. Mindrules explain that on a directly interactive level they cannot be complete, but on a supernatural level we will find the rest of our answers. With supernatural forces at work, mindrules could not possibly be expected to comprehend or come to terms with everything in a proven or reasonable way. Existing mindrules become safe from change, if they have excuses. The conclusion is that reality contains in it supernatural elements that disrupt the normal flow and cause unexpected results. Therefore, we are as accomplished as we could ever hope to be. With mindrules safely assumed out of conscious view, the course of action to take is the study of the supernatural forces. It will become logical to try and appease those supernatural forces, or try to take better note of what they say.

The supernatural has been believed by our species for a very long time, because the strength behind our interaction desire has never waned. Many still strongly believe. There is astrology, devil, god, ghosts, auras, and spoon bending. Surely, so many people cannot be wrong. But mindrules during rapid niche change are easily able to produce such widespread emotional belief in our species. The supernatural reveals to me the power that mindrules really have over the way we think. But it also shows the will behind our interaction desire for something that is complete in understanding, no matter how weird or naive we must turn to find it. I think our desire will win through in the end. It will find that it can exist in pure form, without having to resort to the depths of illusion.

5.11 Religion

Ever since our species evolved it has believed in gods. Even our closest ancestral relatives, the Neanderthal, may have held such similar belief, judging by the spiritual paintings found on their cave walls. All native tribal cultures, including those largely developed in isolation, come up with a god or spirit of some kind. At all times, especially before this century, the majority of the population believed in a god or in spiritual beings. This is an amazing state of affairs when there is absolutely no proof that such things exist. We have launched our rockets into the heavens and none were found. We know that there are millions of species on earth, and billions of planets separated by billions of light years. How could one consciousness keep it all together and maintain some theme of creation or control? How could an ark have contained so many species?

The need for a god cannot be denied. The belief in a god must express some desire in our species that is yet to be filled otherwise. Does the mere existence of this desire mean that evolution itself was convinced there was a god, so that it put in us a desire for god? What is it that people think a god does? A god usually has an overall view of his domain, and all things in the domain are under his control or are connected into a grand plan that perhaps only god understands. But this is the same thing that the interaction desire wants. The interaction desire wants so see a single complete picture in which it can fit everything together. It is the normal requirement of a niche map. Such a complete picture has not been found in our species, due to niche change and the poor state of our current understanding. Therefore, our interaction desire remains unfulfilled. But our desire is so strong that it will not allow itself to remain unfulfilled. Therefore in our species, and perhaps in a few of our nearest ancestors, there remains a strong push to find an outlet for our unfilled desire. It is a push that creates our need to believe in god. In god there would be a grand plan and reason. The desire can then be filled by communicating with that god, and by following closely the complete picture that we imagine the god might have.

Under mindrules, we cannot hope to extend our innermost relatability or soul into all areas. The niche as we know it today is not on equal terms with our soul, and we cannot interact with everything directly. Confused mindrules lose the ability to spread our own complete relatability or soul into the niche. But god can accept such desire and soul. Every level of organisation in our body tells us subconsciously that such level of interaction is possible. Our mindrules however can find no way to satisfy such expectation. While the state of harmony seems beyond our grasp, we still feel that harmony must exist somewhere, perhaps in the realm of a consciousness more powerful than our own. Such a god must hold the plan where all our daily and apparently disrelatable souls and interactions are known and exist in a beautiful pattern that only he understands.

We feel to our soul that complete relatability exists, but rather than admit our mindrules are wrong, we displace the expectation for such soul-like interaction out of our existence into the hands of god. Mindrules have protected themselves so well that they continue to dominate our daily lives by shifting our desire for soul-like relatability towards communication with a god. The interaction desire is neatly packaged and sent off into the heavens in prayer, when it is down here on earth that it would do most good.

5.12 Anger

When we first encounter block, people will usually try to find resolution through hope and love. If those emotions fail, and especially if the block is pressing or painful, anger often follows. However, anger is a most misunderstood emotion. While we strongly link anger with violence, anger in nature is far gentler than the way we experience the emotion. The violence and aggression that we know, arise from an unnatural level of frustration imposed on us by our own mindrule cage of dead-end niche understandings. Anger in the natural world is a positive emotion that assumes it will help create or contribute to the harmony.

Anger creates conditions in the brain where heightened energy can narrow and flow more forcefully through the brain, relieving the pleasure centre and providing the sensation of greater confidence and fulfilment. Anger makes an animal want to take on the block. The animal may be annoyed or irritated by the block, in which case the block is an inconvenience that should be relatively easy to deal with. Alternatively, the block may be overbearing or unjust, and fail to recognise greater need. Against this stayed or stronger block, anger may also contain an element of fear. Anger allows its animal to self-assert until it feels on equal terms with the block. The emotion, and perhaps a contest, may create a new set of conditions for the newly asserted animal. In anger, contestants look for a new compatibility that will be devoid of block. Anger allows an adjustment of confidence and new ability in relation to the block.

Anger begins with the underlying desire to improve bonding, by changing other minds. It does not consider the violent option naturally at first. Anger wants to improve the conditions for wildness. It wants to foster a common desire and maintain a spiritual link within the one shared niche. The alternative of having to destroy to find resolution and agreement is not the first thought that a wild and naturally confident animal will consider. To a mind of high spirits, the violent approach is a weak admission of defeat. It would demonstrate an inability to affect and persuade the fellow forces of the niche.

Anger is an emotion that tries to bring the cause of our anger back into the fold, to our way of thinking or living. We might be wrong, but that will be found out within the anger. It is an emotion designed to bring animals back together, into a position where they can find a new accommodation that is more streamlined for all. They might find a new pecking order, or drive one member from a pack. However, they take these actions to maintain the wildness, rather than for revenge, frustration or to cause damage. This might be in similar vein to those corny westerns where two men enter a fight, and finish up becoming friends. The bond is maintained or strengthened. A mutual respect is found. We have been educated to realise that such a naive resolution is not possible for our species. But in nature, differences are not insurmountable.

Animals use anger to find greater respect, rather than to destroy and fragment the different parts of their niche. They are adapted to their battles, and usually cause little damage. Even if their anger causes death, that death does not happen because they were violent but because they were wild. The difference might seem fine, but it is great. The contact or the reason is not lost. The spirit is respected and the link maintained. Hunter-gatherers did not desecrate the animals they hunted, or the opponents they fought. They considered them with reverence and song. In nature, death does not have to mean violence. It is not violence to the ecosystem, or to the animals involved when they feel so completely attuned with the ecosystem. Death in nature is not tragic as it is for an individualised mind in a lonely world.

Anger is simply an emotion that signals that we want the block itself to make more effort in accommodating what we think is the stronger position. We might think that there should be stronger understanding, better rules, or more attention to a greater need. We become angry when we feel that the other side is not trying hard enough, or that they are being unreasonable. They are not entering into the spirit of what we are attempting. They are using a weaker set of rules to our own, when only one set of rules should exist in a niche.

Our anger demonstrates that we are concerned with the difference and want to put the interaction back on to a new and stronger footing. We want to return to a common set of rules that everyone can follow. If we are concerned about the difference enough, we might tremble with anger or even fight. We cannot find pleasure while such differences remain. However, the aim of anger is still to make the other mind come around and realise what we know or sense. Our anger reveals our desire for closer bonding. It shows that we have not given up trying to find common ground. In nature, animals readily find common ground and harmony through their anger.

When a parent tells a child they are angry with them, the parent does not normally do so with aggression and violence in mind. They want to teach or impress an important learning upon the child. They want to improve the instinctive approach of the child, in the interests of their future skill and harmony. The angry parent shows that they are now serious, and want the child to add an important insight to their fundamental understanding. Anger is designed to improve the level of mindrule attunement between members of a family, or some wider group. Anger attempts to collect the raw energy of our interaction desire, and transfer it directly into the mind of another to impress that mind with the standards we are willing to share. It attempts to force an insight. We do this because the other mind is not trying hard enough, or does not realise what we know or feel. We display anger to try and help the other mind develop, by making a strong impression.

The expression of anger often stops a child continuing their poor effort. If the anger is ignored, then the parent may back it up with discipline, but again, that is discipline to teach rather than to harm or relieve frustration. In nature, anger occurs under the conditions where animals feel the bond of a common soul. They do not let their anger go so far as to break their contribution to the pooled wild feeling.

Once, anger was much easier to use than it is today, because our minds were much more similar to each other in nature and understanding. Our minds were open to receive, or reasonably counter and reverse, the direct alterations of mind asked for in anger. There were fewer fundamental obstacles to stand in the way of simple anger. The blocks were not elusive or enlarged by differences and hidden agendas. Anger could get its results easily, before the receptive link was broken or before any feeling of alienation could creep in. The sets of mindrules in each of us were much more similar, so the requests made by anger did not feel like total upheaval or violence to the soul.

Under natural wild conditions humans would not have to suppress their anger, as it is a positive and useful way to transfer information. It can be enjoyed. But today we must teach against using anger. It cannot get results because of our individual mindrule differences. Therefore, it can readily turn into violence. Anger is the positive emotion that feels most affected by those differences, because it is designed to 'even things up'. It calls for a dropping of pretend differences. It tries to make everyone follow the same set of rules, and is emotional when others resist or claim to be different and not subject to our same code of understanding. Anger wants us to rise above these differences. It is an emotion that expects to be stronger and more impressive than any real differences between people. Therefore, it is not meant to hold itself back, because at some point it could always achieve its even or harmonious result. Within a common niche a result useful to the system would occur before much damage was caused, if any. But when niches are individual and temporary, differences remain, and anger may drive towards the extremes without even realising its folly.

Anger could nearly always settle its blocks in a positive way that would clear the air, and either makes people work together, or else make it clear that someone had to leave the group. Anger is therefore the emotion that is most affected by the differences between our false mindrules. It becomes very frustrated when it cannot make things work harmoniously in the way it was designed. It can only see that differences stand in the way, that are more serious in their desire to be different, than in angers' desire to unite. Anger may try to overcome the differences more forcefully, and if it is duped by our faulty mindrules, it may see the differences as arising from a bad that can never change. Under artificial conditions, anger can become a dangerous emotion that we must suppress because it is so easy to fool.

Anger could be a fun and live emotion for people, pleasurable, if it did not so quickly believe in our mindrules and find itself frustrated. Anger is a natural emotion, and because it arises from the interaction desire quite directly, it is still strongly positive in its efforts to resolve block and bring people together. When love fails, anger can try to capture and resolve the difference, so that true desire will return. If two minds finding block between them decide to share their anger and transfer a new impression upon each other, then they will improve their terms and mutual understanding. Through anger they will find agreement on whose feeling or knowledge is the strongest to share.

During anger, we put all of our cards on the table. We remove our inhibitions, and look for a new level of honesty. The anger looks for a test of will or inner strength. There may be an agreed contest. If one animal is stronger in their chosen field of contest than another, then the fluency and strength they display even under the charged influence of anger should be enough to let them win or at least partially impress the other contestants. The resultant feeling of pleasure gained upon resolution can be as great as any other positive emotion. The minds find the stronger or more fluent position that all can see and share. Anger resolved smoothly can feel enjoyable and invigorating. It improves understanding and terms between people.

However, anger might be unable to find the agreed rules of contest. It is ready to put us to the test, but the contestants might play unfairly. The contestants might feel individual, so any loss will be far more devastating than a loss between like-minds and like-souls. Learnt mindrule differences will prevent mutual resolution and accommodation, because the fundamental differences are too great. We cannot accept any loss graciously, because the loss would weaken our fundamental position, rather than be just a tinkering at the edge. We might fight for our own set of rights, rather than trying to blend what is right with others. Anger cannot get past these barriers to make an impression in the way it was designed to achieve. The clashing niche maps might never be able to merge because of their hidden internalised blocks. The anger must fail before it can even try. Fundamental difference that lies beyond the control of anger leaves the emotion with no real power to be positive. The anger will become frustrated. The anger will become listless and wonder why such differences occur. It will become preoccupied and upset that it cannot find a way in, to display its good intentions and find agreed resolution. Then, the anger might believe its mindrules, and see that it cannot produce results because the other mind is fundamentally bad or alien. The other mind has no real intention of finding mutual accommodation on a merged or instinctive level where it really counts.

Anger that believes in its confused and alienated niche map will usually double its efforts and lash out in its attempt to make another submit to agreement. Anger may forego any link of equality, and try to lower the importance of another until it finds resolution according to its confused understanding. Anger may cause violence. The anger will not flow from a sense of respect, but will fear what could arise from the alien mind if it won the upper hand. If we win, we might feel in control, but we will not find the strength or equality that is meant to arise from anger. The feeling of power from gained from submission cannot be as strong or as wild as the feeling gained from admission.

5.13 Frustration

Frustration is the feeling that we need before we can turn our anger into violence. Anger is an emotion that is designed for a world where block is not permanent and internalised. It is an innocent emotion that sets out with good intention. Normally, anger would be able to resolve block, remove the bone of contention simply, and return desire back to its wild and natural state. Anger is not the cause of social disruption in humans. The source of the disruption is frustration, which arises from our belief that other people are different, and do not try hard enough to find common ground, even after our anger. Mindrules lead anger astray to pursue unnatural options. The problem for us is that we have such poor understanding and ability for receptive accommodation that we can see no way out. Illusory blocks are all about us. This misunderstanding affects us on a deep instinctive level, allowing the development of a deep sense of frustration.

Some level of frustration is normal, and animals evolved a variety of displacement activities to diffuse its effects. They might hit at a nearby bush, stomp at the ground, or frown. Displacement activities help prevent blocks from remaining frustrating, and becoming internalised. The emotional energy can be worked off or taken out on something else. Some office workers might take a similar approach, and hit a punching bag after work hours to relieve tensions. However, we would do better to resolve permanently the cause of our excessive human frustrations.

When we cannot resolve blocks they become internalised. From their internal position, blocks will always be able to maintain a background level of frustration in our species. Frustration will be difficult to avoid. However, frustration wants to be resolved. It arises from a feeling that there is a block somewhere that is stopping the free and pleasurable flow of our desire. Unfortunately, the anger that frustration can generate often has no block to act upon. The source of block is internally hidden, and so we cannot see where the change is needed. The sets of rules between people seem irreconcilable. Anger therefore constantly bubbles away, wanting to get things out into the open where they can be resolved.

We can live with a certain level of background frustration, and become used to it, so that we lose awareness of its existence. However, the subconscious frustration can accumulate until it has to make its presence felt. A background level of frustration is rarely far away. Our mindrule blocks are like a cage, that we are unaware of because they are now a part of our instincts. It makes people snappy and quick to anger, often without us knowing why. Our anger appears often, innocently trying to make our different sets of rules similar. However, they will always fail because the differences are more fundamental than our anger evolved to recognise.

Normally for wild animals the frustration they feel is minor and easy to release. However, if they are placed in a cage, their frustration can increase. They might become self-destructive. They might pull out their own hair or feathers. Frustration keeps gnawing away at them.

Similarly, humans cannot escape their mindrule cage. Much of our frustration expresses the restriction of our hidden mindrule blocks. Our frustration needs an outlet. It can overtake our reasoning. We might find illusory external blocks to fight. People might lash out for no apparent reason, and with no justification.

Frustration can be difficult to account for when it interrupts our mind for minor apparent reason. It can be disappointing and undermining if frustration appears readily, because it indicates some basic flaw in our own basic niche skills. Frustration can lead to the feeling of being denied completeness, of missing out on something, or of not doing enough with our own lives.

5.14 Violence

Violence is common in humans. It is something we fear, yet seem unable to avoid. During rapid niche change our mindrules become inundated with stimulation they cannot relate with directly. We learn to assimilate many blocks into our niche map, and begin to see the world with restricted and alienated mindrule eyes. With such a poorly developed niche map, our desire is continuously thwarted and frustrated on a subconscious level. This makes us emotional, and our frustrated anger will readily convert itself into violence to search for its answers. The violence of our anger can sometimes surprise even ourselves, because we thought we were in control.

Anger produces harmony and resolution in animals, but aggression and violence in us. In humans, the desire behind anger will long continue to feel emotional after its violence, because the violence will fail to resolve at a niche map level. The anger will not let our energy convert back into its original true desire, where it could perhaps see through the illusory bads. Our anger will remain as emotion, and may become excessive beyond need. Because our anger is mindrule directed, it will also act in confused manner. Its effects will fail to be harmonious, and will fail to resolve our important issues in the long term. It cannot free our desire. This compares with anger in wild animals, which is natural and has real and resolvable blocks to face. Anger in animals has much simpler tasks to perform than in our species. For wild animals, their anger can end easily, complete a task, and finish with a result that is harmonious and appropriate for the environment.

We have excuses for our violence, but they all show that we see our blocks as being beyond the reach of the common soul's mutual resolution. The reasoning behind violence is to shift an uncompromising block. The blocks may be a hated person, law, object or animal. If the bad is another race, the violence can channel as prejudice. Emotion will usually not release as violence, unless it feels justified. If it cannot find something to blame it will remain in the form frustration, search elsewhere, or dissipate as nervous energy and displacement activity. An alternative is to produce what has been termed senseless violence. This is frustrated violence that does not wait for an excuse, so attacks for little reason. Senseless violence can be unnerving, because it seems to have no excuse or reason. However, the blocks needed to produce senseless violence come from within. The person has allowed internalised block to overwhelm their lives. A glimmer of reason behind vandalism and senseless violence may arise, if it seems that an impenetrable and insensitive society might change by making it unsettled.

The intent behind violence is always good. Violence tries to remove bads and restrictions so that life will be better. However, the problem for energy that follows violence is that it has fallen for the illusions created by mindrules. That is why violence as I am describing it here does not occur in animals, and why it is always the wrong or weaker option for us. It is not a true desire, but comes from deluded emotion. Violence comes from pent up confused energy. Therefore the act of violence can produce a feeling of relief, but it will not feel right, especially upon reflection.

Sometimes violence can feel good, especially during the time or act when there is relief of built up tension. A person can also revel in the delusion that they are at last doing something positive to make life more streamlined. However, violence will not sit well as a means of accomplishment, especially after thinking about the event. Our feelings might be aware that the act was actually a result of our own weakness rather than strength. The violence will only cut off one more link in our potential connection to the wildness. The feeling of strength gained by understanding a problem will be far greater.

There is never any complete or right excuse for violence. It will always be the weaker option. However, it may at times be necessary to use violence to achieve some kind of balance in the absence of better alternatives. We may have insufficient wit to find the right alternative in the time or knowledge available. However, violence will never be able to fulfil its aim of removing the bads. More bads will always reappear, because the potential for bads comes from restricted mindrules, not reality. The logical extrapolation of violence is self-destruction, because even if all bad people can be removed by violence, the mindrules that produce the potential will still be there, and be forced to turn on whatever is left as its source of bad. The niche map needs bad to keep its pattern of restriction in place. Violence does not succeed as a long term solution, and usually makes the problem worse. Our violence will make us look bad to another. Violence provides people with excuses, and allows mindrules to become further entrenched and defined by their perimeter of bads. Violence makes us lose contact with reality, and our access to beauty, relatability and strength.

5.15 Aggression

Aggression is often put forward as being an instinct and a part of human nature. However, aggression has a different meaning to anger. Anger is an emotion, while aggression is an attitude. Anger is a positive option that desire can use to try and improve its performance, whereas aggression is supposed to be an inherited instinct or adaptation to life. Anger can exist in the wildness, because it does not break the link between the animal and its niche. Aggression is our attempt to label anger, and place a reason behind it that we in our mindrule-restricted terms can understand. We might think that anger is an inherited emotion that was originally designed to make us dominate others. We make this presumption because of our lack of knowledge and experience of what wildness feels like, and our misunderstanding of what evolution entails. We do not see how anger could be a positive drive that can expect to work. We do not know how animals feel when they do their anger, but judge their actions through the frustration and restriction of our own mindrules.

Our anger is always frustrated, because the blocks on our niche map have such an internal hold over us. We might think that violence or domination naturally follows anger. At times we feel our anger wanting to remove the other side. Then, because anger is a natural emotion, we think that the aggressive approach to life is how a well functioning animal should behave. Aggression is seen as an instinct, and as a tool for ensuring survival.

In nature, anger is common but aggression is rare. Anger in the wild is much more raw and passionate than the aggression we know. The desire behind anger is more akin to love and hope. It does not have violence in mind, because the blocks needed to change the tone of anger are not the blocks that a wild animal will normally experience. Violence is a later development of anger that occurs mainly in us. Anger comes to terms with the block while violence tries to destroy the block. Violence requires alienation and restriction of the niche map's soul before it can occur. But wild animals do not feel that way. Wild animals are in fact quite open. Therefore, we need to interpret the aggression that we think we see in the wild differently.

Our regular experience of aggression arises because we have a minefield of internalised block on our niche maps that instinctively turn our anger into aggression. We need to use anger so often that it becomes our attitude or temper. It becomes a blanket response that we use, perhaps even before there seems a need. Mindrules give us numerous illusions to believe, against which our frustration can dupe and send our anger. Mindrules put the excuses for aggression into our subconscious, so that they become how we feel. The illusions they create feel natural to the mind. Aggression becomes an expression of how we feel. Anger now feels like a caged emotion or attitude that is negative.

Some animals may appear aggressive, but they are still only acting within the bounds of doing what they need to do to self-enhance according to the guidelines provided by the ecosystem. They are not using an attitude, but are more responsive and sensual instead. They are doing what is wild for them in their part of the ecosystem. At times they might use anger a lot, when they become territorial, hungry, or in need of a mate. But their anger has a reason that can be met and diffused. Their actions may seem violent and aggressive to us, but their real drive is a wild reason that is more powerful and free. They act because it is what they need to do for the conditions of their niche. When a predator attacks and kills its prey, it is not angry or hateful towards the prey. It is simply a natural job for them to accomplish. They do not have an instinct to cause harm and destruction. Their behaviour is designed to contribute to the harmony. Hunting behaviours evolved to cause least possible harm while still allowing sufficient self-assertion to live comfortably. Animals have no need to continue their aggression beyond this level. They do not have to relieve a frustration.

Similarly, our hunter-gatherer ancestors had a spiritual link to their prey, and did not kill for violent reasons. They would dance for the spirit of their prey, or paint them on cave walls. Violence by modern humans is disruptive and painful to society and all concerned. It uses excessive force and causes excessive damage beyond what is necessary, indicating that we have additional intent or aggression behind our acts. We use our anger for weak reasons.

There are rare cases where animals kill more prey than necessary, suggesting a lust for violence. However, these are mostly phoney set ups where humans have restricted or contained nature within artificial experiments. Some wild animals might not be trained to turn off their developed hunting instincts themselves. For example, a fox in a chook pen may kill all the hens, beyond that needed for food. In the wild, the ability for such an excess number of prey species to escape might naturally keep the excesses of some hunting instincts in check. Alternatively, such examples may be due to a higher predator's need to teach or hone their skills. An important part of learning an instinct is to practise an instinct. The fox may kill all the hens to teach its cubs how to kill efficiently. In Australia, one of the most violent animals to the ecosystem is the domesticated cat. It kills and maims wildlife for no apparent reason. But it has a need to hone hunting skills, even though those skills do not fit here ecologically. This just shows a deeper need to use learnt mindrules, which are normally learnt under natural conditions where they do not go wrong. The nature of the cat is only a problem because it has been placed outside its true niche. Its wild reason is lost. The collection of dead animals bought to the doorstep is not proof that aggression or violence is natural. It is proof that certain instincts can become destructive when they lose contact with their wild niche.

Most other animal behaviour that we judge aggressive occurs between species members when they appear to compete. But the 'aggression' rises and falls according to the flow of their desire for more fundamental needs such as mates or territory. Aggression is not a need of its own. Those animals may be protective or highly assertive only during certain times of the year. They act for reasonable needs. Their aggression is more akin to playing than destroying. They might challenge a dominant rival when they feel confident and daring, rather than hateful. Normally, the challenge will not last long, and the result will be decided without much damage. Aggression is a judgmental label that we apply to what are really just reasonable behaviours. Animals sustain their anger only as far as the wildness will allow. The conditions of the niche determine the kind of behaviour needed to keep a species healthy.

Anger in our species is aggressive because it acts out of attitude rather than wild reason. We use aggression more than needed. It can lead to violence. I would define violence as something that harms the fabric of the niche. It acts for no good or sound reason. It alters the fabric of the environment or society. For example, war has occurred regularly throughout our history, and changed greatly the societies involved. War is usually between different countries, races or religions, where people do not feel they are from the same niche or of the same spirit. Anger in humans is forced to try and break free before it can show its positive intention. It might lash out, and affect the innocent. Anger in animals is not a violence or disruption to the fabric of their niche. They are not trying to break free of a self-imposed cage to which they are blind.

For most of our history as hunter-gatherers we did without wars. If there were any disputes, the protagonists would simply part company. The wild reaction to a block is mostly to leave the block and try to find the wild niche once more. A Philippine tribe of hunter-gatherers discovered in 1971 had no words for war, enemy, honour, glory or bravery. Their words gave beauty the highest value (Farb, 1978: 100). War arose mainly after we lost the hunter-gatherer way of life. Simply parting company during disputes became difficult, because life began to revolve around permanent settlements and agriculture. At least somewhere in the world, war has continued right up unto modern times. It seems likely that it will occur a little while further into our future yet.

Aggression in our species needs to be seen in its right context. A biologist should not study an animal that was under stress to understand its true nature, without also considering the impact of its stressful conditions. The art of biology is to understand a species in terms of its niche, or in terms of its changing niche. The existence of aggression in our own species today does not mean that it is a natural part of our instinctive repertoire.

5.16 Hate

Hate occurs when all hope that a block can be removed seems lost. The block in our niche is a permanent frustration. If the block is such that we cannot turn our anger into aggression and violence, then our emotion may have to turn into hate. In hate, the external block is known and targeted, but it is also immovable and unchangeable. We are fully trapped by the block because of our circumstances, or because it is so dominant, or because we cannot influence its existence. The hate might be for a political party or race of people that will always have some influence over us. The hate might be for a relationship that cannot be escaped. It might be for a person or work partner that is not likely to go away, but will continue to influence our lives for as long as we can foresee.

Because hate can do little against the block, its only chance of success may be to carry with it some hope as well. Simply saying you hate something might be enough to have it go away. In hate we might hope that some ill would befall the hated block. In hate we are often on the alert for any opportunity to reduce the power of the block or hated person. Often, the hate can turn to violence, if there is any slight drop in inhibition, or if any slight opportunity arises to act against the block. Hate can also impregnate itself throughout our niche map to become a part of our attitude. Then, we might not fully understand the source of our block and hate. It will be an attitude, and a person can become a hateful person. They can be ready to put down and be negative over a wide range of interactions and issues.

Hate is not a natural wild feeling. It is only possible when we begin to take the conclusions of confused mindrules seriously. Children are not born with hate. It is something they must learn. They attempt love first. Hate is a caged or unnatural emotion. Hate makes its appearance after mindrules have hardened or become entrenched. To feel hate reveals weakness and restriction of soul and spirit, where the strength to maintain receptivity over mindrules is lost.

Hate is not a natural emotion that animals would normally feel. There is no real expression for it, other than when it is unleashed to become anger instead. Its expression can only borrow from anger. If looks could kill is the closest hate might have as an expression, but this is really just the early expression for anger. Hate is not natural because a wild animal always feels sufficiently confident and accomplished to be able to overcome any block. They cannot be kept down for long. In a natural setting, an animal being routinely inhibited by a block will move away to another place, rather than let its desire or spirit become permanently bogged down in hateful emotion. Only if an animal is confined or caged, will there be hate.

If our mind is in a cage it can hate. Mindrules taken seriously in a changing niche will give us the potential for hate, because the understanding in our mindrules will always be seriously questioned at some point in time. Because mindrules cannot change themselves on their own, without a stronger desire to guide them, they will be left with no alternative but to hate the block they cannot affect. The surroundings just determine the object or direction of hate.

The feeling of hate can be removed by insight. A hateful person should realise that their block is either being misinterpreted, or is itself confused and therefore ineffective and easy to side step through greater understanding.

5.17 Depression

The feeling of depression usually produces a particularly bleak type of mood, because there seems to be no opportunity to improve the conditions for our lives. Depression arises from constant and unrelenting failure or block. We see little chance of being able to improve our situation by using one of our more active emotions. Depression is similar to frustration, however, frustration still leaves us with the feeling that we have some hope of removing the block. Frustration is easier to relieve than depression, because it can lead us more quickly into the emotions of anger hate or reason.

In depression, desire has little chance of finding a way out, so it remains contained and listless in the mind. The desire cannot be fulfilled. Depression will therefore produce a mood to alter the medium of the niche map and find a new track through the altered conditions. Depression is unable to produce an active emotion because it does not know the cause of the blocking feeling, or the block is well beyond conquer, remedy, or reasonable approach. The cause of the depression may be known, such as some recent disaster involving the loss of family or business. The tragedy may end the opportunity for continued interaction or bonding. Alternatively, depression can take hold for no clear reason, and will not be shaken off.

Humans would suffer more from depression than wild animals. All emotions and moods require block before they can appear. The blocks that produce our unnatural levels of depression are the internalised blocks that we place on our niche map. Mindrules under niche change cannot help but produce times of depression. In order to assume a niche map level of completeness when they are in fact mistaken, mindrules are forced to conclude that the reason for their failure is that block is a normal part of our life. If we accept this conclusion, then we must also accept that we cannot escape or reason our way beyond the permanent block. We accept our blocks, and learn to deal with them instinctively. Desire is therefore blocked early on many occasions, before it can enter our mind. Sometimes, the blocking effect is so great that it will produce depression. Depression is the natural consequence of a niche map whose general feeling for life is that it should accept its alienation and restriction.

While the cortex instinct's need to produce a completed niche map makes us accept our niche blocks; our desire will always feel frustrated and restricted by their presence. Our natural adaptations expect to live to their fullest capacities. We evolved to expect life in a niche that is in the vein of wildness. True desires and potentials that would normally have flowed along naturally fulfilling pathways must instead flow along confused pathways that displace and block. All of this is done subconsciously. We are not aware of how much of our desire and spirit is being blocked. The depressed and down-trodden desire can only accumulate and wander in the subconscious. Eventually, it can reach a level that must break into our conscious mind. It can appear for no apparent reason. While we might consciously find a way to release that energy, the potential for our depression will remain while our mindrules reign supreme.

Depression is an unpleasant feeling, so it can lead its animal to turn off and withdraw from its interactions. Reduced interaction will bring less energy to the pleasure centre, so there will be less measure of failure. The fewer interactions, the less stimulation, and the less desire released into the mind. Inaction can reduce the pain of depression. If mindrules have won, and the blocks seem real, then a person may withdraw from society and friends. However, this course offers no way out, because mindrules are the real cause of block, not stimulation with the outside world. If we do nothing to discover and circumvent the blocks, or take them less seriously, then depression may turn into apathy. In apathy, a person does not feel relatable enough to become involved. The person is not effective. Apathy develops if the person learns to live with the blocks, so that the blocks become more acceptable and comfortable rather than depressing. Then, the art of living is not practised. People in a street might ignore and walk by others in trouble. Apathy might cause someone not to bother dropping litter into a bin. They are not really a part of the system anyway.

One known way to relieve depression is to try and turn depression into frustration, by finding or inventing a clear block to conquer. Then the restricted energy of depression might channel into anger. However, the best way to get out of depression would be to look for and expose the blocks and restrictions that we impose on ourselves through our lack of realisation. The bad and alienated things we see are illusions. It is best to wipe the slate clean, and take no impression from the blocks that others see. Mindrules must learn to incorporate all information receptively. It is not true that mindrules are catering to our true potential. There is another being in each of us capable of doing whatever we want to the highest ideals that we want. Wildness is the normal way to be. Mindrules, and the self-identity they have produced, should not be taken seriously. Develop wit until we can take a step outside the boundaries assumed by our mindrules.

5.18 Escape

Frustration and depression are feelings gained when blocks seem insurmountable or at least difficult to overcome. Such feelings are therefore difficult to resolve. Because these feelings offer desire no clear course towards fulfilment, the only alternative available for desire may seem to be what is called escape. The need to escape the realities of life is yet another important difference between humans today and the wild animal. No other animal has a need to escape its niche. However, we often need to escape the harsh realities of our life and society.

An animal in its correct niche has no need to escape that niche. The niche caters to all potentials and desires of the animal. They live a life that is wild. The large variety of escapes that people require today shows that we are not in a wild or true niche. Escape is a need for wholesale separation from the current niche conditions, to find boosted stimulation outside the niche. Entertainment is different to escape, as entertainment seeks additional stimulation within the terms of the niche. However, the escape might not be allowed by society, because it will often look for results outside societies' norms. Therefore, the escape will often need to be secretive. The escape may disappoint other people when they realise how unfulfilled a person really feels. If the standards of the established niche or society are seen as being grossly false or alien, then people might seek an escape that increases their degree of separation from that niche. Two examples of escape are drugs and violent videos.

The need for escape may be seen today as a necessary and normal part of life, however it is important to understand where the restrictions to desire arise. The need to escape comes from restrictive mindrules, not a restrictive society. The most powerful forces at work in our world are the same forces that have always been in existence. Society might seem to provide the excuse, but only a mindrule restricted spirit would use such an excuse. Because it is their nature, mindrules will say that our restrictions arise from outside factors rather than from their own mistakes. From their entrenched and serious position, mindrules can say to true desire that a more fulfilling release is not available. If desire must continue in its spirit of seeking greater stimulation within each of its interactions, then it should look for a way out through escape. Mindrules cannot change, so look elsewhere for what you want. Under this tone, desire can feel trapped by the situation of its own mindrules. Desire might feel like throwing it all away, to perhaps escape through drugs. Desire does not always care that drugs alter or numb the mind, as the mind can see no better alternative for its desire for pleasure anyway. The mind with its strange rules might not always be a friend.

I think that today's mindrules restrict our natural receptivity and desire for wild fulfilment by at least half of its true spirit. Our species realises only half of its true potential, and knows only half of the true forces at work in our world. Some of the evidence to support this view is that we have created so many problems. When we do reach our potential, any permanent block that we see will dwarf in comparison under greater realisation. The restrictions now being imposed on us that might make us want to escape, are rooted in confusion. There is plenty of room outside mindrules to make it all come together. The mistake made in escape is that through them we accept the teachings of mindrules, and take their confusions seriously. However, all the tools that we need to feel complete, in whatever niche we are born, are already in us and were put there for us by nature long ago. Drugs and escape only lead us further away from those adaptations, by assuming that they do not exist or that they are not powerful enough to take control and send our spirit wild. Then, rather than concentrating on the natural mechanisms that are available for finding fulfilment; people will look for boosted stimulation through artificial means. But in the end, the artificial method will always fail in its primary aim. Escape lets us perpetuate a wrong assumption. There is no wildness in drugs.

5.19 Fear

Fear is one of the worst feelings we might ever experience. It is a feeling of surprise or unpreparedness for a situation that seems beyond our means to positively resolve. It signals that we are or could be in a vulnerable position that we cannot avoid. If we realise our fears, we may experience even greater emptiness or pain. The fear might arise when being attacked, standing on the edge of a cliff, looking at a snake, going into a strange environment, or being alone in the dark. Fear can combine all our worst feelings.

It can be difficult to know what to do in fear. The feeling of fear might make us produce an active emotional response. It might make us run, tell lies, cry or hide. Sometimes, we might be so scared that we cannot even produce an active response. We might feel fear, but have no notion of what to do next. We might only be able to express our fear, stand still, and hold our facial expression like a gaze. The expression might turn us 'white as a sheet', as our bodily activities withdraw to hide or avoid the feeling. If expression is all that the feeling of fear can do, then we might freeze. Then we are not really producing an emotional response, but are simply expressing a feeling. At times, freezing can be a useful response. Some predators can only see their prey, from a distance at least, when it moves.

Fear is perhaps the feeling that we least wish to have, because it can be so disruptive and distressing. Fear is the opposite of what the pleasure centre wants to feel. The pleasure centre wants greater possibility out of all our interactions, while fear is the prospect that our interaction will return to us with great emptiness. In fear we sense that there is no common ground through which we can build our bonds of interaction. There will be no bonding or entwining of spirit. Your input is not required, and the events might proceed as though you are nothing worthy of consideration in the chain of events that will follow. Your feelings will have no influence on the outcome. There are no prospects for developing a relationship. Your interactions will end.

There are two main kinds of fear. Our fear may come from something that we know to be dangerous, and may lead us further into terror (fear of pain). Alternatively, our fear may be for the unknown. We may feel fear without being able to specify the cause;

however, its anticipation may lead us further into dread (fear of emptiness). Fear is our reaction to perceived danger from both the known and the unknown. However, there is a deeper concern in our fear than just terror and dread. What the animal in us fears most is the prospect of disrelation. We cannot share in the interaction, and influence the outcome. The pleasure centre can send out its energy with good intent, but will get nothing in return. The animal has lost its niche.

We do not begin our lives being afraid of the known and unknown. Animals are highly adapted to life in their natural evolved niches, so they normally have little to fear. At first, an animal will approach the unknown with curiosity. Normally, an animal's adaptations and sensitivities will enable it to escape or resolve the unknown at the earliest hint of danger. If a species were receiving regular pressure and danger from some part of its niche, that made it uncomfortable sufficient to live in fear, then evolution would have changed that species to become better adapted to its niche. The species' descendants would become better camouflaged, faster runners, or perhaps develop erratic and confusing flight patterns. An animal in its proper niche feels comfortable for most of its life.

Offspring can learn fear from their parents. The young of many species observe and copy parental reactions. From their parents they might learn to fear certain predators, before they ever experience the pain. Similarly, people can learn many fears, such as a fear of spiders, snakes, and height. Most animals do not fear spiders and snakes. Some birds and monkeys view them with delight, and eat them readily. The development of our fears must await the development of our mindrules. Babies and children lack fear, until they experience pain, or are taught to be aware of dangers and bad by their parents.

Proof that fear is learnt, rather than being an inherited instinct, can be found on many islands. Small isolated islands are often devoid of large predators, and the niche is relatively simple. The animal inhabitants usually show no fear, and do not flee from people. They have not experienced the block of pain excessively, and have not been taught to fear by their parents. The dodo did not know fear, and did not try to escape club-wielding sailors. However since that time, many of the remaining island inhabitants have learnt fear. Similarly in Australia, there are few large predators. Most wild animals and marsupials in their pristine environments were relatively tolerant and tame. It is often surprising how close you can get to a wild animal if you respect their niche.

We can vary the amount of fear that is natural to an animal. Sometimes, people might encourage a lack of fear in a wild animal. Protected wild animals fed by picnickers in a national park may soon lose their fear. Similarly, if we release a tame animal into the wild, we might try to teach the animal some fear, so that it will be more cautious within its new conditions, for a while at least.

Fear is rare in animals, because block is rare. Fear is mostly learnt, and it is not an essential natural instinct. It will only arise out of learning or experiencing excessive block. Animals that are potential prey or competitors do not live with a feeling of fear and struggle. They live in comfort. They are probably not even aware that they can die or be badly injured. They don't see their habitat or jungle as a dangerous place where death lurks behind every tree. They can be quite reckless instead. Even while they are being eaten or quickly killed, they probably don't realise they are coming to an end, and I suspect they feel much less dread than we could imagine. More than anything during their end, they would go into a numbing shock of surprise. Nor do humans start out realising that they can die, and that they should fear death, until parents communicate it to them. It often comes as a great shock to children that they and their family can die. Such information cannot be passed between the other animals.

While the fear of pain is common in animals, the dread of emptiness is unique to humans. Dread is fear as a caged emotion. It is a fear that thinks most about disrelation and an end of soul-like attunement to the niche. Feeling individual and alienated increases the occurrence of dread, because we have less in common with other things in our world. Our strongest feelings of dread usually crystallise into our fear of death. In death, our essence will end and there will be nothing to continue our kind. To an individual, death is the final injustice. It is the end of what is essentially you. To an attuned being, death is just a redistribution of the pieces to other forms that already carry and share our spirit. Dread is not felt in animal fear.

Our dread or fear of death expresses our reaction to an underlying feeling of restriction and alienation. These feelings are born essentially from confused mindrules, which is why dread is absent in wild animals. If life seems inadequate and unfulfilling we will fear death because we will not have lived up to the pleasure centre's desires and hopes. Death is the end of our little world, because nothing else shares the soul of our world. For an animal that lives life to the full accomplishment, death does not carry with it the extra emotional baggage of unfulfilled hopes and dreams. It should be possible to look back on ones life and feel as though nothing fundamental was missed. In life today, mindrules cannot fulfil. The body and mind knows it never really quite lived up to the potential that it had. All of our desires will not be welcomed backed into a mother earth, because mindrules kept us individualised. We might carry the hope that with more time, we will feel to our core the spirit of life or a sense of ultimate completeness that we sense could exist. However, our mindrules are not of a quality that will allow this to be achieved. The approach of death can remind humans that they have missed out.

Death is a blow to dead-end mindrules. They cannot in the end make their own little worlds more powerful than the big world that reigns supremely outside their cage. Mindrules consider themselves to be individual, with a precious but lonely soul. Therefore, death will always mean the end to that format of soul. There is no joy for an individual in the idea that the materials of the body will continue to contribute to the universe in other ways and with other organisms. Our body might add strength to a worm, maggot, plant, or predator, and through them, add to the strength of the ecosystem in which we lived. However, if we were not a part of that ecosystem or world, such an end seems bad. There is no harmony or mother earth to which to return. The feeling of alienation wins over the feeling of sensual compliance and involvement. In most civilised cultures, the body is encased and kept separate from the rest of the world upon death. It is put in a box, capsule, tomb or pyramid. It is kept alienated. But in many hunter-gather cultures, the body is hung in a tree exposed to the elements, so that its 'spirit' can move freely back into its environment.

Our immediate ancestral species or subspecies would have begun to develop some sense that their niches were beginning to change. There was an overlap between the time when our cultural evolution gathered momentum, and when evolution continued to change our bodies physically. During this time, some sense of reduced attunement would have emerged. Humans had to find a way of dealing with this growing feeling of difference. Expressing the constant fear of difference would have been damaging within a gregarious society. It would have been inhibiting to show our subconscious feeling of difference through fear and doubt every time we interacted with someone. We had to show that we could overcome our growing sense of fear, with our greater desire to interact positively. We had to be able to change our automatic subconscious reaction of fear into a gesture that was friendly.

Therefore, the grimace of fear evolved into a smile (Morris, 1995). The grimace pulls the lips straight back to reveal the teeth. The smile does this also, but further pull muscles on the top lip and around the eyes to modify the grimace into a pleasant and more overwhelming expression. We turn the initial feeling of difference into a smile rather than a baring of the teeth. The smile shows that we are willing to overcome minor feelings of discomfort and disrelation, in favour of our greater desire to bond. The smile shows that we are willing to believe that the differences we sense instinctively are mistaken or minor. The true smile is absent in chimpanzees, because in natural conditions they do not live with a feeling of disrelation, but feel attuned with their niche. They did not enter a transitional period of accelerating niche change. The chimpanzee can only mimic our smile, but they lack the feeling behind it. Human is the only species that knows the fear of difference, so must smile to overcome it.

It takes some months before a baby can get the feeling that it should smile, but often that feeling is more to mimic than to express any feeling of alienation. The smile is now a natural expression for us. It makes us think immediately of friendship rather than its original fear. The smile tries to signal that there is nothing to fear, and that we are hoping for a positive interaction. It takes some confidence to overcome the initial fear reaction and smile, and so the smile shows that we feel we have the ability to overcome the differences. We are more likely to smile, or force a smile, if we feel uncomfortable or are keen to make a good impression. The smile is often used to try and get us out of fearful situations. Alternatively, we might use it more simply to try and promote a feeling of cooperation and acceptance.

Because fear is such a devastating feeling to have, whenever we feel it, we are probably going to have to make some drastic change in our life to exist beyond its feeling. Surviving fear, or existing beyond it, can be invigorating, as it is one of our toughest tests. Overcoming fear can be a thrill, because suddenly an outlet, accomplishment or skill appears in us that we did not think possible. If we overcome our fear we will have developed a new outlet or realisation. Overcoming fear can give relief to our build up of emotion. It can give us a greater sense of control and participation in our world. The prospect of finding such an outlet or experience can make us try to overcome and master our fears. Doing a dangerous sport such as bungy jumping or skydiving can give us the anxiety of fear and then the relief of accomplishment.

Overcoming fear might require us to find greater insight into our real capabilities, which can be a thrill. It can open up new possibilities. To survive the fear, we must come to closer terms with the real forces of the niche and what we are. We may have to dig deeper and find a new quality in ourselves. Or we may have to come to terms with and understand the feared object or event, and improve our own source of motivation and self-control.

Perhaps the worst part of fear is that we are capable of fear, because it means that we do not feel completely relatable with our world. We are not niche-attuned. However, the depth of fear that humans know is entirely the product of our own mindrules that went wrong during rapid niche change.

5.20 Reason

We generally do not consider reason to be an emotion. Humans have tried to put it on a pedestal of its own. However, a closer examination of reason will show that it has all the characteristics of an emotion. It is different from other emotions only in that the method it uses to try and resolve block is to actively explore the surrounding circumstances of the block, rather than accept that everything about the block is real. This ability to inspect has made reason our most aware emotion. We favour reason over the other emotions, because it offers so much opportunity, especially today when there is so much mistake that is repairable. During rapid niche change, there is much confusion. In this climate, reason often gets results. However, because reason is an emotion, it can only ever be the product of a restricted desire. It is fundamentally trapped by mindrules, and ignores information that is not mindrule labelled. It assumes internalised block, so essentially maintains the status quo of those internalised blocks. For this reason, it is has failed to make large strides into the wealth of wild information that surrounds us all. It traps us in our own fog. Reason has not solved the world's problems, but allowed them to perpetuate. It might eventually work out what is right, but it is slow and indirect.

Reason makes its appearance on one of the higher branches in the tree of emotions. It appears after most of the earlier and easier emotions such as hope, anger and love have failed. When all else fails and we cannot get our way, we will attempt reason to find out why. Reason therefore occurs late in our species. It does not occur in young children. A toddler can be quite unreasonable. Children try other emotions such as hope, love and anger first. Reason begins to appear only in late childhood or in adulthood. However, it will often remain poorly developed in adults as well, in which case those adults might be named irrational, with their behaviour continuing to be dominated by the earlier emotions.

Similarly, reason is an emotion that was not extensively developed by hunter-gatherers, because they were mostly able to resolve their blocks by using the earlier emotions of hope, love or anger. They also had fewer blocks to resolve because they were closer to the wildness, and desire could flow more freely. Only when block cannot be resolved to comfortable levels, do humans move on to the next more complicated and energy intensive emotion. Therefore, reason became most developed in those societies where it was difficult to resolve block in any other way. Agriculture, expanding populations, greater trade, improved means of transport between societies, and permanent settlements all made it difficult for European, eastern cultures, and other cultures, to resolve all of their blocks or simply part company.

Reason requires a well developed neural network in the brain before it can occur, sufficient to allow exploration of side-tracks and surrounding circumstances. It forces emotional energy away from the easiest neural pathways, into less explored side-tracks. It looks for ways to better understand its block.

Other animals can be intelligent, and show awareness about their niche. But they do not gain that intelligence through reason or great emotional effort. They remain comfortable in the use of their brain, and do not try to extend it with reason. They do not put great energy or attention to the reason, but develop their intelligence more naturally. They pick up intelligent information about their niche as it becomes obvious to them. In humans, reason can drive us to find a better world, which is something animals do not need to find.

Reason is able to examine the niche map and look at many of the alternatives on that niche map. It is less tied to the impulsive main highways of the niche map. It does not necessarily follow the most entrenched view. It can examine the more minor tracks surrounding the main highways, that otherwise lay dormant. In so doing, reason highlights those tracks, making them easier to notice. Reason is the most incisive emotion we have, and we can use it to re-examine our experience and things we take for granted. However, it can generally only make minor inroads into our mindrules. Reason occurs in the mind, and uses our conscious information. Unfortunately, the structure of our consciousness is developed for us by the mindrules in our subconscious. Reason therefore mostly assumes our mindrules, unless those mindrules are grossly in error and difference to others. Alternatively, another mind that does not bear the full complement of our own mindrules can sometimes help us to see through some of our own mistakes and assumptions. Other people can reason with us to help us overcome the internalised block to which we are blind. Reason is useful when it is shared by a society.

We have found reason to be a useful emotion. It is able to explore side-tracks in the neural network that will often place what we know into better arrangement. Reason resolves many minor blocks and improves our understanding within the mindrule framework. Because reason gets results, humans have developed its use. Reason is taught in schools, and expected by society. We are trained to divert the energy that we might place into other emotions into reason instead. Reason is more widely appealing to the rest of society. It is the best means of compromise that we have, when minds trapped in little worlds have to compete and balance to find their harmony. Reason can find the most acceptable compromise or pathways around a block. Reason is so well thought of and developed, and our belief in what it can do so strong, that we have placed it far above the other emotions in value, to the point where we no longer consider it to be emotional. However, our species is capable of greater creativity than reason can define.

5.21 Opinion

Opinion reveals more clearly the emotional content of our reasoning. It can take a long time for us to reason out why our world is the way it is. When we at last find our set of reasons, we can accept our world with clearer consciousness. Reasons allow us to acclimatise to our society, and show us how to train our desires in a way that will give them most comfortable passage. We can use reasons to quickly explain an event to our satisfaction. Those reasons that give us most pleasure and explanation become our opinions.

Opinions are the strongest parts in our reasoning. We will personally and emotionally support our opinions. We will argue for them if necessary. They are the result of much emotional effort. They become the conditions or rules of our mind. They are a mark of our individuality. The opinion might be an idea that is pivotal to the way we interpret our little world. Losing that opinion might damage our settled position. We might become so dependent on our opinions that we cannot tolerate anything that does not conform.

Because opinions are born from emotion, they naturally assume our mindrules. Opinions provide us with the reasons for our life's structure. They justify the nature of our mindrules. Opinions become the soldiers of our mindrules.

Some ideas don't get very far on their own. They need extra support before they will be accepted. We offer that support to our essential ideas through the emotion that we can muster in opinion. Humans spend a lot of time arguing their opinions. In their society they have many different positions to defend. It is hard to keep emotion away when opinions seem so right.

While we accept our opinions, others might not. We feel that our opinions should find wider acceptance than they currently enjoy. If people would only agree to our opinions, then the world would be a better place. Other opinions are usually wrong, weak or ill informed. We must fight for and emotionally support our opinions. There are competing opinions, and people cannot always be relied upon to make the right choice.

However, ideas that are true carry their own strength and ability to inspire. Opinions fall into the trap of attempting to drive ideas beyond their real value. They cannot inspire, and then hold back and watch for the wild judgement. Opinions place ideas out of emphasis, which confuses the value of them as ideas. Some opinions contain worthy ideas, but we cannot judge their true value while they remain wrapped up in a protective cloth of opinion. It might be difficult to allow an opinion to cut loose, and drift under its own steam and worth, to oblivion if that is its true merit. We are emotionally attached to our opinions. But truth should be able to fit in with everyone and ring true. Truth can stand up for itself. The only idea that needs encouragement and emotional support is an idea that is wrong.

There is a common belief in our world that we need to argue our point. This shows how completely our species now accepts its mindrule limitations. We shun receptivity. In argument, we assume that because an idea is having difficulty being accepted, we must present it more forcefully. We assume that people are somehow different, and cannot sense a real truth when it is before them. Still further, we might believe that some people are bad, so that against them we should argue even more strongly.

The need for opinion arises when mindrules feel alienated and restricted. Confused mindrules make us feel that the odds are stacked against us. The world is not fair and reasonable, so our good ideas must struggle to survive. Generally, the more individualised a person, the stronger their opinions must also become.

Opinions command great respect in our society. Someone who does not have opinion is often labelled empty or weak. Opinion helps to define a person and give them character. They help describe the attitudes and beliefs of a person, and reveal what type of person they really are. A person who argues reveals a lot about themselves and shows what they will stand up for. An expression of opinion will also help us to seek out people who have similar opinions. Then, we can assemble and mutually pamper our mindrules to our heart's content. Knowing someone's opinions will help us decide whether to bond with that person. It may be hard to get close to someone who has no opinion.

In tribal life when mindrules were similar, the emotions were far more successful at achieving their results than they are today. One way to measure the value of an idea was to see how much emotional support the idea could generate. The more emotional votes obtained, the more likely the idea would help the common niche of the tribe, as judged by the majority. The amount to which an idea was argued might once have been a good measure of its usefulness.

If an idea can generate emotion in a person then there must be something about that idea that is believable and worthy. The idea is more believable than an idea that fails to stir. There must be something pleasing and desirable about an idea that is being argued. Argument often takes advantage of the persuasive effect of emotion. A forcefully and emotionally argued point can often find greater acceptance amongst people than a dead pan delivery. People want to feel the full flow of their desires, so they become very interested when they see someone else apparently channelling their energy passionately.

But the value of opinion and argument has changed drastically today. It often fails to resolve blocks. Instead, our arguments often divide and alienate people even further. Our individual niches are too far apart. Our arguments can drive us back further into our own little worlds, rather than produce resolution and a blending of mind.

Opinions and argument now fail as indicators of truth. Instead, they more accurately reveal the presence of confused mindrules. It is best not to have opinion, or to deliver our ideas by argument. This in itself might seem to be an opinion, but I still try to keep everything listed in this book just idea and possibility.

Ideas should be put forward simply as possibilities. If we do this properly, many arguments will be lost. However, no disadvantage to the person who cannot argue will occur. Arguments can only win over paper tigers and illusions. Illusions have no real impact on our lives. There is a far greater wilderness of ideas to explore than can be caught and trapped within the narrow world of argument. Ridding the mind of opinions will improve our ability to find alternatives. It will improve our receptivity. In the longer term, this process gives a better position than any opinion can create. Rejecting opinions allows us to see the errors of their ideas more easily. Ideas that remain simply ideas are easier to play with and control. They do not have to become personal indicators of self-worth and strength. The rejection of self-opinion allows a person to change their ideas more rapidly, and become more exploratory in thought. The rejection will make our mindrules more pliable.

Our species has to change its mind. One way to achieve this change is through inspiration and insight. Both methods allow a person to realise a world greater than the one they first imagined and tried to defend. No one yet knows the right vision sufficient to inspire everyone completely. However, that does not mean that such a vision does not exist. Arguments can only rearrange the pile of distortion within a vision. They are essentially useless at changing the vision. It can take one simple insight to increase the vision, and bring all the once important arguments undone. There is no need to go through the front door of consciousness where the defences of mindrules are assembled in anticipation. Inspiration and insight can strike through the heart of mindrules at any time.

5.22 Debate

Debate attempts to develop our reason most purely. It is an attempt to drive all of our emotions entirely into reason, so that our emotions become more objective and the resolutions that they find more widely acceptable. It might be thought that if we could properly debate every subject, then all of our problems would be solved. However, the failure of debate to make inroads into our confusion points to the underlying faults and assumptions that bereft reasoning. Debate can lead to bickering, minor point scoring, uninspiring wins and losses, compromise, and an inability to thrill.

The aim of debate is to reduce the clouding effect of emotion, and make that emotion more aware. In debate we are more willing to explore the possibilities. However, because reason is an emotion, it usually turns out to become merely a way of promoting an existing point of view or mindrule world. There can be debating teams, where each side tries to find the reasons why their point of view should win. Debate is often just a more skilled way to argue.

Often in debate the result is a greater acceptance of many different points of view. There is agreement to differ. The subject is seen as being complicated. But from what I have seen, no subject is complicated. There is always a more simple truth somewhere, even if we lack the wit at the time to see it. As with the other emotions, reason fails to recognise mindrule blocks, and is trapped in their terms. Reason can fail to inspire or impress because it fails to recognise the mindrule blocks. It cannot release the desire that is trapped beneath into more pleasurable pathways. Wildness and receptivity produce ideas that are far more reasonable than reason can produce. They are processes that are able to step out of the mindrule ring and cater to desire more directly.

5.23 Thinking

We use our mind by thinking. Like other animals, we can think naturally and follow our instincts. However, if our thought meets block, we can think harder by using reason. Each method of thinking can approach a block or problem in a different way. To understand these approaches more easily, it is worth considering the block to be like a disruptive blot on a grid of neural pathways. The various modes of thinking approach and assess that block in their own characteristic manner and direction. Some ways of thinking are more manoeuvrable and objective about the block than others. Some are more able to remove the block reasonably, because their approach gives them some success at targeting the assumptions behind the block. Other forms of thinking are less successful because they do not look objectively for the assumption that creates all blocks.

Thinking with reason is a way of searching for new pathways on the niche map, so that the outlook can become more pleasurable and understanding. It can occur upon even the slightest doubt or loss of fulfilment. It will occur especially when block is strong, and the other emotions fail. Thinking with reason is an energy intensive process that requires a large amount of attention. The brain can become hot and tired from long bouts of thinking. Thinking can turn our energy towards shallower side-tracks away from the main highways of consciousness, that would otherwise go unnoticed. If the thinking travels over those side-tracks and finds a better alternative, attention will readily give it more energy to explore the new direction, and so entrench the thoughts further into our new consciousness. The new idea might then become a part of the normal flow of our awareness when conscious.

The first form of thinking to evolve was natural thinking. The simplest approach taken by natural thinking is to follow instincts. It is a thought process that other animals can use as well. Its results depend largely upon natural intelligence rather than an extension by reason. This method of thinking uses the least amount of energy, and is least analytical. It follows the same original train of thought so that when it meets a block, it can change only slightly to find solution. It is least able to question any underlying assumption, and has least association with wit. It leaps to conclusions early, and makes little change to the fundamental niche map structure. An example of natural thinking is when a bird pecks at glass to get at seed placed behind the sheet. The bird cannot think to fly around the sheet to gain access. A dog may think similarly when food is hidden under a tin. It may fail to knock the tin over, even though it can smell food. The dog leaps to the conclusion that because it cannot see the food as it usually can at feeding time, the food is unavailable. A dog that does knock the tin over may be more intelligent and exploratory, rather than attempting to use reason. Another example is our assessment of human violence. Natural thinking will try to solve this problem with laws that constrain violence, or that find controlled outlets to relieve the violent emotion in less damaging fashion. It accepts violence as a part of human nature. The real reasons for our violence eludes natural thinking.

Logic is an advanced form of natural thinking that recognises the existence of assumption. It does not excuse instinctive failure, or accept that problem and block are real. It considers that blocks and problems exist because we are making fundamental mistakes. Logic is very good at finding inconsistencies within concepts. Its main method of finding assumption is through extrapolation. By taking trains of thought to their logical or extrapolated conclusion, initial errors within those trains of thought magnify until they become obvious.

If we imagine the block on a grid of neurones, then logic is the thought that will arise when we try to magnify errors by moving forward in a straight line from the block. Logic will imagine as many steps as possible, in line, until the final step reveals the inconsistency. Logic takes a similar direction of thought to natural thinking, but it does not settle for the early conclusion. It draws upon emotional energy to go further, and pays attention to detail. It forces that line of natural thinking beyond its natural conclusions, to help define the errors. Someone writing a scientific paper might be illogical if they jump from one point to another out of order. A person who reacts angrily for no reason can seem illogical.

While logic can make inroads into basic assumption through magnification, it is still largely unable to look at its block sideways or from behind. Logic works forward of its assumptions, so cannot examine its own first steps fully. It tends to rearrange the pieces within an existing pattern, without causing fundamental change. Logic is rarely creative, and often fails to remove large portions of the deeper assumptions contained within each block. Logic tends to accept the general structure of its world, and searches for the least inconsistent pattern within those constraints. It can become trapped by facts. It is less interested in any feelings or broader goals that we cannot define. It might denigrate the importance of other factors to make what it knows neatly consistent. It will ignore feelings that we cannot define in preference to the logical answer. Therefore, logic can at times give a cold view. A robot can be logical, but also miss important information upon which the world turns. A logical person does not necessarily have 'common sense'.

In theory, the more facts available then the less room there is for distortion. However, we can become overly reliant on our facts. Often, the more clearly things are understood, the harder it can be to distinguish or favour certain selected facts. Everything is a fact in some way, so selected parts cannot really be scooped up from the meshwork of information and separated out on its own as fact. Facts are not discrete bundles of truth within a maze of alternate possibilities or bad. There is fact or reason behind everything, which deserves equal consideration. A good understanding does not require the memory of many facts.

If we rule our lives according to the facts, we will let our thoughts and logic dominate our feelings and desires. Mindrules often use facts as reasons and excuses for keeping out the troubling information that we cannot define. Also, different people can view the same fact very differently. While a fact may be true, the interpretation placed about that fact is still subject to mindrules. The fact that a glass has water to its middle means it is half full or half empty. The fact that people can die means life is cruel, or life is generous to let another then carry the baton.

Facts can be useful as a point upon which to focus and think; however, they should not mark the limits of our understanding. It is easy to compare and communicate our facts. But if those facts are used to dominate or exclude other less defined feelings, then it is likely that they will lead us astray into a narrow world. For example, it might seem a fact that evolution is meant to dominate nature, so don't be natural or you will have to be aggressive and selfish. Similarly, if you did not achieve a school certificate then you are dumb, and should not try to broaden your horizons. When we use our facts, we should also consider how they feel. A fact that does not sound or feel right is probably wrong, even though it seems to fit or is said to be proven. In view of the level of instinctive confusion in our species today, I think it is best to view all facts sceptically.

Lateral thinking is a more exciting way to reason. On the neural grid it can view a block from the left or right. Lateral thinking seeks a new angle from which to view the assumption behind a problem. By opening the angle from which we examine a problem, it is well equipped to discover basic assumptions that are wrong. It tends to find simpler solutions to our problems than logical thinking. De Bono gives many examples in his book *The Use of Lateral Thinking*.

During lateral thinking we must approach a problem from often quite obtuse angles. Therefore, it is often the most difficult form of thinking to achieve and control. The process is aided by wit, which makes us more willing to consider the alternatives. If we view the accepted angle or norm less seriously, we will find it easier to view the problem from another, even 'opposite' angle. Lateral thinking might use unrelated thoughts or objects to set off its novel train of thought. It is the most powerful or consistent means of thinking available for confronting fundamental assumption.

Perhaps the optimal approach for thinking is to use a mixture of both lateral and logical thinking. We could construct a good examination of the vertically and laterally connected tracks on the neural grid by working lateral and logical thinking together in tandem. Using these two thought processes we could rigorously examine a problem from many different angles. We could develop a novel idea through lateral thinking, and test it for accuracy with logic.

Still however, both lateral and logical thinking cannot escape their emotional constraints. They essentially can only entertain the information that we can define for them consciously. All modes of thinking remain strongly constrained by mindrules, allowing our deepest internalised blocks and assumptions to remain hidden from conscious view. Thinking is unable to approach internalised block from behind. It does not necessarily let us see the wildness.

5.24 Thinking versus feeling

An important difference between humans and the wild animal is the reliability that each can place on their instincts. Wild animals can be completely reliant on their instincts. Under natural conditions they are free, and flourish with the experience. They feel and sense their way through life. Human mindrules however are inappropriate, blocked and confused. Our experience is that we cannot rely on them, and so our species must instead use a great deal of thinking to try to work out its best course. We cannot use our instincts to feel our way through life, because they confuse so much of what we feel. Our species has come to the point where we must now often decide whether to do what we feel is right, or do what we think is right.

There are four alternative approaches to take. Most satisfying is when what we do both feels right and seems right. Then we can be most sure. At the other extreme, if something both feels wrong and seems wrong, then most people would conclude that they should not act in that way, and would only do so if forced. The remaining alternatives occur when our feeling and thinking do not match. We might wonder whether to yell at someone for doing something wrong, but feel afterwards that we were harsh and wrong. We might hate a race of people without knowing why. We might watch a violent movie or soap drama and feel good, even though we know the story perpetuates false illusion. One part of our mind feels right, while another part says that we are wrong, or visa versa. The conflict can make it hard to know what to do.

Thinking is a highly active state of mind. We think in terms of language, symbols and rules. We use thinking to try and make more sense out of what we feel. Using our symbols, we can order our information into patterns that are convenient to handle and assess. Thinking summarises the information that we sense into a useful pattern that is easier to communicate. However, thinking can only use the information that we can put into words. The simple act of putting something into words entrenches and conforms our information into a pattern of which we are already conscious. Words categorise and draw our feelings into defined symbols. All forms of thinking are trapped by mindrules, and cannot see the assumptions and blocks behind them. At best, thinking can be logical or lateral. But thinking does not necessarily see. Thinking occurs in terms of summary ideas, such as words, that are themselves mindrule entrenchments for a much larger range of experiences.

The information that lies in our thinking can be safe to use. Usually, it has been well thought out, discussed with others, and can reach consensus view. Thinking can be faster, snappier and easier to decide than feeling. It can give us standard answers. We often rely on thinking more than feeling to find safe and defined answers. The more effectively we can articulate our views, the more likely others will accept them. For some, approval by others is important.

The problem with thinking is that it lies entirely within the domain of mindrules. Thinking is done in the mind, and that is the part of the brain that mindrules control. If we rely on thinking too much, we might finish up being aware only of the information that we can articulate. We might learn to believe only in our opinions. If we rely on thinking solely, then our actions become as easy to read as the niche map and the mindrules from which they arise. We can become like switched on robots rather than sensual beings. We become aware only as far as our mindrules will allow. We might block out much sensory and feeling information, to try and keep our mindrule story coherent. We might ignore our true feelings, and replace them with just those feelings of which mindrules can speak and control. The thinking approach might sound as though it knows it all. It might have an answer for everything. But the thinking approach can then make us lose awareness for the things that we could only feel at this stage in our evolution. The perpetuation of our belief in the powers of thinking might increase our reliance on mindrules, their excess discipline, harshness, and fights for principle. Then, thinking might seem right, but it will not always feel right.

Feeling on the other hand contains much more information than thinking. It has information we can simply sense, without necessarily being able to describe its content. Feeling includes the information we can articulate, as well as information from broader nature and 'common sense'. The ability to feel is ancient amongst the animals. The ability to think concisely is largely a recent development in our genus *Homo*. All other animals control their behaviour by feeling and sensing with their natural instincts. Feeling is a method that has been tried and tested over millions of years.

However, the feelings in us today do not all arise from wild and natural places. The internalised blocks on our niche map can influence our feelings instead. We notice many of our feelings after they have been mindrule influenced. Some feelings arise from a wide variety of emotions and illusions implanted within our minds by our confused mindrules. Other feelings may be true and wild. Some feelings can be trusted, while others cannot. Therefore, they can be unreliable and illusory. It is important to determine the source of a feeling, and whether it comes wild from the niche or artificially from a mindrule deflection. Is it emotional, attitudinal or wild?

While mindrules have full control over thinking, feelings can have some independence from mindrules. Some of our feelings arise directly from desire, and will encourage us to look for the wild alternative that is free of mindrules or any other cage. Our desires grew up in natural systems that are based on attunement and harmony. Therefore, the initial reaction of desire is often to look in a different direction to what mindrules expect. We could use the wild feelings of desire to control our mindrules. We should place more weight on the initial aims of our natural desires.

How wide is the gap between what we feel and sense, and what we describe and talk about? The wider the gap the better. If you are proficient at expressing everything that you feel, then you may be strongly trapped within illusion. At this stage of our species evolution, we will not be able to describe adequately what we feel, until we become wild once more.

5.25 Stubbornness

We try to describe our feelings in words. However, if we do not have time to think when we must act, we will find it difficult to express those feelings. We may not have a good set of reasons by which to defend or explain ourselves. We might be asked to do something that we feel is wrong, and not have the reasons to say 'no'. People do not like an inability to communicate. Therefore, to try and resolve the impasse, our emotion can turn into stubbornness. We do not have to explain ourselves with reasons when stubborn. We can do what we feel is right instead. Stubbornness gives us the drive to stand firm and resolute against reason. The emotion gives us a 'thicker skin'. We can withstand the insult, which will surely come, when we fail to share the information upon which we are acting.

Stubbornness is generally cast as a bad emotion. In a mindrule-dominated world, those feelings we cannot speak are discouraged. The species rejects any recognition of the limitation in human reasoning, as we all pretend to be a knowledgeable and articulate species. In this setting, an emotion that recognises the inadequacies of reasoning has a negative effect on the grand illusion.

However, there is some value in stubbornness if we use it to recognise the failure of reasoning. We can use it to help keep our feelings live and strong. It may let us strive for higher levels of interaction than our reasoning currently knows. It can keep the spirits high. A strongly spirited person is often stubborn. Sometimes, stubbornness may be all that you have to get out of doing something that you don't want to do. It can be a useful emotion if it keeps to its original path of remaining more concerned with how we truly feel, than as a means of getting our way. Through stubbornness we might gain the time needed to think things out more carefully on our own terms.

We generally feel little pleasure in having to be stubborn. It is an interim emotion that will normally make us try to find a better set of reasons so that we can explain better how we feel at a later stage. Desire would rather share its feelings through a better set of reasons.

Stubbornness is a problem when it becomes attitudinal. Then, we learn to accept that there are some things we can never explain or share. We think that others can never know how we feel because people are different and individual. Stubbornness becomes a tool of mindrules, to use to defend personal block or mindrule position. It becomes a means of saying no, and loses touch with our desire to resolve our knowledge according to a higher standard. Stubbornness then no longer acts to protect our true feelings. Instead, stubbornness acts on the restricted feeling dished out to us by mindrules. If we allow our feeling to remain bound to mindrules, it can take itself seriously, and think itself righteous in its stubbornness.

5.26 Conscience

The conscience is a further example of what happens to the mind when thinking does not match feeling. It arises when the reason for doing something does not feel right. For example, if we find a wallet and keep the money, our conscience might not feel right. If we use someone for our own benefit, to then abandon them when the task is complete, our conscience may stir. An action that gives immediate relief might leave a lasting feeling of emptiness or disappointment that turns out to be much worse.

The conscience is like a pure seeking standard that speaks against an action or reasoning it feels is wrong. Following the conscience will often make us feel better, because it asks for a higher standard than our actions currently know how to deliver. The conscience usually asks us to be less selfish or honest in our actions than our first thoughts might take us. The things we do should suit a wider forum than our restricted mindrules ask. However, following the conscience can make life difficult in the short term, as it asks us to behave more honourably. It might put us to greater task than otherwise necessary, and make us vulnerable to ridicule for the effort.

The conscience is the pleasure centre trying to operate while under stress. Normally, the pleasure centre directs our desire subconsciously, with little impact on our thoughts. It develops a code of behaviour that rewards the beautiful and efficient things that we do with pleasure. But when our actions become dominated by restricted mindrules during rapid niche change, the desire of the pleasure centre must become louder and sharper to be heard above the confusion. Then as a conscience, the pleasure centre can still strongly influence our behaviour. Its voice can become so loud that it might even force us to confess some dark secret. Often, the conscience must be strongest in those minds with pretend high moral standards. They have learnt their mindrules too seriously. A serious mind cannot have its rules broken. Through the conscience the pleasure centre will try to have its standards heard. However, the serious mind will usually have to reason and wrestle with its conscience, rather than follow a more natural approach.

The pleasure centre only needs to become a separate force of demand in the mind when our reasons fail to live up to the interaction desire instinctively. Early Europeans often said that natives lacked a conscience. But even so, those natives maintained high standards suitable for their niche. The conscience arises only when the interaction desire cannot act naturally, because the mind is being stringently controlled by defensive reasons. If thoughts cater directly and honestly to feeling, the conscience has no need to arise. Conscience is the pleasure centre under stress and strain. Conscience is the pleasure centre under mindrule control, trying to have its say in that mindrule dominated land. Unlike the natural functioning of the pleasure centre, the conscience is rarely free and easy to use. It can become slow and labouring instead.

While the conscience may speak against the first impulse of alienation and restriction generated by mindrules, it can also be wrong about the real cause of those mistakes. Mindrules take themselves seriously, and convince us that alienation and restriction is an integral part of human nature. They will not suspect themselves. Our conscience can only ask for higher standards. It cannot tell us the best way to achieve those standards. It can only recognise when its standards are not being fulfilled. An unaware conscience will follow the reasons of its mindrules to explain why alienation and restriction stands in the way of its high ideals. The conscience can look to its own mindrules for all the answers. Then, the conscience can take on the worst aspects of mindrules. It can become inflexible, and see much bad. It may resist any natural feelings that might look beyond the prison of the mindrules.

The conscience can be captured by mindrules and become their voice. The natural impulsive feelings for fun and simplicity can be squashed. The conscience can become rigid, logical, and warn against giving in to a course that does not conform to what mindrules think is right. The conscience might reason away its compassion for certain things. It might find honour and glory in overcoming illusory bads. Honour and glory are concepts introduced by mindrules to appease the conscience. They describe the standards that the conscience seeks, but also show how a trapped conscience thinks it should achieve its goals. To achieve such accomplishment, the conscience believes that it must overcome difficult odds, usually at the expense of others. It becomes honourable and glorious to defeat the enemy or bad. Once the enemy is quashed, then glory in a better world can follow. However, this is mindrule terminology and thinking. It is not real. The steps that mindrules ask us to take to achieve the honour and glory, the fighting or the war, are rarely able to achieve a position of strength for long. The interaction desire does not find illusion fulfilling.

The voice of the conscience can become strong in the mind. It is strongly influenced by mindrules. Mindrules strongly influence the way we use the conscience. When mindrules plunge us into greater seriousness and confusion, the conscience may become even more detached, erratic and divided. It is common for some mentally disturbed people to hear voices in their mind. The conscience voice can become distorted, and hard to recognise as a conscience. It might seem to ask for strange actions, or any kind of pleasure that might offer relief. The pleasure centre asks for high levels of fulfilment and accomplishment, but it cannot tell us how to achieve that goal. Under the direction of confused mindrules, the distorted conscience might ask us to perform wicked deeds. Strange voices might ask us to murder or torture, to see if there is any fun in how it feels. A pleasure centre starved of pleasure and under the influence of mindrule confusion can give us many strange callings.

Babies seem to act without conscience. They still have to learn their mindrules and their niche map. Their pleasure centre acts naturally at first, and so there is little gap between how they feel and act. Similarly, wild animals do not have a conscience. The way they act is a direct expression of how they feel. There is no gap between their thinking and their feeling. They can trust their instincts.

However when we domesticate and train animals they sometimes develop a conscience. A dog can unwittingly reveal to its owner that it has been stealing eggs from the chicken pen, by skulking around with ears lowered and tail still. It looks guilty. A dog may learn that to us, scavenging eggs is wrong. Our training places a gap between what they know we want, and their immediate feelings of desire. This gap introduces a conscience. The code of training makes the animal doubt the acceptability of its own feelings. It decided to eat the eggs, but later remembered and thought about its training, to feel wrong.

The pleasure centre is designed to rule and guide our cortex and mindrules. If our reasons ignore the pleasure centre to pursue their own immediate ends, then the pleasure centre can turn itself into a conscience. If we continue to ignore, the conscience can make us feel guilty. We feel guilt when we do not live up to the standards our pleasure centre learns to desire. To feel guilt requires a conscience. If we do not do the right thing, then the empty feeling of guilt afterwards can become intolerable. Guilt encourages us to follow our conscience more closely.

Guilt is not the only method that the interaction desire can use to make us follow its standards more often. Simply being aware of the rewards of being able to live with our conscience is often enough. Living with our conscience can make the spirit of our life more pleasurable. Guilt is the back up feeling or enforcer.

At this stage in our species' evolution, we are not naturally accomplished and wild. Therefore, we need and develop a conscience. The conscience can drive us to a higher state of awareness and responsibility than we might otherwise attempt if our restricted mindrules had their way. If we do not have a conscience, then we must also accept a lower level of pleasure for our interaction desire.

Eventually however, we will be better off finding a more natural way to achieve our conscience standards, without the mindrule baggage. Many of the standards set by the conscience are false and mindrule directed. The quality it wants is good, but the way the conscience thinks we need to achieve that goodness is usually false and misleading. A conscience with pretend high ideals might even allow us to commit atrocities in the name of glory and honour. A wild mind does not have a conscience. It can meet its high standards in a way that needs no distinction between thinking and feeling. The pleasure centre can meet desires through its instincts and mind easily. A wild mind can rely on its instincts to judge well. Wild animals embody wisdom.

5.27 Wild feeling

So what should govern our behaviour? Our mindrules confuse us and our feelings today mostly lead us into emotion. We cannot even feign objective reasoning, because reasoning is just another emotion that must eventually bow to its mindrules. The mindrule cage is difficult to escape, which of course is why we have been trapped for so long. But simply realising that we have mindrules begins to erode their instinctive hold over this species.

Before our species can see the natural wisdom contained in wildness, we will have to repair our instincts to the level of attunement where they can deliver fulfilment to our natural feelings and desires. We should be able to use our senses and feelings to tell us what is right, rather than having to think hard for reasons. Reasoning evolved late as an emotional Band-Aid that we use to explain small components within a much larger range of feelings. Reasoning was not meant to be all that we know. Reasons should not keep our wild sense contained within their limited concepts.

Currently, I think the information contained in what we don't know is more important than what we do know. Our species has not been able to solve its fundamental problems through thinking. It is time to move on. Because our mindrules are so confused, there is a great deal of information that they cannot categorise, understand or conceptualise. Mindrules make us instinctively blind to this information. But it is information that cannot go away simply because we do not know how to pigeon hole it with our labels. There is an enormous amount of wild information wafting about, that we could use, if we were receptive enough to allow its entry.

Realising that there is so much missed information comes at a cost. It goes against the grain of mindrules. It shatters little worlds. It means that what we know and are basing our lives upon is inadequate. Mindrules will try to tell us that this outside information is impractical and wishy washy. It is not really important. However, I estimate that we are aware of only half of the true forces at work on us. That outside information is beating itself against the blocks in our head to get itself known. It is free information that is highly practical. The old alternative of trying to make do with what we know seems to me impractical, as proven by a world overloaded with problems and misery.

The best way to tackle our problems is not through thinking, but through something I now call wild feeling. The feeling of wildness as practised by wild animals can lead the human mind to search its more perceptive domain. Only wild feeling can muster and excite the energies of the interaction desire fully, before it steps blindly into the trapped mindrule arena. Only wild feeling produces perfection in its species. Only wild feeling can dare us to wrest control from our frightened and confused mindrules. Only through wild feeling can we raise our spirits to a level that is free of our present niche map constraints. A sense for wild feeling can take our knowledge much further than our reasoning dare go.

Wild feeling can make incisive changes to its animal because it is more interested in the wildness of information than in turning information artificial. It seeks to view information as organised by external forces, rather than trying to make it conform to the internal forces of our own mind. It places no demands on the information, but accepts the consequences of that information receptively. Using this information, wild feeling can view the assumptions behind a block, and wipe the block free from our mind with one simple stroke. Our feelings can be mindrule linked and derived, or they can be wild. One is not prepared to look without the support of earlier experience and guidance, while the other feeling is more daring.

We do not know our outside information. It is something that we will have to feel and sense. There is a whole wealth of feeling information available that our mindrules cannot understand. Those feelings do not give a standard response, and do not fit our mindrule concepts. They are wild feelings. Like a wild animal, the information is timid. It will not go where it is unwanted, because the priority of wild information is to remain free. But that is the information that is most powerful. That is the information that can give us the strength to curb our mindrules. It is outside or wisp information, good lizard information, that to me has proven its worth because it did not need our artificial support to make it exist.

I would rather look for information as it was tested over millions of years of evolution, than as supplied by a lifetime full of mindrule interpretation. We should sense for answers outside the normal thought processes. Nature can lead to inspiration and imagination in areas not human bound. The best way to find wild information is to observe its animals. Another place worth checking is the wild animal within ourselves. We share about seventy percent of our genes with lizards, and about fifty percent with beetles. How do you keep that information out? Why would you want to?

Of course, any wild information we find should upon thought turn out to be reasonable. There is much order and wisdom in the universe, and the wildness searched properly does not contradict that perception. But we will need wild feeling rather than reasoning to find the full extent. Wild feeling can approach the block on the neural grid from behind, to see it all.

Only wild feeling will let us see useful outside information. It is important to get the feeling right. Some feelings arise out of the frustrations of unfulfilled and frightened mindrules. Other feelings arise from external sources, have yet to be processed by the cortex, and so are not yet influenced by mindrules. Wild feeling is a method of sensing that only becomes available if we can separate the interaction desire from its taught niche map. Not all of our feelings have to give their standard learnt response. A feeling can go it alone to find a new pathway. A feeling can remain wild, and explore much more than any other taught feeling thought possible.

Wild feeling does not like to be processed, if that means it is to become trapped. Indeed, it was the last of the major pieces that I was able to name and write into this book. It will always remain the feeling that is hardest for us to notice during niche stress. It is the first feeling to flee when the cortex landscape we offer does not feel free.

Whenever our species feels stress, our feelings will tend to run for cover and reassurance amongst its mindrules. Under stress, our feelings need extra care. Otherwise, they will continue to trigger desires that will only get hurt or become unfulfilled. The pleasure centre does not like that kind of result. We therefore place our feelings subconsciously under the care and control of our mindrules. Then, we can use our emotions, moods and attitudes to protect our feelings. Our desire can jump to our mindrule conclusions and defences early, before it gets a chance to act vulnerably.

It can be difficult to wrest our feelings from the control of mindrules. Mindrules will always present us with excuses of why we should give up wild feeling, and forget the standards that our true desire seeks. Instead, the mindrule will send our emotions against wild feeling and its accompanying information. We will have fears, reasons, loved ones and hopes to consider first, that will all warn against wild feeling. But any danger is an illusion. Wild feeling is compatible with all of our true desires. It asks for the highest of standards, and will give us results better than our mindrules currently conceive. Those results might be unexpected, erratic in their timing, and hard to control and direct, but they are always invigorating.

Most people realise that being wild involves doing what we want. However, it is extremely important to stop our wants from becoming trapped by our mindrules. We need to know what we really want. Do our wants arise from the interaction desire or mindrule convenience? Today, those that try to be wild always fail because they are unaware that this is a point that needs checking. We assume that to do what we want, is to do what we feel like doing. However, if we do that, we instantly fall under mindrule control. We need to penetrate the mindrule barrier using a wild feeling that is far more demanding than what people use today. The first impulse we should follow is one that arises more purely from the interaction desire. Our first impulse is not the emotions, moods and attitudes released into our minds by mindrules.

The wildness of human nature feels very different to the wildness of mindrule nature. Mindrule nature sees illusion, so it cannot tap into anything of substance. A wild mindrule nature cannot accomplish much. It will be self-centred, alienated, false, restricted, and confused. However, a wild human nature is very different. It is a nature that was tried and tested long before we reached the modern mindrule state of confusion. Wild human nature was bought up in a wild ecosystem to have good breeding and credentials.

There is a simple test that will reveal whether we are acting upon true wild feelings or mindrule delusion. That test is whether in our wildness we try to do what we feel like doing, or do we do what we feel is right. The excuses and restriction of mindrules sell the first approach. It lets us use the feelings dished up and processed for us by mindrules. The second approach takes notice instead of the interaction desire and the direct measure of its pleasure centre. We may have to change to make it work. Our interaction desire is most pleased when we get it right, by doing things that are beautifully simple, efficient and wide reaching. Our actions should speak like music. It rewards those actions that are considerate. Giving wild feeling such control over our lives gives us the power to get it right in whatever direction we please.

I cannot really teach how to use wild feeling. It is something that must be felt and experienced to the point of receptivity, and then you know. The best source and most masterful examples of how to use wild feeling comes from the creatures that already live there in the wilderness. These creatures show the kind of organisation that is possible. They reveal a world filled with tolerance, harmony, fulfilment and gentleness for all involved, within natural and reasonable constraints. They produce a system that embodies wisdom, as each creature is developed to their most accomplished state. Their minds and natures show us how to self-enhance. To clear them away would be a blunder.

5.28 Inspiration

The pleasure centre offers a simple way of measuring the quality of our interactions. The initial expectation of the pleasure centre when born is to assume wildness, just because that is the simplest path to take. However, if our world is not suitably organised or accomplished then blocks begin to appear on our niche map. The pleasure centre does not know the point from which to start measuring. It does not know what to expect or what is normal. It leaves such determinations to the cortex. We learn what to accept as pleasurable or empty. What is a pleasurable experience to one might be empty to another. We must learn the standard or expectation against which we should measure our performance. It depends on what we learn as possible. What we realise or conceive, will determine where we attempt to place our measure of quality first. It is where we will spring from to try and develop our comfortable niche. It is what we come to terms with. An unemployed worker winning a world trip might feel enormous pleasure, whereas the same gift to a millionaire might be an inconvenience to a busy schedule. A person used to living in a war torn country, or an unhappy home, will come to terms with a level of violence uncomfortable to another.

The pleasure centre cannot tell us the standard from which we should begin measuring our performance. It can only guide us from whatever point we accept. We must learn the scale or limits that we will measure against. The pleasure centre measures against past experience. It is not born with a ruler in hand or a standard in mind. It can only give us a feeling of expectation. However, our expectations can be controlled and modified through what we learn. Desire is first sent out with an ability to be measured by the pleasure centre. It is not sent out with the knowledge of what to accept. The pleasure centre is not born with the knowledge of whether block should or should not be on its niche map. The amount of block we have on the niche map determines our level of realisation. It sets the limits from which pleasure must then try to arise and measure our accomplishments.

What we are capable of, and what we see as practical, is a function of what we can realise. We need to inspire the pleasure centre to show it what is possible. Otherwise it will not realise its true natural bounds. We might develop our realisation through education, or from peer encouragement. We might accept the status quo, or be inspired to go beyond the normal bounds, to find that in fact we are not within our natural bounds.

Who really knows what level of pleasure and accomplishment is normal for our species? What quality of interaction should we be expecting in our lives? How much does each of us really realise?

If we realise below the level possible for our species, what a tragedy and loss. We will come to terms with a lower level of accomplishment than we could achieve. We will remain bogged down in our world, simply through our lack of realisation. We will set our measure too low. Our level of realisation can become a form of self-imposed restriction. It is important to realise what is really possible, and see the forces that are really at work. Only then can the interaction desire find its true position from which to start measuring our performance and construct our niche map. Only then will we admit feelings beyond those that currently conform.

We require inspiration to improve that realisation. Through inspiration we find the drive to rise above the niche map world, its traps and excuses, to search for something better. Inspiration is a way to make the mindrules within our niche maps suddenly more pliable. It expands the frontiers of what we feel we can realise, so that our mindrules must suddenly realign and reformulate according to the outline of a greater niche map. With a greater niche map to work on, all mindrules in the original map realise they must realign to take up their rightful position in that new world. Mindrules gain new freedom.

Inspiration works by expanding our limits. It does not work by rejecting our past. People cannot really change in a way that denies their roots or what they have experienced. What they have must be built upon rather than removed or dashed. It cannot be denied. We have all had real experiences and observations. Perhaps we have misinterpreted those experiences, but that is different to denying that they were ever felt. Through inspiration we can keep the past, without having to remain bound to its limitations. Inspiration changes our view of the past by putting our knowledge into a whole new context. The pattern of restriction each of us learnt will not change by simply altering one mindrule. We must move from one whole niche map to another instead. The world or context in which we learnt our restriction must expand, if the contents are to relax into a more natural format. People can hide or change feelings, but they cannot really lose them. There is no real point in attacking one belief without replacing it with an alternative that offers a better context. Any course that dashes the hopes of a feeling will only entrench restriction.

5.29 Wild keeper

In some ways, keeping wild feeling live in the mind requires the same skills as keeping wild animals as pets. In both cases, it is hard to avoid a cage, but even so, we should make the contained environment as comfortable and natural as possible for the animal.

Otherwise, the wild animal will die. Also, the wild animal should be allowed to roam free in the mind cage. As it approaches the fences, the wild keeper should draw those fences away so that the wild animal never sees them or feels inhibited by them. It is the job of the keeper to make the landscape for the wild animal or wild feeling as natural and free as possible, so that it can live as it wants according to its true nature.

We can give the wild animal in each of us a safe and free mind to explore. We do not have to touch it or stop it, as that would only influence the wild animal and turn it artificial. If it starts to go where we would normally not dare, don't banish the wild animal. Instead, set about rebuilding the mind cage so that its fence pushes back and away so the wild animal does not begin to doubt its naturalness and think that it should have turned for shelter. Our mind cannot help be a cage, but we can at least move its fences and expand its size, following and making room for the wildness. To become wild inside we need to let wildness tell us what it is, rather than us tell it what it is.

To give room in the mind for the wild animal to roam, we need to remove the internal blocks and cage bars as far as we can see and whenever they appear. It is important to keep to the wildness, rather than give into weak excuses and mindrule fears. If wildness does find a block, at most those blocks should be offered as a curiosity for the wildness to inspect. They should not be something of fear and seriousness.

To remove blocks we must actively look for their signs. One way to find internalised block is to look for the things that make us emotional. The cause of emotion is always mindrule block. We can therefore use those emotions as a way of detecting the blocks. Whatever we hate, detest, are revolted by, depressed about, or frustrated with, is illusion. This is hard to believe, but it is amazing how consistently it works. All things are there for a reason, and that reason can be fitted into wild format in a reasonable way that reveals a stronger context. We have blocks and bad because mindrules need them, but even more, because our spirit has relinquished its control to mindrules.

To see that blocks and bad are not real, we must try to see the good in them or behind them. Often we must see past them. We must get them on our side before their greater strength of wildness can shine through. This can be difficult because we emotionally detest blocks and bad so much. To see the good in the bad often requires a great deal of exploration and understanding. It forces us to consider areas previously not dared. This does not mean that we have to finish up agreeing with the bad or allowing it to have its way. But we must go to that side, to see the block from that angle, and through the test gain the strength needed to rise to the next level. Any hates, revulsions or fears must be attacked internally, to find an arrangement that drives them from the mind so that they no longer arise in us instinctively. It might seem like a dangerous game, but if we keep our wits about us, we will always find a way to reach the wild perfection that is free and more instructive beyond. We are natural animals after all. We will not be able to view the reasons of blocks and bad receptively until we can see the mistake with them.

Mindrules have a characteristic nature of assumption and categorisation about them. To reduce assumption we should try to begin from the basics as often as possible and work it all up from there. Also, we should be much less ready to categorise. Get into a position where we can take the time to sum things up slowly. We should aim at dismantling all our opinions, categories and attitudes, especially those that we have about ourselves. The biggest delusions we are under are usually the concepts and ideas we have about our place in the scheme of things. Because mindrules confuse us we should attempt to reduce that confusion by continuous redescription to try and get closer to the heart of the matter. We should describe until what we have feels right and interactive, like peeling back the layers of an onion.

As far as they allow me to be aware, I have been experimental and ruthless to the mindrule blocks and smug niche map that continually tries to establish itself in my own mind. Mindrules see their world as completely packaged, and take themselves seriously, so I try to reject this position and apply wit instead. Do not believe in anyone's assessment of reality today, including your own or mine of course. They are all phoney. But of course, it is easier to see this in others than in ourselves.

After seeing the style and wisdom of wild animals, I decided to try and donate my mind to the same forces that shape their world. I am not sure that I fully understand all the processes involved, but I think that most often I apply the following steps. First, I remember or sense wild feeling. I can do this by viewing or remembering wild animals, lizards, insects, bushland or forest. This inspires me, lets me see perfection, and makes me realise that I do not know it all. It places a higher standard of measure in the mind. It raises the expectation of the pleasure centre. This feeling is the strongest I know. I try to match the class and style of the wild creatures that have had the grace to share their information with me. With their standard in mind, I begin to take what I know less seriously. Everything that humans know seems to me confused. Even the things I write, I expect to be able to change quite drastically in the future. The only reason I don't see the mistakes now is for the blocks in the mind that I fail to realise. This lack of seriousness in the state of organisation of the human mind, I assume, returns mindrules to a more pliable state. Their blocks and excuses pail into insignificance under the desire released by wild feeling.

Reducing mindrule blocks improves receptivity, which is the state of mind needed before wildness will enter. Then sit back and observe or encourage, and watch the information, thoughts and feelings that appear. We will be on the right track of wildness if the feeling we get seems to grow in power and pleasure. Any feelings of alienation and restriction should subside as well. Do not accept any restriction or negative thought, as there is always a more positive thought available to control them. Only allow yourself to be driven by inspiration, and only accept thoughts that paint a more beautiful picture. Anything less will lead to mindrule nature rather than wild nature. Ultimately, reasons that link it all should begin to take form and shape. Use the interaction desire to judge the standard of these thoughts and actions. Take more notice of desires and dreams. They desire and dream for an evolved and tested reason, and are not wishful thinking. If we cannot see how they can work, then change the mindrules not the dreams.

All of this probably sounds a bit flowery. But I am attempting to give an image of what to do, rather than necessarily knowing or being able to accurately describe how it is done. Of course as always, don't take any of this too seriously. I always enjoy keeping some of my mind in reserve for scepticism, to mock and name as false anything that I come up with. Perhaps wildness is only safe to use while sceptical. This lets me withdraw if needed; though I have not been bitten yet. It also helps keep the mindrules pliable for next time. The fun is in feeling the wild forces have their way, not in finding the conclusions upon which we can rest our laurels.

The wild keeper process is something to do when you have the time and feel comfortable enough to cope. I would not try it while under duress or the influence of emotion, as that would be like trying to start on the wrong track. Let wildness have its way, but when you have to get back to the realities of this society, go back to doing what you feel is best at the time, rather than following what you have found. If what you have found is of any real value, it will settle out and gain greater control in your life naturally by itself, without us having to force it to take up some false position. Only accept and use information that feels right. If an idea is true, it should be able to stand up for itself without artificial protection. That is the real test for a wild idea. Life was meant to be fun, not serious.

I let wildness in by watching what it feels like, rather than doing what it feels like. This lets me hold some wit in reserve, that I can use to encourage the wildness to move into new areas where I want more answers.

5.30 Accurate description

One problem with wild feeling is that it is untrained and tends to wander if it is not interested. It may not tackle the things that we want to sort out. One way to gain some control and hasten the results in a certain area is through attempting accurate description. This process does not train or tell wild feeling what to say, but tempts wild feeling to roam in certain areas. By thinking about a subject, and describing it, our attention highlights the area and its surroundings sufficiently to make it more interesting to the wildness. Wildness often goes where there was most recent activity or scent. By simply observing or describing the area, we make the area more interesting and pliable. The description should not attempt to form its own conclusions. It should wait until wild feeling is sufficiently happy to move in and find the pathway for us.

While wild feeling can sense much outside information, its results are difficult to implement unless they can be converted in our thought and named. Accurate description is a process that I use to try and give structure to wild feeling. To use wild feeling, we must eventually try to home in on what it is trying to say, but in a way that does not suppress the feeling in the attempt to name. Accurate description tries to spring directly from the feeling, rather than trying to fit in with previous knowledge. It is a continuous process of getting the description closer and closer to the feeling, like peeling away the layers of guff. You know you are getting closer when the description we come up with still stirs that same wild feeling. The description has not detracted from the feeling, but should rather inspire the wild feeling to go even further. Knowledge should give wildness more freedom.

Accurate description is the process of trying to describe rather than interpret. It is a way of holding back the willingness that mindrules have to interpret, and the keenness of the interaction desire to have an answer. It requires patience. We must think about the circumstances and surroundings of the subject. A subject must be put into its right context. The description should proceed until it has stripped away interpretation to reveal what should be simple basics and motives. We should try accurate description again and again, until assumption is stripped away to reveal the truth, or until what we say at least feels right. Accurate description involves continually redescribing a subject, and all of the surrounding outside influences that impinges on it. We should do this even when there seems to be no need.

A sign that we are describing a subject better comes when that subject begins to join together with many other related subjects in a simple and logical way. The subject should be redescribed until it feels right. For example, is violence a part of human nature? It is widespread and common in our species, so we assume it is a part of our nature, and a natural animal instinct. Many things in our society would be explained if it were a part of our nature. It would explain why we seem unable to live without violence. Perhaps we should accept violence as a way of life, and concentrate on finding ways to give it controlled outlet. Then we could diffuse our need at the early stage, before it builds into rage. We could build our society around ways to please our violent instinct, rather than waste time trying to ignore it. However, does violence really feel right and strong? If not, then describe it more accurately. What are the different types of violence that can be found? What are the circumstances that lead to violence? What do we hope to gain by violence? What is the true desire behind violence? Is there really no motive behind senseless violence? How important and durable are the things that trigger our violence? Are the things that trigger our violence really bad? Why is something bad to one person, and not bad to another? All of these questions must be answered properly, before we can reach an accurate description of the subject.

A good way to promote accurate description is to list as many possibilities as we can imagine. To find all possibilities, we must usually uncover more possibilities than we previously realised. We also need to list our questions. These can provide novel angles that might help to reveal the inaccuracies of interpretation in our subject. As our attempt at accurate description proceeds, we should continue to add more items to our list for consideration. Eventually, the description should be able to keep the feeling, and also explain many or all of the items on our list in a beautiful manner. Wild feeling senses more reason and beauty in an area than we currently realise. It rejects all doubts and fears that say otherwise. Accurate description must therefore home in on how this wild feeling could possibly exist or work under our presented circumstances.

The wild animal lives comfortably and properly by developing its instincts. We fail, because our instincts are now so poor. We have tried to improve our lot through emotions, reasons, and thinking, but still fail. Life for our species is complicated. However, life would be easy if we could trust our instincts. It would give us better judgement. We should follow nature to develop ourselves fully. Wild animals show us how to develop a true nature to its full potential. The target we should hold up as guide to our mindrule's evolution is wildness. We need to be able to tie our adaptations together in the most interactive way possible, as judged by an interaction desire that understands the standard of the wildness.

6. The nature of the universe

6.1 Complete relatability

When we remove the blocks of the mind to make room for wild feeling, something fascinating happens. A better understanding suddenly seems to fall into place of its own. Finding a good idea to replace the illusion that blocked our understanding is amazingly easy. It is as though the better understandings are out there already, just waiting to jump in and take the place of the confusions that we allowed previously to grow in the mind. It seems that important answers come not by trying to think harder, but by simply removing the blocks and assumptions that keep out the obvious.

Wild feeling does not require complicated or exhaustive reasoning for it to have an impact, because it is such an effective means of information transfer. Wildness is interactive with its creatures, and willing to share whatever it has. It requires very little effort on our part to obtain its information, just receptivity. Any reduction in internalised block improves receptivity, and allows wild information to snap into place of its own.

After a while, this process leaves an impression about the world that wildness would have us share. The results of wildness are always enlightening and invigorating. This suggests that the world of wildness is filled with a strong understanding that is highly interactive and transferable. All we have to do to see it is to break down our own internal barriers by removing our mindrule shields and blinkers. The understanding then available is so strong and obvious, that it moves inside us freely by itself, as though we were a natural part of its system. The revelations that appear after removing mindrule blocks are always so simple and far reaching that one gains the impression that in the true nature of things, there is a deep natural order and beauty.

That impression made me look for words that more accurately describe such a feeling and the order of the natural world. The word that sprang to mind was that the universe is relatable. The world that lives outside our minds is highly interactive and available. All of its parts relate together into a highly ordered and compatible structure. They all interact together well and for good and fair reason. All parts impact on each other and fit together neatly to strengthen understanding. The more parts that we can relate together in the one picture, the stronger our understanding will become. This is strongly suggestive that all of the parts in the universe have a common basis. We could dare to look anywhere.

This impression is quite different to the one that mindrules would have us believe. Under mindrules, the world is divisive and complicated. Reasonable understanding cannot spread throughout its realm because of differences and individualities. There are areas where we must not look, because they are bad, emotionally sacrosanct, or because it would question tradition. In a world as large as the universe, we are unimportant and liable to be quashed by more powerful forces that are incompatible and have no interest in our well being. Chaos rules. We must be guarded and defensive.

The difference between the impression of the world gained by wild feeling, and the impression gained from mindrule reliance, is why it is important to gain some wider knowledge about the nature of the universe. Without such an understanding, mindrules can keep us fearful and closed.

It seems that everything in our world can share in and be a part of an understandable structure. All parts in the universe are relatable, and have the potential to be understood. For example, we could understand the movement of all the planets in our solar system according to gravitational forces. The tides can be understood in terms of both the sun and the moon's gravity pulling on the seas. Terrestrial animals probably evolved from marine creatures that lived in the tidal zone. The reason why thousands of insects look like their host plant can be understood through evolution. The reason why humans have problems can be understood in terms of their conflict between human nature and mindrule nature during rapid niche change. The reason why those humans and insects could exist at all is because of the way our planet orbits the sun. The reason why humans evolved is because other adaptations for survival such as camouflage did not always work. The DNA of humans is made up of the same four amino acids as in insects, and we know that amino acids first appeared on our planet before there was life. There may be other planets in the universe with pools on their surface containing the same amino acids. There are many reasons that impinge and help explain another, because all of the parts are relatable.

Now that we have a word to describe how all things fit together and interact we need to find out why relatability is universal. Why should everything be relatable? Why should everything be understandable? Is there no line that we cannot cross? A simple way to imagine this question might be to consider two billiard balls approaching one another on a table. This can be a model of interaction. If the two balls collide when they meet, and change direction, then they have interacted with each other. The balls exist to each other. They must be relatable. A reason can transfer from one to the other. The reason one ball is moving in a different direction to the direction we originally gave with our queue, can be traced back to an interaction that it had with a relatable object or ball a few seconds earlier. Quite simple really. Conversely, if the two balls did not change course when they met, but kept following their original directions, then we would have to conclude that those two balls were not relatable. They did not exist to each other. They could not touch or affect the other. They are not a part of the same understanding, and no reasoning in one could transfer or affect the other. If we were one of those billiard balls, then we could safely ignore the alternative, as we could never relate with that alternative and alter its course. An alternative that we have no means of relating with cannot exist to us.

So let us concentrate on the two billiard balls that are relatable. If the two colliding balls do interact, then they must share a common part within them that can affect and exist to the other. What might that relatable part be? One ball might be made of ceramic, and the other of plastic, and yet they can still interact, even though on superficial observation the two objects are quite different materials. We will therefore have to look internally to find the relatable parts. While the materials of plastic and ceramic are different, some of the molecules or atoms that make up those materials might be the same. They might contain similar carbon or nitrogen atoms. If not, then both balls will at least contain the same protons and electrons. If we look closely enough at any two relatable objects, we will find that at some internal level they share a common part. This is what makes them relatable. The common parts can transfer an impact between each other, and cause an interaction.

If the balls had nothing in common so that they could not interact, then they would simply pass through the other as though each did not exist. There would be no need to consider the other, as the two would never meet. There are some high pitched noises that we cannot hear, and yet a dog can. To us, those noises did not exist, until modern science was able to build electronic meters that register their impact. However, in an indirect way through our pets or instruments, we can interact and relate with those noises. At some point, we can find a way to interact with those noises. Conversely, there may be non-relatable aliens walking about us right now, without us having any way to sense or know that they are there. Such aliens will never exist to us. If there is no technology or relatable way for us to bridge the gap and interact in some way, we will never know. There must be something that is in common or relatable before two objects can exist to each other. An interaction must be able to go from one part to another.

If we trace this inward spiral further we might find the original source of our universe's relatability. What is the smallest part in any object? It is possible to break all matter such as wood, rock, and living tissue, down into about 103 different kinds of atoms. Atoms in turn will break down into three main subatomic units: the proton, neutron and electron. However, even these are made up of smaller particles, which themselves are made of smaller particles again. In physics, the smallest particle that cannot break down any further is called a fundamental unit. Fundamental units are the most basic building blocks upon which all other things in the universe are made.

It is from fundamental units that relatability in the universe begins. Therefore, it is important to gain an understanding of the nature of those fundamental units. One important consequence of being a fundamental unit is that they should be uniform in composition. A fundamental unit cannot have different parts; otherwise it would not be a fundamental unit. The most fundamental units in existence must be those that cannot be broken down into anything smaller.

We can take the principle of relatability even further. As all fundamental units must be uniform in composition, when two fundamental units meet, there can be no separate part in them with which they can vary their interaction. The entirety of one fundamental unit must be able to interact with the entirety of another fundamental unit. There is no region on each unit that could allow for anything in-between. They either can or cannot interact. This means that all fundamental units from the same existence must be completely relatable. They must all be able to relate or interact, no matter from which angle they approach, or which other fundamental unit they meet. If all fundamental units in the universe are completely relatable, then this probably means that all fundamental units in our universe are the same. There must be only one type of fundamental unit in our universe.

Scientists are already investigating the inward spiral that will lead to complete relatability. The approach of trying to explain everything in its simplest terms belongs to the realm of physics. There have been many discoveries in this field. Einstein showed that matter and energy are the same, when we look at them in their simplest form. They can inter-convert according to his famous equation. Today, physicists can place most physicochemical forces within the one theory. One such theory was the grand unified theory. Then physicists found that the superstring theory could explain even more. Physicists expect that one day we will be able to explain all things in simple terms within the one theory. Many of them suspect that there is just one fundamental unit in our universe (Witten, 1988: 92). When we understand the nature of that fundamental unit there will be no exceptions. Its context would never change, and everything within it would seem reasonable. There seems to be a logical explanation for everything, which could be converted into simple mathematical principles (Schwarz, 1988: 87). A reasonable approximation of ultimate truth is that persons are important and all bound together in a universal relatedness (Harris, 1967: 214).

Presumably, each fundamental unit has its own universe. Within each universe, the one fundamental unit would be able to create for itself great reason, strength, harmony and diversity. And all of its parts within that universe would be completely relatable. This must be a simple defining law for any universe, including our own. All of the components within a universe must be completely relatable. This simple law has universal application and importance to us, because we are one of its parts. It means that certain things are and are not possible. This law will allow us to see through certain illusions easily. If everything is completely relatable, then everything is within our reach.

The law of complete relatability has affects that are far-reaching. It explains how the universe can be so large and complex, and yet remain intact and constructive in the development of its diversity. It is as if a house must be built from the one kind of brick, rather than having walls dotted in brick, rock, twig and straw. It offers a law that can bind everything in the universe together and that can explain it all in the same simple terms. There are no parts that can break away and become different in nature. As soon as two units interact they must share whatever they have. This makes everything grow out of a common basis or stem. Any building done in the universe must have a tree-like structure. All things must share in and strengthen the common basis or stem before they can progress any further. All things must be well founded. Only then will they grow and branch out to make further creation in the universe. From this branching pattern, things will always be able to feed back into the common stem whenever any part needs more strength. This same fundamental reason explains why one day we should be able to understand everything.

6.2 Seeing good

There are no parts that are different within a fundamental unit. Therefore, the fundamental unit cannot react differently to anything, because there is no way to build those differences into its structure. It has no way of storing and assessing the interaction. The reaction of a fundamental unit is either all or nothing. Fundamental units either relate and interact, or they cannot relate and so do not exist to each other. There is no in-between. The fundamental unit has just one reaction to give. They have nothing in reserve, no separate part in which to consider things differently. They cannot find a way to give a variety of responses that could either help, join, build, avoid, block, damage or destroy.

This is an important feature of a universe that is completely relatable, as it means that there is only one way in which anything can ever really happen. Whenever two fundamental units meet, there is only one response that each of those units can give. The fundamental unit can survive in this way because it allows only one possibility to exist. The fundamental unit does not need to have several responses in reserve where it could defend or reveal itself if necessary. Instead, it can give out the same response to all things. Also, because the fundamental unit does not need to choose which response it should give, it does not need to conceive of itself or find a position from which to make a choice. It can be wild, and follow its single response with confidence. It will always interact freely with the other fundamental units in its universe, because they are all completely relatable or the same.

The structures that the fundamental unit builds in its universe will carry this completely relatable nature into all of its manifestations and in all directions. There are no alternatives possible in the detail, because there is no possible origin from which such differences could arise. The fundamental unit keeps its same basic nature in whatever form it creates. This feature makes its universe very strong. The fundamental unit has made everything about us. It is completely reliable, and cannot be defeated or undercut by another existence. It puts a common thread through everything.

For each interaction, things can turn out only one way. Similarly, for any series of events, there is just one course that can ever really be followed. There is no choice, because only one reaction was possible. This means that there is no room to alternate between good and bad. Neither the universe nor any of its contents can switch from following one course to another. Bads are mindrule illusions. There is only one force and one way for things to happen. Fundamental units are completely relatable, so there is no difference between them that would lead one group to react in good principle and another in bad principle. They can only react according to the one set of principles.

If only one kind of reaction is ever possible in our universe, how should we describe that reaction? Humans need a descriptive word, to make it easier for us to understand the process. I think that the best way for us to understand this single reaction in the universe, and realise its full implications, is to describe it as good. The only reaction ever possible in our universe is one that is open, direct, and creative. The only reaction ever possible in our universe is good.

It might seem as though I am getting carried away in this discussion with words that might sound nice but are not practical. How could we begin to apply this premise when so much that is bad and different surrounds us? Indeed, it is a tough test, but it is one that we must meet if we are to advance to our next level of achievement or wild niche. I have already given some clues on why our mindrule nature makes us see its illusions of bad. It is a test of strength to see beyond this, but I will discuss that later. First, how else could we name the single reaction or theme that permeates through our universe?

An alternative view might be that we should see in the reactions neither good nor bad but nothing. The reaction simply happens, and it should not touch us personally or force us to make simple conclusions about its performance. When we add salt to water, and one of the chemicals dissolves in the other, we need have no emotional link to the reaction. The simple physicochemical reactions that occur between fundamental units, or chemicals, do not seem particularly good or bad. They are simply reactions. But there is something fascinating about how all components in the universe interact. If you take the time to look more closely at the reactions happening about us, the possibilities, it can fire the imagination and then it does seem good. Some chemists actually get excited about chemical reactions. Is that because they are wrong, or because we do not see?

Good becomes more apparent to us in reactions when they occur at the higher levels of organisation. When the extent of interaction is higher, and its impact spreads more widely, the nature of the underlying reaction becomes more obvious. We can see reactions on such a large scale by watching the weather, nature, or the movement of the stars. Wild forces at play can be a source of inspiration. There is a way of looking at these interactions, and seeing them all relate together into a common theme that seems creative and good. Imagine all of the forms in the universe working and moving together according to the same unifying theme. This must be good. To describe it as nothing is to be uninvolved, which in itself is a false state to claim. In some way we are a part of those same events.

The reason we should class the single reaction possible between all forms as good is that we are included within that same reactive process. If we were not a part of the universe, and were not included in the complete relatability, then we could claim non-involvement. But we cannot claim such a position. It would be an illusion. I think that we must view the true nature of all things as good. Good is the term that we use when we see how things relate to us in favourable manner. Anything else is impossible. Anything that we see or understand that seems less than good, must be a mindrule illusion.

The nature of the universe and its fundamental particle permeates through us as well as it does through any of its other creations. The good is in the beauty and efficiency of our bodies, and the tolerance and vision available to our minds. The good that the nature of the universe puts into all of its creatures is very strong, and it occurs in them at every level of organisation. In us, the dominance of good in our minds has been engraved and ensured. It is the standard that the pleasure centre likes most, and one that in the end we will be unable to resist.

By seeing the good, we will come closest to seeing the true pattern that flows through all things in the universe. We will gain a strong and accurate understanding or 'basic unit view' of the universe. Through it, we will also see best the radiating edge of creation as it continues to develop. Certain things will become clear.

6.3 Ugliness

In a completely relatable universe, everything is good and beautiful. So where do all the ugly people come from? While the interaction desire is strongest in our species, sexual desire is also strong. Therefore, our appearance or level of attractiveness to others is usually of major concern.

In the same way that it is possible to see good in all things, it is possible to see beauty in all people. We need to ask our mind what position it needs to reach before it will see that this is obvious. It is something that I think a completely wild and free mind could see, even though it is difficult for us now.

The view people have of beauty depends largely upon what they are used to, and the level of confidence they have at being able to leap courageously from the standard vision to see something wilder. We judge beauty today mostly through the eyes of mindrule nature, which is a nature that seeks to contain wildness within its own restricted set of parameters. What we find attractive and beautiful is mostly an expression of the restriction that mindrules make us feel.

The clearest sign that currently we judge beauty through restriction, is that many of the features that we see as being important to beauty are in fact determined by what is average. This is the sign of a restricted mind that lacks the strength to see past the majority or average position. It conforms to the established view, as that is the safest course to take for an overwhelmed mind. Therefore to be beautiful, height, weight and shape should not vary too much from the average. Someone too short or too thin, or with chubby or thin arms or legs would be at a disadvantage. Another important factor to a defeated mind when judging body size is some hint of physical prowess. This is especially important to a mind that sees so much bad and danger in its life of struggle. For height, this might make somewhat taller men more attractive. But tall does not always work for women however; who in the conforming view should play a more submissive role. While some might favour more than the average height, the same does not apply to weight, because that can mean the person is unfit. Under the delusion of 'survival of the fittest', thin and lean athletic appearance is essential for beauty. However, during mediaeval times, a chubby figure was considered more beautiful because it was a sign of affluence rather than poverty and starvation. Another example of the need to be average is in ear size and shape. To be beautiful, the ear should be not too small or large, it should not press too closely to the head, nor should it protrude out from the head beyond an average angle.

Another important influence on beauty is our memory of more carefree times in our life. Mindrules made us comfortable towards a certain set of conditions that we learnt when young. When those conditions change, we find things more difficult. Our ease and pleasure of life, eagerly sought by the interaction desire, is harder to achieve during rapid niche change. The older generation becomes less relevant and attractive to the new order. While restriction seeks its averages and dominants, it also seeks a fresh start where life might be more fun. Therefore, it will also see more beauty in people with certain childlike features. Features lost by some people upon maturing from the child to adult are blonde hair, blue eyes and small noses. These features are also the standard ingredients for modern beauty. Upon growing up, these features can change. Hair often darkens, blue eyes often darken, and the nose can grow and change its average child shape. Certainly, our sense of beauty can rarely extend to features such as baldness, grey hair and wrinkles.

Sexual selection occurs in some species. For example, mature male peacocks have display gear that must be cumbersome even hazardous to survival, yet they develop elaborate plumage to attract mates. Often, the displays are an attempt to show how accomplished an animal is at being able to live even with the burden of outrageous plumage or bright colours. Animals are attracted to those attuned and wild enough to be able to display comfortably. Therefore, in the animal mind there must be some perception of variation in beauty. Most often, the choice is for the animal showing peak signals of maturity and health. Juveniles often lose in contests for mates. Choice will also often be influenced in some animals by their mindrules. A female duck reared by and imprinted to a human will not be attracted to even the most splendid male of its own species. It will look for human company instead.

Minor variations in the perception of beauty can occur within some species that have reached a functional level of wildness. However, evolution does not seek to produce ugly members in any species so that they could not find a mate. Sexual selection would have removed ugliness from its species long ago. Each species contains a natural variation of faces, but there would be no reason to produce consistently an ugly variation that could not attract a mate. When evolution acted on our species, mindrule restriction did not contain our minds, and we would not have seen such ugliness in our own population. The reason humans have such a variety of appearance is that we are a social species, and must be able to identify readily the various individuals in the group. This is very important for a social species that must identify its members to help formulate a cohesive plan. The species had to create these variations to aid identification and survival. Those variations were not designed to be variations in beauty. They were variations to aid identification, within the scope of beauty.

Similarly, the physical changes that occur in our species upon ageing were not designed to be a cruel loss of attractiveness. On the contrary, the process of becoming bald and grey was designed to improve and enhance the position of the aged. In the stable niches under which our physical appearances evolved, aged people were associated with being highly attuned and wizened in the ways of the niche. They had a well developed understanding. They could foresee much, through their experience and accomplishments. They would know the conditions of the niche that are the best source of fun or comfort. In times of trouble, people would seek the aged for their experience and advice. They would not go to an inexperienced juvenile for guidance and wise ideas. Indeed, evolution allowed them to advertise the possession of age and wisdom by developing characteristics such as baldness and grey hair, perhaps as a counterbalance to failing strength. Hair grafts and colourings are a modern invention, needed only while our own species does not know what it wants.

Unfortunately, wisdom in the aged today is lacking in a world where niches change so rapidly. Understandings attuned to our current temporary conditions are more likely in younger people. The advice of the aged is often not relevant, and does not express the feeling of the day. For the aged, only lessons in wit might remain true.

Mindrules were designed to give us an easy set of rules that we could rely upon and follow instinctively. A part of the mindrule forming process is to give ourselves a self-image. The image that we have of ourselves has an important affect on the expressions that we give out from our face and body language. The expressions of the face closely reflect how a person feels about themselves and the world. The human face is highly evolved to reflect its feelings. Therefore, a serious and restricted mind can produce a face of similar appearance. Mindrules under stress can develop attitude, and this can leave a permanent appearance in the face, that is not necessarily the natural face of a person. The attitude and emotions can also almost uncontrollably affect the body weight of a person, as they become more thin or fat than is natural or comfortable for them. I imagine that the face would to some degree grow into and reflect the attitude of the mind. The body is designed to find the most efficient way to produce its expressions, and so it will grow to take on certain expressions, if that is their standard. I think that a hateful or restricted attitude can grow into a face, whereas a more natural and easy disposition can give a face and body greater calm and freshness in appearance. Similarly, a tall person might develop a permanent stoop in an effort to be of more average height. I am not sure how far this state of mind influences our appearance. It would be hard to do controlled experiments. However, it is often not hard to imagine a supposed plain or ugly person looking beautiful. Certainly, this theme has often worked in stories such as Cinderella and its modern versions. Mindrules have such a hold over our species that it makes me wonder what we all really look like.

Beauty is in the eye of the beholder and is a reflection of the state of mind. A snake can look ugly to some, but beautiful to others. A city in lights can look beautiful to some, but artificial to others. It is possible to look at all human heads and see them as being quite funny or ugly. It is a large irregular bulb speckled with odd fleshy flappy lobes, bearing on top a mat of thin tough strand. And then there is a deep central cavity bordered by a circle of pink red that conceals hard chips of white until the pink red is peeled back spasmodically in supposed smile. However, beauty comes from knowing the functioning behind such forms. If the forms evolved for a reason then the form fits into a larger picture where it will seem more beautiful and true. This is why understanding increases the amount of beauty that we can see. The same items might be involved, but when we see them properly, their beauty is revealed. Seeing ugliness is the trademark of a restricted mind.

6.4 Whose creativity?

The universe is thought to have started as a big bang. Just before the big bang, all of the fundamental units in the universe had compressed into a single sphere about the size of a ping-ping ball (Mather, 1986). In the split second after the big bang, the fundamental units were thrown and dispersed into a certain pattern. This single major event was the beginning of all originality and creativity in our universe. During completely relatable interactions only one outcome is ever possible. If we could know the exact position of each fundamental unit in that original pattern then we could predict the entire future of its universe. We would know which unit would react with which, because of their position in space. All events would follow an inevitable path that could not be altered. The creation set in place by that single original event is the only play that can be acted out. Davies and Brown (1988: 7) allude to a similar view, where they note that 'there would be no need for experiment as we would know it all'.

This programmed view of the universe, and of the events that occur within it, means everything that each of us does is predictable. Another way to say this is that everything we do is for a reason. We rarely know enough to be able to predict, but after the event we have more clues so can often see the reason. We cannot claim our own start or beginning because what we do was set in motion billions of years ago. Because we are not a universe unto ourselves, there is no possibility of our having become detached into a position where we can now do what we want through claiming our own creativity and originality.

Claiming our own creativity is something that mindrules under stress would like to believe we can do, but it will always be an illusion. The universe is very strong and does not let go. There can be just one creativity per universe. We did not suddenly and unexpectedly invent ourselves and our own intelligence. The standard of good that we seek is more highly expressed by other animals in their wildness than in us. The path that our species now takes is an entirely predictable creation that nature set in train very early in its wildness. Our path into high moral standards is not ours to claim. Being entirely original is an illusion, as all things arise today through the effort and support of past interactions. The course that humankind is now taking, and the reason it has done what it has done, is that it was the only alternative open to us. It is a course that we must see as good.

Variety and difference in the universe might make it seem as though there must be many different creators. This is one way to produce variety. However, variety in a universe where all the building blocks are the same can also arise through the simple redistribution of its particles. Where a particle happens to find itself in space and in relationship to another will determine the next creation. After the big bang, the fundamental units would have started to clump into nearest neighbour groups. As these groups developed, differences between them would have occurred such as size and timing, and the level of organisation achieved. As the numbers within a clump rise, mass and energy increases, new laws of gravity come into play, and further differentiate the clumped groups. As the branches of creation move further away from their main stem they find greater differentiation. However, all variation is still due to opportunity rather than originality.

What we now create does not arise from our being able to detach and separate from our environment to do something better. We create by tapping into existing forces, and by following through with what they make us feel. If we look at the creative process in our species, the dependence that we have on our environment for that creativity is apparent. Many of the great discoveries made by our species were made concurrently by several people because the time was right. The new things we find either already exist, or are the next logical step in the progression of the universe's branches. Science does not create new laws, but finds them out. People and science discover things that already exist or will exist due to logical laws. They do not really create anything new or impossible.

Often we need inspiration to create or rise above what we now know. Creativity in us is a means of transferring a feeling or inspiration, which we gain through interacting well with something outside our own bounds. Creative people might be different to what the majority of people think and so appear independent. However, creativity comes from ignoring the limits imposed by people, and instead listening to some of our outside information. The reason creativity seems to require independence and originality today is that society is in an illusory position. Therefore, to tap into the creative universal forces we must become more independent of that illusion. A creative person might be more sensitive to the outside information, rather than being hardened and set in the human ways.

Whatever we create or think cannot be original. Good ideas are obvious, and they float about in plain abundance throughout the universe. The things that we come up with as novel are not really our own creation. They contain contributions from the completely relatable forces at work on us. The creative things we do are due to the original creativeness of the universe, not our pretend ability to rise above or find difference to the universe. Creativity is not ours to claim, but it is for all of us to share.

6.5 Freedom

Freedom is the ability to pursue our wants in whatever direction we wish to take. There are various levels of freedom, and some freedoms can be taken away. A prisoner is not free in body, but could be more free in spirit than his jailer. Freedom implies a need to be free or independent of containing and restrictive forces.

The loss of our illusion of being able to make our own independent creations as we like might seem constraining. It could make life boring. So much fun today lies outside the conventions of the standard human mind, that it can be hard to see how attunement to a programmed creation could be fun. However, the same view will reveal how to achieve our full potential and meet our full range of desires. We would no longer have to feel as though we are at odds with so many things, but instead feel as though we are an intimate part of the universe and its nature.

In a completely relatable universe there is no need for a concept of freedom, because in its reality there is nothing in the structure of our lives that we need escape. Freedom to pursue our best path is automatically available to all forms that follow their true nature. If we can be wild, we will be free to do what we want. In complete relatability all forms are free and can operate according to their true natures and desires. It is only in the illusion and confusion created by mindrules that freedom becomes restricted. Trying to be free assumes that we need to find an independence from other things. To be so independent we must deny relationships to certain things that we feel are constraining. This will reduce the range of interactions that can feed into us to give us strength and wholeness. Therefore, in a completely relatable universe, seeking independence and freedom will only result in restriction and alienation, the opposite effect to what we originally sought in freedom.

Despite what we think, the desires of freedom are already fully catered for, and can be achieved with ease. The ingredients are already there. Nothing external needs to change for us to feel free. It is only mindrules that need to struggle for their freedom, because the universe does not know how to cater to their illusions. Concentrating on finding freedom can be a distraction, because it makes us assume that we must fight and overcome opposing forces. This further exacerbates the mindrule illusion.

Currently though, our society needs to legislate for freedom. No one today knows how to behave receptively and according to our wild and true nature, and so there are many competing interests in our artificial world. The forces of mindrules often seek to impose their natures, and deny the importance of others. So we need laws that believe in the equality of people for protection. Each little mind world needs some freedom to explore, and hopefully create and develop their own positions further until they can join into the reality. Each person needs to feel comfortable before they can undertake such an expansion.

However, it is important to realise that legislated freedom will not serve as an end in itself. It is only a temporary balance mechanism needed during the species' transitional stage of mind evolution. We must value freedom in others, before we can feel free ourselves. The ability to be free must arise from within. Otherwise, mindrules will create illusions of bad so that we will never achieve the freedom we seek. The level of happiness people seek out of freedom will only come by finding true wild nature, as this will lead us into the freedom created by complete relatability.

6.6 Chance

There is enormous variety within the universe. If we knew the full detail of each fundamental unit we could predict the path that each creation in the universe will take. However, in reality we could never hold that much detail in one place for sufficient time. We could not store enough knowledge to know the full course that the universe will take. It would take another universe to memorise all the information, and we could not interact with that other universe anyway. The programme set in train at the beginning of the universe must be acted out.

Sometimes with good understanding we can make predictions, and be right. To see the entire pattern that is in the universe, we do not have to look to the fundamental unit every time. Soon after the big bang, basic units began to react and merge into more complex forms. They produced things such as minerals, radiation, planets and life. Each of those forms has reached a certain level of organisation. We can still understand them as being part of a completely relatable nature. However, we can also understand them with laws that come into play just for those levels of organisation. Those laws are often just as useful to us for understanding the nature of things. They may be less accurate and universal than if we knew the original position and plan of every fundamental unit, but the approximations that they give are often all that we need to function optimally. Chemists would not waste time trying to describe solids that form in a test tube by describing the state of the component superstrings. They would describe the atoms and molecules instead. Taxonomists would not try and publish the description of a new species of mammal based on the arrangement of its molecules. They would describe the general appearance and shape of tissues containing masses of molecules instead.

However, while the laws found in different areas of science are useful, they are not always completely reliable. When they fail to see the good and the beauty, they near the point where they are no longer able to accurately describe what they see. Their value as a rule diminishes. They might even become confusing.

Sometimes the detail we need to know to be able to predict is so great and varied that it is beyond our means. To cater for these circumstances, we have invented the concept of chance. Sometimes, chance is as close as we can get to describing the forces at work, and so it becomes a description or way to say there are too many interactions involved for us to know. However, the basis of chance is human expedience, rather than a model of reality.

Chance is when we cannot predict the next event. We must wait on chance to see what happens. In its simplest example, chance is letting things determine their own outcome, rather than going through the effort of trying to understand all of the circumstances that would then make the event predictable. However, from these simple beginnings can emerge the idea that chance is some real force of its own. Then, this force would actively prevent certain things from being predictable, even if we did make an effort to understand the full range of circumstances. Chance might suggest that understanding and reasoning is futile.

Chance implies that there is another set of rules operating that we cannot fathom. The only way that we can then influence chance is through inventing an opposing force called luck. We might be lucky. Chance can act as an unsettling force in the universe that moves according to its own whims, and cannot be controlled. It produces strange and unexpected results. It controls the destiny of some of our actions. Understanding can be so poor that chaos might seem to dominate the universe. The outcome from the roll of dice is up to chance. The outcome of being selected over others in a job application might be up to chance. Chance might determine how a speech will be received, or if a proposal will be accepted. Whether the human species destroys itself or not might seem a matter of chance.

While chance is often expedient, it can be overly used to the point where it becomes an illusion. There is a strong drive within mindrule nature for us to believe in chance. Mindrules can use chance as an excuse of why they cannot understand and allow us to achieve wildness. While it can be expedient to let chance determine the outcome of some things, mindrules can transform this expedience into 'some things cannot be predicted because they are controlled by chance.' Chance gives mindrules another excuse not to change when they make mistakes. If some outcomes are up to chance, then no amount of change is likely to influence the outcome. It is more a matter of luck. Because the pattern explored by chance is haphazard, our mindrules could not model that pattern anyway. Therefore, our mindrules can stay as they are.

In a completely relatable universe, disrelated and inconsistent forces like chance do not exist. Complete relatability produces a harmonious meshwork where every event can be understood and incorporated into the one universal pattern. Every event is understandable, and could have been predicted, if the need was important. There is only one way that any event can ever really go, and that outcome is not the subject of chance. It is the subject of complete relatability.

Chance as typified by rolling a die can seem real. However, if we knew all of the circumstances surrounding the event, the numbers that come up would become obvious. Of course to do this, we would have to know a great deal. We would need to know the exact atomic composition of the dice, its centre of gravity, mass, the earth's gravitational effect, wind direction, the table's level, the table's surface tension, the fitness of the throwers arm, the orientation of the dice in the hand, and much much more. Might as well just throw the die. However, it is important to realise that chance is just an approximation. It is not a true force of its own. Chance is only a word that covers those events where the contributing factors are too many or difficult for us to know at any one time.

6.7 Strength

The universe has great strength. The breadth of its creation and the time scale of its existence show this strength. Strength holds the universe together. Strength is the ability to have lasting influence over a wide range of forms. A person able to lift a heavy weight has strength over that form. Being able to exert influence on the outcome at a conference table shows strength of knowledge or persuasion. Being able to inspire another shows strength of understanding and accomplishment. Being able to produce numerous levels of organisation, and cram each level full with a diversity of life and creation is another sign of strength.

The source of the universe's strength is its fundamental unit. These units even have the strength to hold together at the end of a universe's term, for a time at least, in a form the size of a ping-ping ball. The fundamental unit produces strength naturally because of its completely relatable interactions. Any interaction has a domino-like effect that can reach out and impact on any other part of the universe that is within reach. One reaction is completely relatable so can spread to whatever is nearby. If anything was weakening, the universe will spread out to meet it in a completely relatable way to make it strong once more. The reaction can ripple on to the edge of creation and fill any gaps and needs within the developing structure. If there are no needs, then it can create something new from its solid basis. Any new form created will further strengthen the structure of the whole creation, by becoming another arm that can brace the structure. The whole structure of the universe can continue to build in strength, because its reactions freely transfer from one to another. Strength does not need to be proven or advertised, because it is not unique but common to all things.

Such an open sharing of strength occurs under the natural conditions of wildness. Wildness is where complete relatability is free, and where all forces in the universe and nature are most real and direct. In an ecosystem, the continuation of this process ensures that nature will fill any opportunity that appears. If there is a gap in a niche, then evolution will create a new species. The new species can then further buffer the ecosystem against the elements. It can contribute to the microclimate of the ecosystem, and improve its harmony and strength.

Under the state of wildness, strength in a completely relatable universe can flow from one form to another anywhere within that universe, whenever there is need. This produces what I think of as a shared pool of strength. Sometimes, we feel this strength when standing in a forest, or when gazing upon the expanse of stars in the night sky. We can draw strength through such forms, to inspire and rejuvenate. Each form in the universe has access to the pool of strength. Complete relatability ensures that whatever strength is available is shared. But where has this strength gone in our species?

Strength should produce security and harmony in our species. If we could interact properly with other forms we would be able to draw upon the pool of strength freely. The network of forms surrounding us should provide us with support and options. However, for our species to draw upon the pool of strength, we must first become completely relatable by joining in the wildness. Mindrules do not allow us to do this. They do not recognise that there is strength beyond their own reach and field of containment. They assume that their present format can already reach all available strength that is practical and nice.

Once when our species was wild our mindrules were able to tap into the pool of strength. Now we are artificial and taught. Whatever strength we have is locked up within our individuality and soul, where it has withered to a shadow of its former self. It can do little. Strength is most powerful when it is free to flow in any direction. Only wildness allows this to happen. Strength must be freely transferable to create its solid foundation. However, mindrules block out certain areas from this free flow of energy. Mindrules can so individualise our arena of interaction that the strength left in that arena reduces to become ineffective and unrecognisable as strength. It may turn into weakness. The strength harbouring in a person's circle of interaction or niche map can languish in obscurity. Then, strength will not be seen, and the reason things do what they do will remain a mystery.

We become weak when we start deleting things from our picture of good. Those things that we think do not belong with the good, we reject or modify. We certainly do not accept them with receptivity. However, we need to put everything together on the same terms. Otherwise, strength cannot flow into the rejected areas, and it will remain incomplete. We cannot make real contact with the things that we blame, trample over, or exploit. This loss of contact will eventually weaken our position. Being able to dominate and ignore does not make us stronger.

The test of strength for our species is under how many circumstances can we see the good? The distance we can see everything as good, is the same distance along which we will allow our strength to flow and return. Life would be easier if we could see the good behind everything. This is a test to apply every day, and on each interaction. The more progress we can make in any direction, the more strength we will be able to draw upon, and the easier the test becomes. It will strengthen our understanding. At times, seeing the good can be very difficult. To do it we will have to gain control over our minds, rather than leaving the job to our mindrules. This can be testing. However, the test of seeing good does give us a direct measure of the size of our own circle of relatability. The bigger the circle, the more access we have to the pool of strength. Maximum strength would come if we could achieve complete relatability with the universe through wildness. To see the good in everything is the ultimate test of strength.

6.8 Equality

Before the strength known by the universe can flow into us freely, we need to be able to include everything into our relatability. We must know equality, before we can feed from the strength. The more equality we see the more strength that can transfer. It is perhaps sensible that the universe would only offer its strength to those parts that are in its complete relatability. Any foreign body that was not so equal, would not gain its strength, and could not prosper and spread. It will ultimately fail to exist or expand in the universe.

Equality is a term that feels right to say, but what it means is poorly understood. By equal, are we trying to say that all things are the same? Plainly, they are not. In mathematics, the equal sign is used when two sides of an equation add up to be the same. But one side of the equation may be very long and complex, and the other side of the equation might be just one numeral. Even though both sides of the equation are equal, one side might be very complex and have numerous steps to take before we find its solution or better understanding. This side might be like the complexity of a human being. The other side might be a single digit. We could think of that digit as a single celled amoeba. While both sides of the equation lead to the same point or understanding, the level of complexity or number of steps involved on either side of the equation can be very different. It can be as different as a person and a single celled amoeba. All sides of the equation need not be the same, but when you work them out, they are all equal. You do not have to be the same to be equal.

In mathematics, there can be many different equations, but the equal sign still has only one meaning. Also, in a completely relatable universe all parts are different, but they all add up according to the one equal sign. By the time you do the sums, steps and processes involved in all people, all animals, and all other creations, you should begin to realise that they turn out to be equal. Another way to say this is that they all share in the wildness, or all share in a common soul.

This feeling of equality has been described in many ways within our various ancestral cultures. In the past, people have seen common spirits or souls, or have felt a direct relationship with their surroundings. A more recent saying is that we are all equal in the eye of God. To maintain the equality, our actions must be for a reason that also feeds totally or equally into the same original tree. Our reasons must be equally reasonable to all. Therefore, if we were in that position, we would do the same. We cannot use reasons that are not a part of the common tree or soul. We cannot cheat or consider that we are more blessed than another, so that we can find our own self-contained path. Part of our reasons cannot be a blend of common reasons that all can see, and personal or special reasons that only apply to us. All reasons must be equal. Our reasons need to be able to survive in the wildness, where we must test them without shields and artificial requests. They must pass the test of equality, as judged by all other creations that live in the wildness.

As long as we do things in the spirit and knowledge of equality, then we can do what we must to self enhance. As long as there is a good reason to what we do the spirit of the other equal creations in the universe will pardon us, and even expect us to behave in our way. They will see or sense the equality of our reasons in themselves as well. If we have to kill a wild animal to survive, then that will fit as long as we do it for good come gentle reason. However, if we kill for no reason, then we are not being equal. We are not sharing our highest strength of reasoning with whatever we kill. If we over-populate and ruin the land, while not sharing in the spirit of good reason, then we are not being equal. We cannot raise ourselves above other creations by ignoring their reasons, and by considering ourselves superior and different. That course will only make us weak. In older cultures, it was common for people to consult with the spirits of their prey in reverence, and to explain. We are more aware now, and know that spirits do not exist as their own mystical entities. But those older cultures show the feeling of equality or respect that should still be driving our actions.

Mindrules have confused the universal feeling of equality in modern times, because such a free flowing ideal is beyond their comprehension. They look to impose their alienation and restriction instead. No longer can our reasons be equal, and they cannot pass the test of wildness. Our mindrules are in fact quite unreasonable. They find little acceptance and strength from the outside world. Instead, our mindrules must retreat into their own worlds of self-imposed alienation and restriction. This is a world where they can be equal, but only to their own illusions and limitations. Without universal strength to draw upon, we will have to become emotional and hard working to keep our worlds live. But we will always be plagued with problems, and fail to live life to the full.

All creations and people have equally powerful reason for being how they are. They are the best creation that could have been produced by the equal forces that we all share. It is a matter of being able to put yourselves in others' shoes. Unless we see their equal reason, we might think they are not trying hard enough or are not equal to us. However, this conclusion is false, and a sign of weakness in our own understanding. No creation can be denied or disrelated. All creations are equally in the best spot to fill the next step before them. They will all best develop the pool of strength or total creation in their area. They cannot be denied. All creations should be able to see the opportunity to develop their own part of the creation in their own wild way.

The basis of equality is not that all forms should look or act the same. Its basis is that all forms should be allowed to drink from the same pool of strength directly. Equality is in terms of equal access. The pool of strength looks the same from every angle. It is equally available to every form within the universe. Anyone who attempts to deny a creation its access to the pool of strength by interacting with them with weak reasons, will damage their own access, and become weak themselves.

People are born with equal access to strength. However, mindrules determine the degree to which strength is allowed to connect and survive within us. Strength and equality should be an automatic ingredient or signature of our daily lives. It is only mindrules that inhibit this realisation. The true nature of people is the same, even though individualities seem different. If we do not give a form its equal relative due, or see its equal reason, then the restriction and weakness we know will feed into the pool of strength. From there, it can come back to haunt us in some other way. Before our species can find the strength it needs to live well, it will need to understand that there is a common system in the universe where all forms need to be able to practice their own true natures. We will have to give up our individual mindrule natures. We will have to act according to our true nature, for good and equal reasons.

In a completely relatable universe, all things have fundamental unit value. Everything feeds into the same pattern, and makes it strong. The completeness of this strength fails if any part that feeds into it becomes devalued or lost. We cannot deny or weaken any part without the loss trickling through to the rest of the universe. A loss in one place will eventually carry through in the pattern to become a loss in another place. Therefore, we cannot disregard and alienate things without reducing our own strength. Our species has lost its wildness to become isolated and weakened. We pretend that we do not have to join in the wildness and become equal. Such a weak approach within our species has begun to spread its decay through to the rest of the planet, so that our world is now in a sorry state. Thousands of species are becoming extinct at a rapid rate, and our own future is unsure and perhaps hard to read, all because of our weakness. However, because we are a part of a universe that is completely relatable, strength will eventually return to our species under natural processes of which we have not been fully aware. Then I think will we find the strength needed to allow other species to live.

6.9 God

Many of the characteristics that I assign to the nature of the universe others assign to a god. Throughout human history gods have been portrayed as strong and powerful, complete in knowledge, and ultimately good and creative. They act according to reasons that exist on another level above the one we currently know. This shows to me that humans have a feeling for complete relatability, even though we have been unable to describe or understand it properly. Therefore, to cater to the feeling, we invent a god. However, there is an important difference between the two possible explanations for order and strength in our universe.

The fundamental unit organises its universe in a way that is different to a god. The fundamental unit has no need to be conscious to keep everything in order. It can create its universe by merely existing and reacting according to its single self-organising nature. It perpetuates its own goodness to the exclusion of all alternatives. All of its creations can build upon each other to give its total creation an enlarging solid basis.

The way we conceive of a god is strongly moulded by the conflict that we feel between our human nature and mindrule nature. For example, our gods must usually protect us from bad or evil. This reflects the alienation that we feel through mindrule nature. Our gods must punish our true and base desires. This reflects the restriction and weakness that mindrules make us feel about human nature. The freedom of the mind to think wildly is forbidden and classed as evil temptation. It reflects the fear and dread mindrules have for the things that live outside their own little world. We cannot reach the ultimate pleasure that our species can imagine, but must serve our time as sinners before we can reach heaven. This reflects the confusion and lack of effectiveness that we feel with our mindrule natures.

We might see the workability and harmony of the universe as proof that a god exists. However, a completely relatable fundamental unit can build such a universe as well. Through its nature, workability and harmony are inevitable, and requires no external organisation. The building blocks of the universe are self-organising. Their impact on each other is lasting and direct. A completely relatable fundamental unit can create strength and beauty simply by organising according to its nature.

In science, when two plausible explanations are proposed for the same event, the simplest and least complicated explanation will gain favour. The theory of evolution has already partly dismantled our belief in a god because it explains better how all of the species in nature were created. A god was not needed to create them. However, we feel uncomfortable about applying the same natural principles of nature to ourselves, because we do not know the full picture of nature. We only partly understand evolution, so it provides us with a poor and uninspiring example of what the realities of nature are about. Evolution portrays the realities of nature as a struggle for survival and a survival of the fittest. Where are the beauty, strength and equality in that? It is not what we feel or desire. Perhaps until now we did not know about the wildness, and the complete relatability that wildness lets into the picture.

Who made the universe? Is there a being that lives outside the universe? The big bang creates and perpetuates its universe under its own steam. It goes through a cycle of expansion and contraction. Our universe is currently expanding, but scientists think that gravitational forces will eventually cause everything to contract into a small ball once more. This form will eventually explode again to send a new wave of creation through the universe. There may have been already many other expansions and contractions, or other existences for the universe. God does not need a hand there. The nature of the fundamental unit will keep this process turning over forever. We could ask, who made the building block of fundamental units, and injected them with good? Did a god put the building blocks for the universe into existence in the first place, and then allow the building blocks to self-organise because the god also gave them strength and complete relatability?

But clearly, we could ask the same questions of a god. Who made the god that made the universe's building blocks? We could pose the question equally to both sides, so the ability to ask it does not favour one side over another. What came before the universe? What came before the god? If one was always there, then which one? This is more of a problem for the universe as a whole than a problem for us. The only thing that can influence us is the universe. We are now removed from the influence of whatever put those fundamental units in place. If a god did give our universe its fundamental unit, then after that work was done the god could have gone home, safe in the knowledge that all was well. All interactions that occur after that initial creation could be organised and handled by the fundamental unit on its own. To stay and watch the predictable outcome to a god might be boring. To influence its outcome after the initial input would be to admit or consider initial failure and weakness, which would also be dull.

The existence of a god might be too big a question for us to answer. What existed before the fundamental unit? It may be that the fundamental unit itself lives in its own existence or ecosystem, along with many other fundamental units. In that world, perhaps each fundamental unit produces its own universe. Then, for a fundamental unit to exist perhaps it must prove its value and worth by showing how completely relatable it is, through the creations that it makes. A fundamental unit that was not completely relatable could not produce a universe and could not exist. However, would those imagined myriad universes ever know each other, or could only a god see them. Does a god allow an existence to occur where different universes can meet? This is a world outside our universe, shielded from us by the strength of our own fundamental unit, and so perhaps it is academic as we could never know or interact with them. It may be something that will become clearer to us when our species becomes wild, and can see and feel all of the true forces that surround us more clearly. Then we would be in a better position to answer or pose the questions.

6.10 Life and its meaning

The difference between live and inanimate objects is grossly exaggerated. There is overlap between both states. 'Live' cells took millions of years to evolve from their primordial soup of 'dead' organic molecules. However, there is no clear distinction to say precisely when one complex organic molecule that at times could self-replicate became a life. Similarly, viruses bridge the boundary between life and inanimate chemical compounds. At times viruses act as though live. They feed and self-replicate. At other times some simple viruses perform like a chemical. They can solidify into crystals, and have no metabolic activity. In future, scientists will probably be able to create life from pre-historic strands of DNA. The DNA is not live, but could become live through purely laboratory procedure. In some ways, life is simply the speeded up and more complex state of the inanimate. Life is essentially chemicals and chemical reactions.

Life is made of the same basic stuff as everything else, and does not have a super-natural component or anointment that makes it answerable to another set of laws. The spirit of life is not a mystical or special force. It is simply the excess energies that cellular reactions within a body produce, that combine to give a structure a unified theme or purpose.

Is there a meaning to life? To ask this question, and to expect to find a special answer for life alone, reveals an assumption that life should have some special meaning above all other creations. However, after our discussion of equality, it should be apparent that the same kind of reason passes through all things. We are equal to all things, including those that we class as non-life. The meaning of life therefore should be the same as the meaning or nature of the universe. We will find our meaning for life when we see the world of complete relatability. The pathway that gives most meaning to life is easy to see when wild, because that is when we see true forces most directly. The meaning of life only becomes confusing and difficult to contemplate when we allow our spirit to become dominated by mindrules. However, the meaning of life should be the same as the meaning for all creations, whether live or inanimate. The common soul goes through all creations.

We might hope that if we found a special meaning for life, we would also find a sure way to raise the fulfilment that we can feel to a new and satisfying level. Indeed, there are simple and clear ways available to enjoy life. Those pathways lie in becoming more accomplished in as wide a realm as possible. We will find our meaning through wildness, and the recognition of complete relatability. Wild animals demonstrate how to live according to the meaning of life, and in reward they have diversified and strengthened to produce stable ecosystems that contain millions of species. In nature, wild animals take what they are, and make the most of it. They can self-enhance within the wildness.

Life on its own makes no particularly important sense. Life that feels alone and individual will wonder why it was created, only to vanish upon death. However, life that is a relatable part of the universe finds meaning and reason. There is no single great ideal that life needs to believe to make itself meaningful. No ideal can be isolated from the rest of the universe, to become more important than the universe. Life is meant to be another part within the meshwork of creation. It is meant to self-enhance, hold up its end, and enjoy itself in a wildness that will ensure that it remains at the forefront of the radiating edge of creation.

The reason why the universe should produce life and then leave it to simply enjoy its true nature might be that life is the natural product of the universe's nature. It is a further progression and consequence of a completely relatable nature. Without the flourishment and celebration of such a nature, a universe of extensive proportions would not be created. The production of life and its associated levels of organisation are a reflection of how far the simple basis behind the universe can go in its creation. It is a result of the strength and potential beauty contained in the fundamental unit. The fundamental unit will always produce such things, universe wide, and never fail. The universe that we are a part of cannot help but produce interactions that are good and exciting creations of its own true nature. Those creations must tap into the same nature of the universe, to feel the life in their meaning. Therefore, we will find our meaning in life when we can see the good, and have the grace to enjoy what we see. We are meant to be a part of the universe, or one with our surroundings.

This might be as far as it goes, though a further speculation is why a universe needs to be so active and completely relatable sufficient to produce life? Perhaps universes need to be this active, their interactions direct and sticky, for them to exist? Perhaps only universes that can create will gain a place in existence? Even for universes there might be a selection for existence. An even more remote possibility is that universes need to produce life to ensure their own continued existence in some form. A universe may need to create life that knows its nature, so that when a universe comes near its end its life can perform or trigger some universal event to enhance its own evolution or next creation. After the reversal of the big bang, and the eventual contraction, could some of the life that it created escape to a position where it can influence proceedings? Is there a way to programme the big bang, so that its life can at last play god, and after their death, set in train a series of events that will create the next universe?

6.11 Choice and decision

An animal could live by exploring the possibilities. It could find its pathways by following its desires and whims instinctively. It could explore the options available by sampling each option a little, and discovering which was most pleasurable or likely to take it to the next step of desire. Then the animal would not really be choosing its course, but following its whim. If that whim arose from solid structure and wisdom, then the pathway followed will usually be best, even though the 'decision' was made lightly or imperceptibly. But if there are any impediments to our exploration, or if other considerations need to be taken into account, then the decision becomes harder. A choice may have to be made.

We have choice when there are two or more pathways to take, upon which we have to stop and consider. We do not know enough to see how the possibilities will unfold, or we cannot be responsive enough to change our course upon better whim or instinct. We might therefore suffer a loss by taking one path over another. We must make a decision.

A choice can be easy or hard to make. This depends on how important the outcome or loss will be, and how much we already know about the alternatives. The choice of which video to watch or scent to wear is simple. These simple choices can be fun, because the alternatives are known, and the outcome is not crucial. There are many simple choices to make while shopping. Each item for sale can fire the imagination of what we could do if we had those items or the money to buy them. Then there are the choices that can be stressful. These come about when we know that the alternatives are going to have long term impact, and might affect the basis of our lives. Deciding on a deal that could shape the future a company might be stressful. Choosing whether to take out a mortgage on a house, with repayments that might prove too much to bear over the years can be stressful. We have little control over the outcome of these choices, because we cannot control the state of the economy in five year's time. However, if the result is successful, and the stakes were high, then the result can be satisfying.

Whenever a choice is to be made, we must stop what we are doing for a while and think about the options. This pause slows the interaction process. Choice introduces a delay between stimulation and response. We do not have an instinctive response to tell us what to do. Delays in response are often harmful to survival. The time that an animal takes to ponder its choice can leave it vulnerable. Not knowing which way to go can be stressful. Trying to decide whether to hide or run or fight gives a predator a better chance of making the decision for you. Evolution does not favour choice. It seeks to develop animals to their full potential so that they can explore and know what path to follow instinctively. Animals evolve to know their niche well, and become attuned to it, so that their course of action will be clear. An animal at its full potential already knows its capabilities and acts accordingly. It is not natural for an animal to have to make hard choices, and it is something that other animals rarely have to do. It is only when an animal is out of its niche, that there is a need to decide things regularly.

By making decisions, the brain tries to return us to its natural instinctive state where we no longer have to make that same choice. Making a decision reduces the need to face that same choice again. If we remember the gelatine model described earlier, a choice is like two alternative courses to take on the niche map. When we make a decision to follow one course and not the other, the mindrule mechanism of selective stabilisation will entrench the chosen course. If the result goes well, we will not need to make a decision at that point again. We will follow the deeper course more naturally and instinctively. In the future, the options will no longer seem equal. However, if the result did not go well, then our emotional energy and thoughts may revisit the decision. We may make a different choice next time.

Decisions are therefore mindrule forming. They turn a course that was once part of a choice, into a mindrule, so that next time we can treat the same event more instinctively. Evolution does not lead to choice. It seeks to make our behaviour instinctive. Once we make a decision between two equal paths, the thought and energy that flows along the chosen path will have it reinforced and entrenched. Even if both pathways lead to useful information, we may ignore an alternative in favour of making a decision. If the energy that helps us make the choice is particularly strong, such as during emotion, the path we take can become even more assumed and blind to the alternative.

When we need to make a choice energy builds at the crossroad to await an outcome. If that choice is particularly important, emotional, or it takes a long time to make, then the amount of stored energy at the crossroad will become great. When we finally make a decision, there will be a flood of energy through the chosen course. This can be a relief, but it will also entrench and impress our mind even more deeply with its mindrules. We might forget the value of examining the other possibilities. The equality that was once seen between two pathways can be lost. A person who once understood the plight of another, and had a difficult choice, can become hardened against them after a decision. A working class person who once understood the conditions of their mates, might become a boss who has to make many management decisions. Eventually, they might forget or turn against their working class. The more decisions we must make, the more single-minded we can become. The energy released through decision can select an ever narrower set of pathways for us to follow, which begin to think more strongly that they are right and others wrong.

Choice can be useful and pleasing to make when the current arrangement of mindrules is not fulfilling. The opportunity to choose can promise a way of relieving pent up energies. It might lead to a new or smoother life style. People therefore see it as important to be able to make choices. It would be a way of improving their lot. The feeling that progress is being made, and that an important life style is being developed, can be gained by apparently making choices through life. It can become important to make choices on a regular basis. An individual needs to make many choices to keep their world fresh and alive.

There is great social pressure to make decisions. People do not like a pragmatic or unresolved approach. They want a solid niche structure, even if it must be created before it is right. However, because decisions are mindrule forming, it is better to look for those pathways that do not require a decision. It is better to find the pathway where the answer becomes obvious so that there is no need for choice. That pathway will keep receptivity alive longer. It takes great strength to be able to hold back the desire that we give mindrules to snap shut. However, wild information will have more room to play if we can keep life undecided, but responsive instead.

What we like about decision is that it can lead to a commitment that makes common ground between people clear. Decisions can set the rules in place upon which we can then build. However, it is the commitment or spirit to work together rather than the decision that people need. With each decision, there is a winner and a looser. We decide to ignore one course over another. However, all information has value, and all information is compatible in a completely relatable universe. The belief that we should make decisions throughout life is just another of mindrule's grand illusions. A decided person might seem to have greater strength and less doubt. However, they gain this only by restricting their minds into a narrower world of what is acceptable. They ignore, so their world becomes weak and easy to topple. It will lack universal support, and will survive only while they work hard and fight.

Our species thinks that it has choice, because it assumes that we are moving into uncharted waters. It thinks that we are creating and deciding our own future as though we have greater power than the world about us. However, in a completely relatable universe there is only one way in which anything can ever go. We have no real choice. Even the outcomes of our present choices are predictable, and therefore not really the subject of choice. Of course, to be able to predict which course a person will take requires great knowledge and understanding. Some couples know each other so well that their choices are already predictable to each other. However mostly, our knowledge is insufficient to predict. Therefore, the course that a whole species is following is probably easier to predict than the course that one of its individuals will follow. Individuals show greater variability about the mean.

Stages come and stages go, but the course that our species is following is still right on target. Our species has decided that slavery is not the way to go. It is no longer natural to think of another race as being lowly enough to be owned by another. In the eighteenth century however, this principle seemed to be a matter of choice. In hindsight we now know that it was never really an option. The war against Vietnam a few decades ago was to try and stop the spread of communism. Today, communism is running out of steam through its own devices. The USSR has crumbled. Vietnam is looking to integrate more of the free enterprise system itself, even though it won the war. It seems that divesting personal influence and power to a centralised state was never a real option for our species. While we are in the midst of transition, the course open for our species can be hard to see. We might even become deluded into thinking that we have a choice.

6.12 Will

While it would be safer to act by waiting as long as possible for the right answer to become plain, that answer might come too late or not at all. In theory we have no choice, but in practice it would take another universe to know sufficient detail to predict every step of creation. We cannot always wait or expect to foresee our best option. Often we will have to make a decision, even though the habit will develop and harden our min-drules. One way of reducing mindrule rigidity during decision making is to develop will. We can make our decisions more lightly by including in it will.

Will lets us try to achieve the right result by strengthening the resolve of our inter-action desire. Then our intention can become our will. Sometimes it is simpler to act according to will than to delay our action and wait for the safe prediction. We could choose our course lightly, because if we are men and women of good will it becomes clear that we are trying to act with good intentions. Through our will we can set the stan-dard of what we expect to achieve without necessarily knowing how. Its a creative 'lets make it happen' approach. Through will we can signal that we want things to go well, even though we do not know all the answers. Mistakes can be forgiven, because a per-son of good will can usually be trusted. We can change the course of our decisions more easily, because the outcome must fit in with our will. A person must be confident to use will, because it signals that we expect a good outcome in the absence of full knowledge. Will can become the faculty by which we decide what to do. It can become the action of a brave volunteer.

Having a will or strong spirit is the sign of a healthy animal. A wilful animal will usually be confident enough to explore its niche. Will lets us live in a way that is not constrained. It can let us self-enhance to the level we want to achieve. By using will we do not have to check with everything before we act. We do not have to wait for everything to be perfect, or check that nothing will be offended. Our will, while it is responsive, could take care of any small misunderstandings and problems along the way. If our decisions lead to mistakes, we can return more easily to our original intention through will. Will lets us act more freely and responsively. We can move ourselves for-ward to become an active part of creation. We can use our instincts and senses more quickly because we can trust the spirit behind our will. Without a strong will, we might cower and feel insignificant. Will or spirit is important in wild animals as well. When keeping wild animals as pets it is important not to break their will. It is important that they do not lose their will to live.

Humans sometimes try to change their will from this responsive and confident approach to something more forceful and dominant called will power. Humans can be deluded by their mindrules into thinking that their will should have power over others. Then will becomes more hardened than responsive. We might think ourselves superior with our will power, and try to become dominant to the point where we can no longer listen. Our will power might even attain mystical heights. We might think that our will power is strong enough to bend spoons, move objects or change reality. Such abuse of will turns it emotional. Then will becomes similar to hope, but more concentrated and self-determining. We will things to happen, and expect them to occur through our power rather than by being responsive and interactive.

In humans, a wilful approach can develop further into a positive attitude. A positive attitude is the best attitude to have, especially if it can remain responsive and does not become deluded. It is certainly better than a negative attitude. It can be surprising what a positive attitude can achieve. It might let our interactions happen more efficiently so that we achieve more simply. Sometimes, it can even help us recover from illness more quickly.

6.13 Questions

Creating and exploring under free will can be fun. Even though an understanding of the universe shows that our results are predictable, effectively, we must create and explore under free will if we want to remain wild and current with the radiating edge of the universe. Then we could make our choices without having to decide, because what we did would be compatible with the developing wild system. Our 'choices' would be compelling, and follow a clear and sensible course. We could follow our desires and true nature directly.

But today unfortunately, the choices for our species are overwhelming. Our problems are many. Our choices often lead to decision. We must often come down hard and decide to leave something out of the world or system that we are creating. Our species cannot be wild the way it is structured now. We cannot trust our mindrules, so our free will and good intentions go astray. Our responses are slow, and have taken us away from the leading edge of creation into artificial appendage.

Many choices can become stressful or problematic. There may be too much choice, too many problems, and we need some answers. Free will may not be able to cope under the strain. Our standards may drop, and we will accept less strong and beautiful answers just to get some of the problems resolved.

When the question of which choice to make becomes problematic, we need to improve the structure behind our will so that it becomes more realistic and easier to use. We need to improve our understanding. As described earlier, all events in the universe are predictable and obvious. All of the answers to the big questions that affect our species and guide our course should be obvious. They are as clear to see as the main branches on a large tree. Only the tips and leaves, the fine detail, should be hard to pin down and define. It is easier and more fulfilling to live and experience the detail than trying to predict its outcome. That is the area where free will is meant to work. Free will is not meant to work on the main branches or structure of our world. We should know those parts instinctively. They should be the basis from which free will can then respond.

At times, choice, problem, question and decision intermingle. So what is their order of appearance? There are several stages to the unanswered question. When we do not know what to do, we may at first try to explore by asking simple questions. If those questions are difficult to answer, they can become a problem. If the problem remains insoluble amongst its people, it may produce a variety of opinions. We may consider that we have found a set of pathways that are a matter of choice. We will then be deluded into thinking that we must make a decision.

Choices can be exciting when their many possibilities open before us. We could come to terms with those choices through our good will, and explore them for what they are worth. We can remain live and responsive to our choices if we act under good will. However, often the understanding behind our will is not pure or wise enough to remain responsive. Often the cost of seeing many choices is that eventually we will have to make a decision. When we decide, something or someone will miss out. We may decide to fall heavily into one camp or another. We will have to decide which side to support. Upon decision, our mindrules will have to entrench our minds into taking one path over another. Then in the future we will not have to face that same choice again. Our decisions allow the mindrule illusion to prosper. We allowed the problem to grow within our minds. For example, our decision to follow one political party or religion over another can eventually entrench until their ideals become a part of our self-identity. In some cultures, marriage between the two sides is forbidden.

Thus, it is important to try and answer our questions while they are simple and open to exploration. Otherwise, each step that we take from the original question will plunge us deeper into the world of mindrule illusion where we cannot see the other side. We should recognise that any problem we think we have, or any choice we think is ours, is really a signal that we are failing to see with receptivity and open eyes. We are failing to see real and obvious forces at work. We should explore more freely and get carried away with the possibilities. The appearance of a problem or choice, the demand on us for decision, signals that we are trying to answer our questions one or more steps too late. Instead, we should be driving ourselves deeper into simple question. It is important for us to repair the complexity of our minds by making our questions simple once more. Only when our simple questions penetrate the mindrule barrier, will our complex questions begin to find their answers. In a complex society, we need to develop a complex and varied array of laws to try and answer the varied and competing requests of its population. In a wilder society, we could discover that the similarities in our true nature would let us solve our problems intuitively. The proper answers on how we should live and interact should come more simply from within.

In a completely relatable universe everything follows on from the nature of the fundamental unit in a simple and reasonable way. Under such organisation, complicated answers do not occur. Questions only arise when we do not properly understand their basis, and so we cannot see how things naturally fall into place. Questions reveal an acknowledgement that we are finding something difficult to understand, and that we want to improve the basis of our understanding. A simple question seeks to improve the learning, and shows that the mind is receptive to an honest answer.

Admitting confusion in our minds is a necessary step to take before we can improve the basis our minds. People are not used to questioning themselves so deeply, because we generally assume that our mindrules are a part of our true nature, and therefore out of bounds. They hold our soul. However, we learn our soul, while our spirit is the centre of our being. We need to take control of our mindrules and inspire the spirit out of its mindrule cage.

The best way to solve a question is to examine the basis that produced the question. Looking for some elusive answer will only confirm the view that the universe is complicated and partitioned. It will not solve our problems. Such answers only enshrine the mindrules. Our species has postponed its simple questions long enough. We have delayed, only to have our problems compound. We need to question and remove the assumptions that protect mindrules. In other words, we will find the solution by asking the right question, rather than by finding the right answer. The right answer generally falls into place once we ask our question properly. It is best to seek the position from which the answer becomes obvious. We can do this by questioning as many previous steps leading up to the problem as possible, because that is where the assumption will lie. We should take our simple and undermining questions through the layers of the mind to its core. The right answer will then distinguish itself for us. It is the one that reveals most simply the harmony and strength that our interaction desire wants. It should also provide new insights in other areas that previously we thought unrelated, such is the branching nature of the universe. The answer will feel right. Science also recognises that the best answers are those that are the most simple and widely applicable. Similarly, the pleasure centre will help guide us through to the right answer, because it is most pleased by simple yet far-reaching solutions. It likes music after all.

The best way to answer a question is to leave it unanswered or undecided for as long as possible. Otherwise we will settle for early answers that do not feel right, and make decisions that encourage the consolidation of mindrules. The best way to find the right course to take is to go back and reanalyse the events leading up to that point. A mistake must have been made somewhere along the way for things to seem as though they do not fit or are a matter of choice. Examine all possibilities more closely. Describe them more accurately. If we do this with receptivity, we will see the true motives that lie behind apparent motives. True motives are compatible, because the universe is completely relatable.

6.14 Paradox

A paradox occurs when two converging laws or rules meet, but reach a gap that cannot be bridged or resolved. Reason cannot flow between the two, so that the event or other side remains unexplained to either party. One side follows reasons that are different or conflicting to another. Paradox suggests the existence of a different nature or alienation. We might even think that it reveals a supernatural event that cannot be explained.

While this is what we imagine a paradox to be, no true paradox has yet been found. Science has shown that we can eventually solve all supposed paradoxes according to some natural law. All things strange that we have come into contact with have been explained if it is within our reach, and if it occurs frequently enough for us to experiment upon. For example, spontaneous generation was once used to explain the spoiling of meat or the growth of mould on bread. People thought that such simple life could appear spontaneously. We now know that the growths that can appear on our food arise from spores too small for the naked eye to see.

Some people still claim that paradoxical events can occur in the supernatural. However, the claimed events are usually designed to keep one step away from science or any real means of investigation. Paradox might dwell in space, where we have not been able to explore fully but can only imagine. However, even black holes and other odd phenomena are on the road to explanation.

In a completely relatable universe reality radiates from an original beginning. It moves in a radiating direction, and cannot cross over to produce paradox. A branch cannot grow into or through another branch, without interacting and coming to terms. All of the forces and reasons in a universe are relatable and begin from a common source or fundamental unit. A paradox can never really exist in a universe. If a paradox were to exist, then it would suggest that there are two universes acting according to their own forces in the same arena of existence.

We can use paradox to show fault in reasoning. Mindrules give different views or angles to the same world. Confused minds can see the same world in many different ways. Therefore, a mind governed by mindrules will often see paradox when its angle of view crosses the angle being generated by reality. Mindrules will prefer to see paradox, rather than interact in a way that might make them change their position fundamentally. If we want to resolve our paradoxes then our understanding must change, until we can see things from a better angle where the paradox disappears of its own. In place of paradox we should be able to find harmony.

6.15 Balance

It is often thought that to achieve harmony we must live in a state of balance. Then we might gain the harmony that we can see in nature and elsewhere. However, that harmony is not the result of compromise between competing forces into a state of balance. Everything goes its own way at full pelt. There is no real attempt by wild forces to hold back and balance or compromise with the other. Each form has only one way to go, and for most they do that to their fullest ability. Their balance is reached because they are naturally compatible and of common soul. They are supportive of each other, even if we don't see how.

A universe that is completely relatable demands interaction whenever possible. It all seems very sticky. Two forces cannot remain apart in balance. They have to interact and find a common outcome. They must alter each other until they find the combination where they can work together as one. They must be prepared to change fundamentally. All true natures change upon interaction into some new form, whether slightly as in growth, or greatly as in the formation of a new galaxy. The new form that emerges from the interaction continues to develop the common soul at full speed. Those forces did not need to compromise. Their result is stronger than the originals, because it is the product of two forces that joined together.

People probably believe in balance because some reactions take thousands even millions of years to complete. The slowness of these reactions makes them look as though they are in balance. For all intents and purposes, it may be easier to think of those events as being in balance. Over a relatively short period of time the error from making such an assumption might be small. However, during times of confusion, mindrules can take hold of small assumptions and push them out of emphasis until we lose the understanding behind the convenience. For example, the universe contains a multitude of galaxies that seem to be in balance. Over the history of humankind, the relative positions of the various heavenly bodies have changed little. People made star charts that were reliable. To us, the universe is in balance. However, science has found that the universe is actually slowly expanding. It is not in balance. Eventually, the relative position of the various galaxies will be very different to what they are today. Similarly, in our own solar system, the planets seem to orbit the sun in balance. The years and the seasons seem constant. However, the true reaction controlling the planet's movements is not in balance. The Earth slowly creeps further away from the sun every year. Eventually, strong forces will fling the Earth from our solar system. The time scale involved is so long that the effect on us is negligible. However, it is worth remembering that the balance we see is not real. The balance we see is not due to compromise but compatibility and necessity to interact.

Natural ecosystems seem to be a further example of balance. Each year the population of an animal might go up or down somewhat, but over one hundred years the population closely follows some average level. The general conditions within an ecosystem, its species' composition and their populations can remain almost unchanged for thousands of years. Rainforests are particularly stable. An ecosystem finds an average set of conditions that it will return to regularly. We could say that on balance conditions are constant. In this instant what we mean by balance is the same as on average. However, the average or balance of ecosystems does change over time. It is estimated that some 90% of all species that ever existed on earth are now extinct. Ecosystems are constantly changing and evolving, though slowly.

Nor do the species within an ecosystem try to keep that balance. Animals do not try to balance themselves and compromise. They make no agreement to stay away from interactions that would cause them to change. They live wildly instead. Two or more species have not found some equal position between them where interaction can end and they can remain in equilibrium, to maintain their own little worlds. The average 'on balance' position found in natural ecosystems is harmonious because to get there the inhabitants interacted together at full potential. They found one common way to work together. They did not find their harmonious position by abstaining from interaction. They are unselfish and willing to make their changes to their very core upon the interaction, even if that means their own death or extinction. They accept the rulings of the wildness.

Even the existence of our man-made balances is not proof that a balance can exist. If two items are placed on a set of scales in balance, and left that way for millions of years, eventually one will decompose or change at a rate slightly different to the other. The two items will be shown to have not been identical and therefore precisely balanced in the first place. They might have a slightly different number of atoms, or vary in combination of superstring oscillations, that makes them change at different rates. There are no two identical forces in the universe that needs to find balance. Similarly, there are no two identical forms that at their most basic level can balance into a state of stayed interaction. The only things that are completely the same and relatable are the fundamental units. There is only one species of fundamental unit in our universe. That species of fundamental unit likes to interact.

Mindrules like balance, and it is easy to see why. If balance is possible, then they may not always have to change their position upon interaction. They do not always have to accept their information with receptivity. They could hold their position, similar to the other independent and balanced forces, and find their own balance. Then they can create their own worlds. In the confused and alienated view given by mindrules, the world is divided up into different independent entities. Therefore, for all of those entities to exist in harmony we must find balance or compromise. For example, a universe might need to find a balance between good and evil. However, if evil is an illusion, where is the need for balance?

Normally, harmony is produced when true natures and full potentials react together. At the moment our species can perform neither. Human society has to work from a large variety of temporary niches that cannot mix. If people cannot agree, the next best option for improving harmony is to find balance. If we do not know our true nature and if we lack the will to find its wild position, then we may have to try and pragmatically live within our imperfect set of rules. We will look for balance and compromise. Our world is full of compromise. Indeed, this is probably the safest way for us to live while we cannot change our mindrules. We need our compromise to avoid conflict between so many different cultures and religions. Our willingness to find balance and compromise shows that we realise that each side, including our own, is not completely right. Our balance shows that each side has the wit to realise that they are not so far into the right that they should try and dominate all others.

However, the balanced position that society finds cannot last. It is only a temporary measure. It readily breaks down. Wars are common when one side thinks they might be able to alter the balance. At the moment people think that there needs to be a balance between the economy and the environment. However, eventually there should be no balance, as the economy will need to come under the complete control of the environment. The economy must become completely relatable and sustainable for our species to survive. Although the adjustment process has begun, the environment is still mostly seen as being at odds to the development of our economy.

Other ideas that arise from a belief in the existence of balance, are cycles and opposites. A cycle is a movement around the point or centre of balance that allows each side at some stage to have it all their own way. This lets a person believe they should hang in there without changing, because one day their time will come and they will be right. Permissiveness is often seen as a cycle, where the level reached must eventually return to a more modest level. Permissiveness in Roman times is often cited as an example of the cycle that led to that empire's downfall. We can also find cycles in nature, such as the seasons, and the carbon cycle. However, even with these, there is a net change. The perfect cycle does not exist. The relative amount of time spent in each season does change very slowly over the years. In the carbon cycle there is still a net throughput. Not all carbon is recycled. Change will have to occur eventually. The cycle will have to move along, as it cannot return precisely to some past point.

If there is balance, then the opposites are the ends in the equation that must be kept separate to achieve harmony. Opposites are another of mindrule's illusions. Mindrules can claim that the reason for mistake is not fundamental error, but the existence of opposites. We might be prepared to make changes for mistakes. However, there is no point in us trying to please or unite the opposites. Opposites exist because we impose our view on the range of events found in reality, to conveniently divide them into groups about a mid-point that suits us. While we have imagined many opposites, they are all false. There is no good and bad, only good. There is no hot and cold. All temperatures can be measured on the same scale. On the Kelvin scale, there are no minus temperatures. It is only when we impose our view of what is comfortable for us on that scale that a hot and cold emerges. However, if those temperatures had a consciousness, they would not feel opposite to each other. They might feel as though they all exist on the same scale. There is no opposite sex, only another sex. As an embryo, we start out the same. It is only through some later hormone production that we differentiate into two sexes. All embryos begin with a clitoris, which simply becomes enlarged into a penis for those embryos that become male. Similarly, the behavioural differences between the sexes are exaggerated. Women have proven that they are not helpless and incapable as their opposite tag might once have suggested.

Mindrules think they can get us to maintain their positions by finding balances, cycles, and opposites. Then to achieve harmony we compromise to find these positions rather than letting ourselves change fundamentally. However, the variety of cultures and individualities that we have today in balance will not last. Compromise does not please the purest standards of our interaction desire. Our interaction desire wants to be able to relate openly with all things. Eventually, all players will have to interact fully. We will have to emerge into a stronger but all inclusive cultural instinct. One animal, one instinct.

6.16 Maturity

A species does not naturally question its mindrules. An animal will normally assume its instincts. The ability to distance ourselves from our taught instincts will only happen when we begin to perceive that our assumed behaviour carries some fundamental flaw. We must be able to detect fault in what we do at the instinctive level. It takes time and experience to realise the faults, and learn that our first reaction can sometimes disappoint or be misinterpreted.

Normally, the interaction desire expects to be able to follow its mindrules closely. However today, our good intentions can get lost in the confusion. When we cannot deliver the good that we feel, we come to a critical point in our approach to life. We face two possible explanations of why the good that we feel does not shine through. Perhaps our expectation for good is unrealistic, and should be dampened. This path makes us retract from the true aim of our desire and spirit. We allow ourselves to be overwhelmed by the failures. The soul withdraws into a realm of individuality. Parts of what we feel dies, as a way of reducing the high expectation of our interaction desire. Emotions and attitudes develop strongly to cover up the internal restriction that we feel.

The second approach is to try and make the good that we intend prevail. We can try to keep our standards high, but then we must also find an explanation of why our intentions fail. This makes people question the behaviour of themselves or others. There must be a mistake somewhere that we can overcome. This approach can lead to maturity.

Experience teaches us about our failures. If our spirit can persist despite those failures, the mind will learn ways to come to terms with those mistakes. It will learn how to deliver a finished product that is good, no matter how mistaken our first attempts might be. Maturity lets the original standard for good persist. When we gain maturity, we learn not to worry so much about the bad and the wrongs. We learn to control our emotions, so that we can remain open to correction. A mature person recognises mistakes, but is sufficiently self-assured to rise above those mistakes and take control of their own behaviour to make it right.

At first, the pleasure centre will not like the mature approach to life because it prefers to be instinctive and wild. But our mindrules in their current state cannot reveal our true nature. Maturity does not always accept the first impulsive view. It is not quickly overwhelmed. It gives us time to look at things from a variety of angles. It looks for a wider common sense. It makes us prepared to change our behaviour when our actions cause unwanted harm. It lets us feel less threatened at being wrong. It is learning how to make our behaviour work, by gaining experience about the views of others. It helps prevent the insanity and self-perpetuating illusions that could arise if mindrules had everything their own way. Today, maturity is needed more than ever because of the increased potential for confusion in our mindrules.

The things that a person must do to act maturely vary, but there are generally some essentials. For our species to act maturely and deliver the good, we must also generally learn other qualities that strengthen our ability to control our own instincts, and act beyond their inherent errors. Self-discipline, self-assurance, confidence, grace, wit, honesty, responsibility, a down-to-earth approach, can all contribute to our ability to be mature. Like the production of wine, it can be a long process. However, despite the twisted, alienated, restricted, confused and mistaken set of mindrules that we all learn during the stress of rapid niche change, we can still turn out to be descent people through maturity. Maturity can turn the self-perpetuating and illusory tendencies of mindrules under stress into a workable package.

There are many mistakes that a mature person can still make. A mature person might become too mature and controlled, at the expense of natural exuberance. They might deliver the good in their world, but that world might become narrow and small. All that is outside their world might be treated with intolerance. To prevent ourselves from taking this path, it is important to include wit with maturity. Wit reduces the claim of knowing the only right path. We should not expect to impose our own self-discipline and controls on others, because the mistakes might still be our own. Wit will make it easier to search for alternatives.

6.17 Wisdom

Wisdom is the ability to see things as they really are. Therefore, wisdom also allows us to predict more outcomes and see things more simply. In our species, wisdom must come after maturity because mindrules naturally prevent us from seeing things as they really are.

Things come easily to a wise person. Only they can know how easily. The basis of their knowledge is that they see reality more closely. They seem more attuned. Wisdom can often offer a new and simple idea that has obvious qualities once spoken. How would we go about improving our own level of wisdom?

The greatest source of wisdom that I have found is in wild creatures. I watched them closely to see how they did it. Of course, wild things do not consciously express their wisdom in language. It is built into their very being, and it is most easy to see when they are in their natural habitat. They do not have to go through a process of maturity to become wise. I could see strength and wisdom in the intricate forms of insects, and in the behaviour of reptiles and amphibians. Wild things are the embodiment of wisdom. They can do so much with what they are. They might be a lizard or insect, but they behave extremely sensibly, given what they are or the level of organisation they have. They operate at their full potential.

Our own species is not wise, even though we might think we are. We are actually the most stupid species on earth. We make inefficient use of our adaptations. We do not even know the point of our adaptations or what we want. We think we are wise, because we can control other things and make tools. However, this ability is a display of our gifts rather than our wisdom. Strength is having the power without the need to use it. We do not put our technology and our tools to wise use. Instead, the earth is dying under our care. Not very wise. Wisdom must start from within. We call ourselves *Homo sapiens*, wise man, and yet the ant crawling on the footpath embodies far more wisdom than we can imagine. We cannot even dare to put our actions to the wildness for a fair vote.

Wild animals are wise because they take what they are and make the most of it. They do not have to be aware of opposing forces or bad things. They do not have to be highly intelligent and manipulative. They do not have to struggle. They can be wise by being themselves. Because the universe is completely relatable, all that they have to do to get the most out of their life is self-enhance. They have to put everything that they are to its full potential. Anything that can become accomplished sufficient to be wild will find a place in the universe. This is an easy path to take, because making the most of what we have is also the most pleasurable thing that we can do. Our pleasure centre evolved to show us the way. The path is lit up clearly in neon signs. Only our mindrules stand in the way.

Before our species can become wise it will have to become aware of its mindrules. Then we will need to use wit and receptivity to make them pliable once more, and to place them under the direct control of our interaction desire. Mindrules trap us with the abilities that they learn for us, whereas wit allows us to renew our abilities. For our species, wit opens up the pathway to wisdom best. Wit encourages us to keep our options open. It makes us more responsive as the events unfold, rather than allowing us to assume that we are clever enough to make rules that are worth following.

7. Human adapting

7.1 Introduction

So how wise could we become? How well could we know our species and ourselves? Could today's events look sensible? Could we be wise enough to foresee our species' future?

The way to be wise is to take what we are and make the most of it. But where are the assumptions in this? Mindrules always assume. The first assumption is that we think we know what we are. However, for the question of our future, we really have to tackle the assumptions about what makes our species our own. We cannot tread lightly but must get stuck into it. We have to know what the make up and true nature of our species is, before we can see where it will lead. We cannot assume that we know the answer to that already, but must delve deeper beyond the mindrule illusion, to where we can feel more at home with our answers. Perhaps then we can live up to our self-anointed name of *Homo sapiens*, and at last display some semblance of wisdom.

There is much more natural strength and fairness in nature and in our own species than is currently realised. Millions of years of evolution have combined to produce a finely tuned species that is inherently capable of seeing the wildness. Our biological problems arise now only because our species' niche is changing rapidly. They do not arise because of some devious need or strategy in nature designed to pit animal against animal in struggle. We no longer live in a wild niche, but our adaptations and instincts are geared to grow up in their scenario. Our adaptations are expecting a natural connection that cannot appear. All other animals develop their instincts and adaptations within the context of a wild niche. They undergo a process of attunement that produces for them a deep sense of fulfilment, stability and natural wisdom. For our species however, the ground rules constantly change. It is difficult for us to attempt any fine-tuning under these conditions. We cannot rely on wild niche interactions to draw out the best qualities and arrangements for our instincts. We will have to find another way to know ourselves before we can experience the sensation of the wildness. We will have to work out our own true nature for ourselves. Perhaps with that knowledge and under-standing our species will once more achieve the credentials needed to become a part of the wildness.

Human nature grew out of an evolution that was shared and supported by the other species. From that process, we now carry many of their influences and share much of their nature. Two of the most important ingredients to our current behaviour have already been described. We are strongly influenced by the interaction desire, and by the development of our mindrule instincts. However, both of these forces are widespread within the rest of nature as well. They probably occur in all mammals and vertebrates at least. They are two forces that combine under natural circumstances to produce a highly efficient animal, for whatever species and niche is involved. The interaction desire makes animals want to combine whatever they experience into a simple and effi-cient pattern, and mindrules combine to make those efficient patterns our second nature. Our second nature used to match well with our first nature.

What makes each species different are the adaptations that these two forces must tie together in the cortex to produce a well coordinated control centre and mind. Each species has a different set of starting points from which to begin the process of niche attunement. The simple physical differences between a lion and a rabbit will demand different combinations of efficiencies and different sets of mindrules. The different claws and feet, body size, teeth, and brain structure lying outside the pliable cortex, must all combine in a way that will make the most of the attributes available in each species' category. To understand ourselves better, we should first look at our physical adapta-tions. This will show what our interaction desire and mindrule mechanism must work with. How could they tie it all together?

7.2 Our survival strategy

Each species today is the most specialised in existence for the niche they occupy. If they were not, they would soon lose their place to another species. We need to work out our own direction of specialisation. Then we will also learn more about our true niche, and better understand our adaptations. We must find the direction our entire being evolved to achieve. There should be no detour or side show in a species' plan for life. An animal cannot do two things at once. Evolution calls for total commitment to a niche, or it will find another species with the commitment to take your place.

To work out our strategy for life we need to gain clues from our adaptations. They will point towards our natural talent. There have been many contenders. Our ability to use tools, to be aggressive, to be selfish, to hunt in packs, to use weapons, find social kinship, altruism, intelligence, creativity, and consciousness all have been put forward as reason for our species' sudden advancement. However, I propose that our primary aim in life is to understand. All of our other adaptations fall into line to enhance this one strategy for life.

It may seem hollow claiming that understanding is our strongest adaptation, when one look at human history and society today seems to reveal anything but understanding. However, it is important to realise the conditions under which our species' was meant to develop its deep understandings. Our brain evolved to be very successful at learning and understanding niches that change slowly over thousands of years. Our brain did not evolve to cope with niches or contexts that change repeatedly within one lifetime. We can no longer rely on a wild niche, or anyone else, to show us how to turn our nature wild.

We share many adaptations with other apes. Our closest animal relatives are the chimpanzee, and our extinct ancestors *Homo erectus* and Neanderthal man. These species and sub-species already had our adaptations of a grasping hand, three dimensional stereoscopic vision, upright posture (for chimpanzees this is found in infants), intelligence, and a variety of adaptations that promote close social bonding (Farb, 1978: 84; Lambert, 1987: 14). Our ancestors had the intelligence to learn, and to hunt in cohesive groups for large mammals. They lived in family groups and tribes, and cared for the aged and sick. They could build shelters, use fire, and make clothing tools and weapons. Also, they must have had some ability or mind for conscious thought. Our immediate ancestors had jewellery, cave paintings, burial ceremonies, and possibly religion. All of this suggests that our ancestors had an ability to think about and conceive of themselves. But their species did not enter an evolution of mind that could change their behaviour at a rate faster than the slowly changing environment. An adaptation operating at another level must have emerged in us.

7.3 Understanding or intelligence

Our most striking morphological difference to the modern apes, and to our own ancestors, lies in the brain. Compared to our near relatives, the human brain is much larger and its interconnections more numerous. The main difference lies in just one part of the brain, the cerebral cortex. Yet despite such development, at least three-quarters of the cortex has no specific function to perform apart from learning (Farb, 1978: 63). No other species has placed such an investment into simply learning. Such investment signifies that a part of humankind's adaptive strategy is to produce an uncommitted and unspecialised brain, which is then open to learn about its niche. With this strategy, humans could live comfortably within the wide variety of niches into which it was to be born or emigrate. Our species spread from the equator to the Arctic, the sea to the mountains, and the jungle to the desert. Evolution could not predict which instincts we would need for each of these new environments, so it gave us a brain that could learn its instincts instead.

The ability to remain receptive and learn about a particular niche, was achieved in part by maintaining throughout childhood a brain growth rate well beyond that of any other primate. A prolonged brain growth rate could have come about through neoteny. This is where the embryonic growth rate of the brain does not switch off but continues after birth into childhood (Wilson, 1980: 36). While the brain keeps growing, it is easier to continue learning and adjusting new instincts. Brain growth continues very late in humans, and may not end until about age twenty-three (Morris, 1967: 30).

The human brain has a high memory capacity. It can store many facts and become highly intelligent. However, this ability on its own does not always ensure comfort or survival. Intelligence is useful only if it can find a niche where it is relevant and effective. Abstract intelligence or perfect logic may not always help. It is more important to understand the available niche than to be intelligent. Understanding seeks to unify knowledge and intelligence into a useful system of interrelationships. The neurones in the cortex have a highly developed network of connections between them. This allows a great deal of cross-referencing to occur, and is what understanding needs before it can develop. It is in understanding that we are designed to excel.

An intelligent brain is capable of storing many facts, and of recalling facts to provide answers and solve problems. However, unless that brain can link its facts into a simple system of understanding, it will expend a great deal of energy maintaining the separate positions of those facts. Intelligence needs to keep its knowledge conscious and within reach of attention for it to be recalled. Understanding allows us to bury knowledge deeply into our being according to an ordered instinctive structure, so that we do not have to remember and consider as many facts. The effects of understanding can be cooling. Understanding prefers to take knowledge and find ways to assemble it more simply. It is in our biology to make our understandings instinctive.

The pinnacle of intelligence is the genius or those with high IQ. However, it would be a mistake to think that only some are capable of such intelligence. Everyone has it in them to be the genius. The highly intelligent brain that can solve complex mathematical calculus, or design space rockets or perform brain surgery, must still use what is essentially a cave man brain. No matter how intelligent the cleverest mature cave man was, they would still not be able to do or learn such things today without the ability to understand first. Understanding allows us to build upon the gains of numerous ideas and experiments over thousands of years into a simple framework.

7.4 Insight

A good understanding is much more valuable than intelligence. Intelligence can add to understanding, but it is not the only contributing factor. If relied on solely, intelligence can become foolish. Without real understanding, intelligence could think that it was the most special creature in the world, and that it can keep six billion people on a small planet happy.

We can find the proof that we evolved to understand, when we look at what is needed to achieve its result. Understanding needs a large brain to absorb the information and assemble its intelligence. This we have. Our species has the largest uncommitted brain known. The other contributing factor that is needed to make understanding is insight. Most of our remaining important adaptations evolved to make us accommodating to insight.

Insight is able to give us unexpected but better understandings. The insight process allows the sudden switch from one way of looking at things to another (De Bono, 1969: 177). A brain that was purely seeking intelligence could find a perfectly logical explanation to the many facts it knew, but at the same time be drifting away from a workable understanding of the niche. The intelligence would often need to be bought back to its main role of correctly understanding the niche. Intelligence cannot be left to wander off on its own. It could develop in a tangent of its own without even knowing. It might become irrelevant, but continue to grow within its own self-perpetuating structure. Any species that let intelligence become more important to it than niche understanding would have died out long ago. Intelligence is only useful if insight can turn it back into understanding. A scientist might be highly intelligent, but lack the understanding of how to organise life at home, or of how to survive in the bush. An engineer might cleverly plan a vast project to dam a river, and yet fail to see the long-term environmental devastation that results. Scientists might try to build a giant mirror to orbit earth and reflect light on landscapes during the northern winter, but alter some of the natural cues to which certain species have evolved.

Insight has to be able to catch intelligence by surprise for it to have an impact. Intelligence might try to resist insight and keep its own structure and theories intact. Unless we have a backdoor or insight entry into that intelligence, the intelligent structure could self-perpetuate into a world of its own. Insight must find a way to bypass the predictions made by intelligence. Insight needs to be unexpected. However, the benefit we gain in understanding is so great that we have evolved to appreciate and seek the insight surprise. Often, it will make us laugh. It opens up new possibilities that we did not realise. It improves our understanding for the situation at hand, and lets us interact more directly and sweetly. It makes our neural pathways so much more efficient and accomplished, and brings us back to the reality or meaning of the situation. Insight can be exciting. Some might call out eureka. It might come as a flash of inspiration. It can feel as though the penny has dropped. It may take the form of a religious experience, revelation, or liberation.

A species that needs insight to enhance its survival strategy of finding greater niche understanding would benefit by living communally. Insight has to be unexpected for it to have full impact. Therefore, it will not always happen when we would like, and cannot be on call. Insight will occur in its own time. A really keen insight might come rarely. All an animal can do is to try and improve the chances that insight will occur. An animal living on its own might never get enough insight to live well and develop good understanding. An intelligent hermit could become quite strange. It might take generations to accumulate the insights needed to build a strong niche understanding. Therefore, a species that has a life strategy to understand should also be gregarious. Otherwise, it would have to discover and learn all of its understandings over and over again.

The members of this gregarious species would also have to bond closely to each other for them to share their insights willingly. If the species members were tightly bonded, they would happily pass on any insight that they found while roaming the niche to affect the group similarly. This would make the group more cohesive and well adjusted. Humans have many adaptations that seek to make bonds intense, intimate and lasting. The more intense the bonding, the better shared the insight.

While our most distinctive adaptation lies in the brain, almost all of our other distinguishing adaptations exist to make us bond tightly with each other so that insight will flow freely. Humans have an unusually long childhood. Most animals are mature and sexually active within the age of two or three years. Humans do not reach puberty or maturity until the teenage years. This adaptation allows bonds in a family to become very strong. It avoids sexual complications that might interfere with family trust and purpose. A long childhood gives a person the time they need to learn their understanding. Children need the security of a close knit family or tribal family to give them the confidence to explore and make mistakes, and still know that they will be accepted afterwards. The development of the cortex into a well-tuned map of niche understanding requires much trial and error. We can experience many minor blocks and bumps while growing up, which can be unpleasant and draining. Family and social bonds act as a back up during this time of learning.

There are also many adaptations that make ours a highly sexual species. We are the only primates that can have sex on almost any day of the year (Morris, 1967; Farb, 1978). One of our important adaptations is the suppression in females of heat or oestrus. Sexual activity in other primates is strongly regulated by oestrus. It generally lasts only a few weeks each year, or for a few days each month. In other primates, sex stops upon becoming pregnant, unlike humans. In other primates, the female apparently does not have orgasm, whereas our females can. Our species can view the facial expressions of another during intercourse, unlike other primates. The species is naked of thick body hair, possibly to increase the sensation of touch. Other primates have secondary sexual characteristics that only appear during oestrus. Our species display these characteristics permanently when mature. For example, lip colour or enlarged female breasts do not vary noticeably throughout the year. Also, our species has a relatively large penis, for a primate.

These remarkable adaptations go beyond the simple need to reproduce. They were not put in us by mistake, to make us wicked, or to let us have a good time. They contribute strongly to our strategy for life. These sexual adaptations seek to make our bonds intimate and lasting. They seek to make us put time and effort into developing and maintaining those bonds. Any increase that we can make in bonding will improve our opportunity for insight swapping. Insight swapping becomes automatic upon intimacy.

The more bonding adaptations our species evolved, the more concern it had for the welfare of others. We have achieved a level of altruistic behaviour not found in any other species. We needed our bonding adaptations to evolve to this degree to help us take understanding to its limits.

The strong development of our survival strategy turned the aim of our sex from simple reproduction to insight exploration. Now, the primal aim behind sex in our species is to find insight. It aims to produce total interaction and honesty between partners, so that insight can transfer more easily. Sex becomes dirty and unfulfilling when it lacks this associated sharing and honesty. Unfortunately, during rapid niche change our understandings develop so poorly that we have no real insights to share. Also, mindrules inhibit our receptivity to such an extent that we are unable to transfer the honesty and wildness normally possible in sex. This failure and strain can cause our sex to lose sight of its most romantic and fulfilling aim. Sex might reduce to simple relief, with little or no contribution towards the pleasures sought by our interaction desire.

A further adaptation that evolved to help bonding and insight swapping was the emotion of love. It is an emotion that we think might be less developed in other animals. It is a state that goes beyond the needs of reproduction. It strengthens the bonds, and can make us crave for more of everything about another person. The main function of love is to make us more attuned to another, so that between the two we can find the best way to live. Love can act like an insight. It can totally change the behaviour and nature of a person. Love is an important back up emotion for a wild animal that needs to understand. If the interaction desire cannot be totally wild some of it will turn into emotion. For humans, one of the first emotions to appear on the tree of emotions is love. If the interaction desire is not being filled well, then love will generally help us to bond with another, and give us the drive to care and work harder towards finding a life more comfortable for both. Love can turn us around and give us the drive to find more pleasurable conditions in which to live.

Some of our adaptations for bonding and sex are designed to make us want to share our insights. We also have another set of adaptations that improve our ability to express those insights. We are highly adapted in our ability to communicate; thereby increasing the value of the information contained in our insight messages. Humans have well-developed vocal cords that allow us to form complex sounds such as speech. We are also able to produce many different signs and gestures. The muscles in the face are unusually mobile. We can produce a large variety of expressions such as the smile and frown. These expressions can convey our honest feelings even before we realise what they have done. Their appearance can be difficult to mask. To do so is unnatural. It takes conscious effort and practise to hide them. And there is great social pressure within our species to interact honestly and freely. This further helps ensure the spread of insight, when it appears, amongst our species.

At first, an animal will obtain most of its insights from the niche or its partners. However, our need for insight made us evolve further. We are now able to generate many ideas for possible insight ourselves.

The brain of most large animals can summarise its vast array of information into a more useful map. This will put the information in a simpler form that is easier to read. The map to the brain was placed in the mind because that is where it would be easiest to read. The mind also had to be able to concentrate on certain parts of the map rather than trying to view it all at once. To be able to focus on certain areas of the map the mind evolved attention. Attention could then roam the mind map, pick out what it wanted, and request more detail if it found a need. Attention is the most energetic and active part of the brain. The direction that attention takes in animals is strongly influenced by their most pressing need, and by niche interactions.

Our need for insight made our mind evolve further than it did in other animals. One-fifth of our total energy now goes towards running our brain. We increased the amount of information that the mind can view at once. We can give our attention to two or more ideas at once. We are not necessarily drawn or confined to the most pressing task at hand. Our minds can wander and look for alternatives. We can think about one idea and compare it to another. This increases our chance of finding insight. It allows us to evaluate either idea in more detail. We can hold one idea still while using the other to dissect it and see how it works. Also, the ideas bought up for comparison can change rapidly until we find one that produces insight and a clearer understanding.

The attention we can give to several ideas at once means that we can make many comparisons throughout our lifetime. Eventually, we would notice that some of our ideas do not change. They would seem to us the most accurate ideas. These ideas might make us feel good, or some might be unpleasant. However, if they seem to give insight on a wide range of issues the mind will still learn to return to them regularly. Those stable ideas would become a characteristic of the mind itself. They would become the mind's self-identity. From the variety of comparisons that the mind can make a picture will build of how that self-identity fits in with the rest of the world. The mind will become aware of its position in the niche.

The increased awareness that the self-identity offers allows humans to become far more conscious than any other species. The self-identity gave us a constant reference point from which to view the niche and compare and dissect its many components. It was because of our great need for insight that the comparative ability of the mind pushed forward to give us our self-identity and keen sense of consciousness.

Besides understanding, other qualities are often put forward as being our most distinctive. Our species seems unusual in its level of perception, abstraction, imagination, and humour. However, each of these falls under the umbrella of what we need to do to achieve greater understanding. They are not very useful on their own. There is not much survival advantage in being abstract, or in walking around with just a good sense of humour for protection. The value of these other characteristics comes from the improvements that they can give to understanding. Understanding is a life strategy that evolution can favour and select. It is a strategy that can grow slowly over thousands of years, as even the smallest gain in understanding can enhance our specialisation.

Understanding can transform the mind into a new state of awareness so that it becomes more effective. It can do this independently of any opinions we might have that thinks such change is not possible. Insight can catch our opinions unawares. We gain insight in a variety of ways. It can come from perception, abstraction, imagination, humour, bonding, consciousness, the keenness of our senses, and from a pair of hands that are adept at exploring. The understanding that an insight can lead to is rarely predictable. However, our species continued to evolve ways to find insights more easily because insight improves our understanding.

Our strategy to understand explains most of our unique adaptations. Our adaptations cannot lie. Only what we think can lie. Our specialisation into understanding explains our brain size, lack of inherited instincts, bonding behaviour, and level of consciousness.

7.5 Change and potential

Our species' niche is changing rapidly. The things that we can include within our understanding grow continuously. Each day we can find new items or knowledge to consider. All other animals develop their understandings within the contexts of their niche. Their understanding is a process of attunement. For our species however the ground rules constantly change. It is difficult for us to attempt any fine-tuning under these conditions.

At first niche change for our ancestors was slow. Now it is gathering pace and momentum. Such level of change is unusual for animals. No other species can change the way we do. We can change niches within one lifetime. The niches of our children are different to the niches into which we were born. The way they do things is different to the way our parents and grandparents did things. Why should our niches be changing in this way? What is the real reason for the change?

Any prolonged change that happens within our universe always occurs within the framework of a new potential. There must be surrounding reason and structure before any change can occur. We might like to think that we are creating our own change, but if we want to understand that change, we will have to see that it is the universe that allows us to move. We will have to see ourselves as just another creation undergoing natural reactions within the universe. We are not under any particular difficulty or problem. The circumstances of our progress are quite simple to understand.

Potentials can arise in two ways. Either the environment sets up a new potential for an object, or the object initiates its own potential. In the first case, the changed environment provides a new end for the object to pursue. In the second case, the changed object provides itself with a new start that must find an available end. If change occurs, then the object embarks on movement through the potential towards its new end or position. Once the potential is filled, the object will stabilise. The big bang set up the ultimate range of potentials for our universe.

Examples where the environment sets up a new potential for an object are: The position of an electron (the object) in a wire will change if given the potential. Placing an electrode at either end of the wire can set up this potential. A ball will move to a lower position when the tube it rests in tilts. A species of termite that feeds on woody litter on the ground can gain the potential to feed on floorboards if a house is built nearby. The influenza virus can become deadly if it is given a potential new niche. Natives on islands in the eighteenth century were often prone to this change, because they had no immunity to the virus. In these examples, the electron, ball, termite and virus have not changed structure. It was their environments that changed to produce their new potential.

The second way to find new potential is through internal change. The influenza virus can gain a new potential to infect by changing its surface chemistry, rather than by being transported to an unsuspecting population. This internal change gives the virus a new potential to by-pass developed immunities. Once more it can sweep through a population as though a new niche had suddenly become available. In this case, it is the virus not the environment that changes structure to set up the new potential.

Our species' development is simply another example of the change that will occur under the direction of a potential. As in the last example, it is a potential that was induced by some change in our own make up. Therefore, we have three parts to consider within the framework of this change. There was a change in our form in the past that set up our potential, a niche must exist that can draw on that potential, and within that potential we have the transition stage. We are currently in the middle of our potential. Our world is temporary and filled with the influences and legacies of the two niches at either end of our potential. There is no requirement for us as the moving object to be aware of the external structure of the potential along which we now move, at least not until we fill that potential.

It will only be a matter of time before we find the knowledge needed to fill our potential. We shift from one niche to the next. When we complete all the change that our species is capable of making, what will our new position be like? I think that it will be best described as our wild niche. When we can use all of our adaptations to their full potential we will be in a position where we can know what it feels like to be wild.

The wild niche is the potential position for our species. We could step into that position now because it is already available. The world and the universe do not have to change any further to make our wild niche real. We can take up our rightful position any time we realise. Each time we learn a little more about our potential, we move further towards it. We slowly step from one temporary niche to another. The only reason we have not jumped straight into the wild niche already is that we need to learn still more understanding. However, the potential is there. Our travel through those temporary niches is accelerating at an ever faster pace.

The wild niche is what fashions our change today. The presence of its structure draws us out of our present temporary niches to make us change. The wild niche is no longer a niche that nature can confine. However, nature is really only the product on earth of universal forces. It is more accurate to describe the wild niche as universe provided. It might seem strange that a species can etch out a tight little niche for itself in something as large and expansive as a universe. However, simple laws make up the universe, and it is those laws that provide the framework of our wild niche. To think of niches as also occurring in the universe, rather than just in nature, expand its definition slightly. A niche is any comfortable interacting position within which an organism finds itself. Our species has only one wild niche available to it. All of our problems come from trying to make do with a variety of temporary and false niches along the way. Most people realise that we are not yet living at our full potential, and sense that we could do better.

It might seem paradoxical that unfilled potentials can occur in the universe, where everything is supposed to be completely relatable and interactive. Potentials exist because in a completely relatable universe all events fit together as meshwork in a predictable pattern. The growing edge of creation is itself in various stages of completion and interaction. Not everything can interact at once to spread the strength of the universe evenly. Potentials can develop at the radiating edge when simple physical limitations arise and impose gaps on how quickly interactions can occur in the time and space available. Creation occurs in a radiating pattern. The tips of creation can for varying times branch out on their own, before the universe can even things up again. Potentials are really just delayed interactions.

A potential is not proven until it has been achieved. However, the end result can still be obvious if we know the surrounding framework of the reaction. In a completely relatable universe only one outcome is possible. The task is to find the position where we can see that outcome clearly. To see the potential we must understand the outside structure in which the reaction is taking place. The power of this outside structure makes the potential appear as though it is a hole ready to be filled. Once the potential is set in place, it can be less important to the surrounding structure whether the potential is filled immediately or with time.

Most reactions occur immediately, so there is little point in thinking of their end results as potentials. But when the reactions are slow, as with our mind evolution, the recognition of a potential becomes useful. There are simple limitations on the rate at which we can change, because our change has to work at a rate that is comfortable for an animal and within reach of our mindrules. Before the potential appeared, we did not have to know how we were being influenced and programmed by our mindrules. But now they are the only impediment to us reaching our potential. Our new wild niche is calling on us for greater understanding.

We are approaching our wild niche through discovery and insight. Different times arise throughout our history when the potential or push for a new discovery builds. Humans make their discoveries because the time and potential are right, rather than because of some human ability to create its own path. There are many examples in our history where two or more people made important technological discoveries almost simultaneously (Jewkes *et al.*, 1960: 227). It surprises me that no one else has already written a book similar to this one (which might suggest that I am wrong!).

Sometimes we feel the power of our potential and describe it variously as fate and destiny. Fate tends to be a pessimistic view of potentials, while destiny is more positive. Whether we can predict such potentials will depend upon how well we understand the initial course of events, and the structure that surrounds the potentials. It would require great wisdom to know our own fate and destiny. It would require a level that none can truthfully claim. But it is easier to predict the potential for a whole species, than it is to predict the future of one individual.

7.6 Universal understanding

The life strategy developed by humans is to understand. If we trace the steps along which this strategy might lead we should be able to find the one last step that launched us into our mind's evolution. With one more step into understanding a threshold appeared that revealed before us a whole new potential.

Our adaptation to understand reached a point where it became the start of new opportunities beyond the confines of our ancestral niche. We had reached the point where any small gain in understanding began to find much wider relevance than our starting niche could contain. Our thoughts pushed outwards. We were able not only to understand the niche within which we lived, but parts of a universal structure that exists beyond our niche. We continue to discover more pieces to this universal structure through our science.

Our ability to understand has reached a level that gives us the potential to understand the universe. This threshold level of understanding I call universal understanding. It is our latest adaptation.

Our early ancestors had no idea that such a universal structure existed. It was not the aim of our strategy for life to understand science and the universe. Our species developed its capacity to understand with the aim of functioning better within its earthly niche. It was only when our understanding reached a certain level that its broader implications began to fall into place. We stumbled into the beginnings of a new world, when it was with our ancestral niche that we were really trying to come to terms.

When our species reached the threshold to universal understanding our further physical evolution slowly ground to a halt. The broader applications of our understanding allowed us to change our mind and habits when the need arose, rather than having to wait for a physical evolution to make the changes for us. The speed of change available within the potential began to take hold. Our new found ability to change makes us move too quickly for natural selection to act.

However, our new potential also gave our species its problems. Our ancestors could sense that things existed beyond their comfortable niche. We tried to explain the feeling away with spirits and gods. But natural limits fell away, and change was always available to those who were sufficiently curious or daring to explore. The species dispersed from Africa to most other continents. Some further physical evolution into races was possible before universal understanding could apply the brakes fully on natural selection. Our ability to understand has bought further physical change to a halt. It is our understanding that now evolves, rather than our physique.

In some ways, universal understanding is similar to the niche understanding that our ancestors were able to find. Both kinds of understanding can organise the knowledge that exists within their real or potential niche. They do this by searching for common underlying factors. What makes universal understanding different is the way in which we can now look for those common factors. We can look for patterns to the things we experience by imagining into the abstract. We can think in areas outside the confines of what we first knew. The comparisons we make to find insight can be very unexpected and novel. The more imaginative can be the brain the more insight it might find, and the greater the impact insight can have on our understanding. Our imagination can search into the abstract for its insight. This move would often allow the mind to organise its memories better. There would come a time when the amount of abstraction possible gave insight that was so perceptive, that understanding could move beyond the bounds of its original niche. This is why our species now experiences rapid niche change.

Threshold adaptations are not rare. Some animals have reached important thresholds before. However, those animals have always been able to fill their potentials through speciation rather than through mindrule evolution. When other animals reach new potential they continue to evolve slowly into a myriad of new species. A good example is flight in birds. The ancestor to birds, *Archaeopteryx*, was an ancient dinosaur that could jump and glide short distances. It evolved its gliding abilities until eventually it reached the threshold of flight. However, one species of bird-like dinosaur did not then occupy all of the skies throughout the world. It could not do all things such as fly marathon distances, hover, fly at night, survive in the desert or the cold, and fly at high speed. Instead, this one ancestral species filled its potential through speciation. Over the years, physical evolution turned that one dinosaur species into the thousands of different species of birds that we see today. The difference for humans is that our threshold adaptation does not allow us to fill our potential through speciation. Our threshold adaptation makes us change more rapidly than physical evolution can act.

7.7 Transition

Our mindrules were designed to produce good niche understandings. They were not designed to accommodate the changes bought about by our latest adaptation of universal understanding. The leap for them is too great. However, while we do not know about our mindrule limitations we will continue to perceive that problems in our world arise externally. Our species will continue to go through a series of steps that must strike a balance between the demands of our potential niche, and the ability of our mindrules to cope with being prised from their current teachings. We move through a series of temporary niches that change us slightly with their greater context. This process will continue until we have filled our potential niche. In the mean time, any niche understanding we find is destined to become undermined by a bolt of insight sent by our final wild niche.

During this transition stage, our history will be dotted with times of temporary cultural stability followed by periods of disruption. Our species has gone through a series of unexpected but inevitable changes in context. Discovery and insight constantly disrupt our various cultures and societies. No culture is able to withstand or control the change. The important changes for our species do not come about through the logical progression of our cultures. Important change occurs with the unexpected lateral expansion of new ideas. With change, our species finds a new and broader context from which to view things. Our change can be both unexpected and overwhelming. An extreme example of this kind of change is when the industrialised world discovers some new tribe of hunter-gatherer. The hunter-gatherer would not have conceived of the things we know. They would have assumed that they already knew the limits of their world. The new understanding that they should learn can for them be overwhelming.

A more recent example of the way our species changes is the awareness we now have for the environment. Two or three decades ago people thought that there was no stopping the logical expansion of our society based upon resource exploitation and population growth. People thought that new technologies could be found that would clear land faster, grow food plants bigger, rid us of the world's insect pests, find limitless nuclear energy, build taller buildings to house the people, and so on. All of this is now suspect. There is now a broader view that says we cannot live on our technologies alone. A society built on a broader understanding of our environmental world is important after all.

These two examples show that change does not occur in a way that a culture can predict for itself. The standard view that arises within a culture does not predict the basic change that will befall it in ten or twenty years. Real change happens unexpectedly. Real change comes as unexpected insight that opens up new concepts and contexts. Only when we can see our wild niche will our discoveries and insights seem logical and predictable. Once we find universal understanding, there will be no more insights available to disrupt the framework of our understanding. Our understanding will model complete relatability so that anything else that we learn will find a place on our model of understanding. Upon reaching the end of our potential, we will enter a prolonged period of attunement that will turn us wild.

Because the universe is completely relatable there is only one path available to us throughout our transition, although I cannot claim to see all its turns. The path our species took throughout history was the only option ever really open to us. The universe gave us no other choice. The single course available for our species remains true today. We must still be following the best and only course available for our species to fill its potential of universal understanding. I cannot imagine a better script. It looks to me as though we are rapidly heading towards our wild niche. I predict that we will have a workable or 'instinctive' understanding of that niche within three hundred, plus or minus one hundred years. In that time I think that we will achieve a functional level of wildness.

However, there is no real reason why our species could not complete its change within a matter of days. All we would have to do is realise the understanding that lives at the end of our potential. We are a highly social species with well-developed communication skills. If anyone found such an understanding, and it was real and they could communicate adequately, then it would soon spread. Natural reactions can happen quickly. Any real insight will spread, aided by natural forces for which mindrules have no control or understanding.

Unfortunately, the quest for our stronger and more just world usually turns humans phoney and delusional. We start so poorly, and our patience is short. There are many new age religions, philosophies and gimmicks that try to explain our world. I always thought that there would be more chance of finding answers where thirty million other species have found them before, rather than anything human invented. But then again, perhaps the theories in this book will turn out to be just more human delusion.

It seems our species cannot think of the big issues without buckling under the strain. We actually do such a poor job of trying to understand the big picture that it is not worth the effort if we are then going to take what we find seriously. If we become serious, then the inevitable delusions we find make us trapped rather than free. Therefore, it is important not to take ourselves too seriously while tackling such questions. The mindrule trap for our species is still far too strong and hidden to think that we might have escaped. And besides, there is no harm in being sceptical anyway. If an idea is true it should be able to stand up for itself without artificial protection. That is the inherent quality of a wild idea.

I have not tried yet to work out the various stages that our species is likely to go through during its transition. I will just mention a few steps that I think we will need to pass through in our mind's evolution. One of those steps is population control. Although our species could keep breeding to our heart's content, we will have to limit our population for the sake of our surroundings. Will have to find the strength and grace needed to control our own population growth. We will have to get it right within the population that we have. When the species discovers the wit needed to limit and reduce its population to respectable levels, the home run to our wild niche will become clearer.

Another important step for our species will be when we start to return much of the earth to its natural state. We will learn how to live more efficiently in our cities, to the benefit of millions of other species. This might seem wishful thinking in the face of the human juggernaut. But with clearer understanding and more direct access to internal motivation, I think such a change will only be a matter of time. I imagine that our species will also try to return to life many of the species that we made extinct during our transition. Their return will help us to see the wildness. Scientists will eventually be in a position where they can recreate life from DNA strands. The DNA strands of extinct species might come from the carcasses and pinned specimens stored in museum cabinets, the gut contents of those specimens, gene banks, or by mathematical calculation that determines the sequences of the 'missing links' that were never human known.

As humans we have learnt a great deal. We have built monuments, climbed Mount Everest, shattered the atom and moved into space. But for now, the sum result of these actions has been death and destruction. What we have done to the Earth so far is failure. None of our achievements will count for anything until our species can be wild once more. Only then will we become an integral part of the universe where what we do can contribute to the radiating edge of creation. If we let ourselves remain governed by min-drules we will remain several steps away from that leading edge. We will be moving according to rules that are old hat and of little consequence. We will remain dead inside like programmed robots. Our work will fail, and all we will do is create a void that something else in the future will have to fill and repair.

7.8 Our wild niche

Having identified our latest adaptation it should be easy to see its full potential. It will give us direction. We will reach our full potential when we have made absolutely full use of our most recent adaptation, universal understanding. So where does under-standing end, as from there we will be able to view the surroundings of our new wild niche?

We can gain an idea of what our wild niche will be like by looking at the limits to understanding. Earth does not confine our understanding. We can understand the ways of the universe. There seems to be no reason why we should not be able to understand the entire universe. This does not mean that we must know all forms and facts. All we need to do is find the right working model. Our mindrules could then learn that model as its niche map. This may seem to be an enormous task, but understanding is efficient. It can link a multitude of forms into the one system. Then rather than remembering the detail of every form, we can remember just one understanding. With understanding, forms become merely variations of the same basic nature or context. While we might not know each form, we will know their nature. We will have a working knowledge of how to live life, without needing to know the detail of everything. The discovery and experience of that detail will become the spice of life. A good understanding can always branch out further to connect ever more detail into its structure. There may be a limit to what intelligence can remember, but universal understanding has no limit.

We will achieve our greatest accomplishments when we have made full use of our latest adaptation. Then, we will have earned the right to be wild once more, and we will be able to interact more directly with other forms in the universe. There is no reason why our species could not be wild, and no reason why we would choose to be other-wise. Wildness is the state where we become most accomplished in all our interactions. Wildness makes the most of our adaptations. Wildness asks for wisdom in its creatures. For our species, the wildness is asking us to find universal understanding.

As for other mammal species, we will probably reach a functional level of wildness when about ninety to ninety-five percent of our desires can remain true. After reach-ing that level, I am not sure what level of wildness our species will move into to embrace. It is within our potential to become one hundred percent wild. If we choose that path, then we would feel as one, feel of common soul, and know each other's mind and desires. We would have no need for emotion or expression. However, in evolution our bodies became used to some level of emotion and natural block. We have adaptations that naturally cater to these emotions and their expressions. Perhaps we will choose to live according to our ancestors' natural state of attunement, and remain just ninety to ninety-five percent wild. Then we could still play with our emotions. Alternatively, perhaps we will move from one state of wildness to the other as the feeling takes us. It is too far ahead for me to see the 'no choice' option. However, I do know that wildness is a very powerful attractant.

I have not yet worked out how we might behave in our wild niche, its structure or economy. However, I can imagine the nature and spirit of the people that will live in such a time, and what living in a wild niche might feel like. I think that we will be in our wild niche when we can look at each other and see ourselves. We will not feel restriction, alienation and individuality. Instead, people will feel the same. Our view on life and the environment will be governed by a sense of beauty and strength. We will learn methods of attunement and harmony where we can live comfortably and find ways to fill our desires simply. It could turn out to be quite different to what I imagine, however, I would be happy with whatever a truly wild society found to be true.

By now you should see that the potential for everyone is the same. No one is fundamentally any better or worse than anyone else. The differences we see amongst ourselves today are rooted within the illusions created by mindrules. We could all reach our species' wild niche. Indeed, no one could honestly go there on their own without taking the rest of the species with them, such is our gregarious nature.

The real battle for our species lies within. Humankind is born with prized biological gifts. It has a good interaction desire that if properly trained can double as a fairly astute crap detector. The species also has all the adaptations needed to achieve universal understanding. The only real problem facing humankind is how to bring out our best during these times of rapid niche change. Our other biological gift, the efficient imprinting of niche understandings as mindrules, did not evolve to cope with the rapidly changing niche. Instead, that biological gift now imprints our minds with dead-end instincts that so complicate our lives, that we have become the most confused, miserable, and destructive species on the planet. But the future of our wild niche is not so far away. All it needs is for each of us to find the strength and wit needed to search for the solution to our common problem: the slowness of the mechanics for implementing our latest adaptation.

8. References

Andrews, G. (1995). Australian and NZ J. of Psychiatry 29: 394-402.

Barnhart, R.K. (1988). The Barnhart Dictionary of Etymology. The H.W. Wilson Co., New York.

Bateson, P. (1987). Imprinting as a process of competitive exclusion. In, Imprinting and Cortical Plasticity. Comparative Aspects of Sensitive Periods, John Wiley & Sons, New York, pp. 151-168.

Blakemore, C. and Cooper, G.F. (1970). Development of the brain depends on the visual environment. Nature 228: 477-478.

Blakemore, C. and Greenfield, S. (1987). Mindwaves. Thoughts on Intelligence, Identity and Consciousness. University Press, Cambridge.

Borden, A.R. (1982). A Comprehensive Old-English Dictionary. University Press of America, Washington, D.C.

Changeux , J.-P. and Danchin, A. (1976). Selective stabilisation of developing synapses as a mechanism for the specification of neuronal networks. Nature 264: 705-712.

Crook, J. (1987). The nature of conscious awareness. In C. Blakemore and S. Greenfield, Mindwaves. Thoughts on Intelligence, Identity and Consciousness. University Press, Cambridge, p. 383-402.

Darwin, C. (1859). The Origin of Species by Means of Natural Selection or the Preservation of Favoured Races in the Struggle for Life.

Darwin, C. (1871). The Descent of Man. John Murray, London.

Davies, P.C.W. and Brown, J. (1988). Superstrings. A Theory of Everything? Cambridge University Press, Cambridge.

Dawkins, R. (1976). The Selfish Gene. Oxford University Press, Oxford.

De Bono, E. (1969). The Mechanism of Mind. Penguin Books, Harmondsworth.

Denning, J.V. (1987). Aids: The Real Truth About the Aquired Immune Deficiency Syndrome. Dr J.V. Denning, Dorking, U.K.

Epstein, A.N. (1982). Instinct and Motivation as explanations for complex behaviour. In The Physiological Mechanisms of Motivation, Ed. D.W. Pfaff, Springer-Verlag, New York, pp 25-58.

Farb, P. (1978). Humankind. Jonathan Cape, London.

Gallup, G.H. and Newport, F. (1991). Belief in paranormal phenomena among adult Americans. Skeptical Inquirer 15: 137-146.

Habermehl, G.G. (1981). Venomous Animals and their Toxins. Springer-Verlag, Berlin.

Harris, T.A. (1967). I'm OK-you're OK. Pan Books, London.

Harris, J.E. and Wolfe, U.K. (1955). A laboratory study of vertical migration. Proc. Royal Society of London B 144: 329-354.

Jewkes, J., Sawers, D. and Stillerman, R. (1960). The Sources of Invention. MacMillan & Co. Ltd., London.

Lambert, D. (1987). The Cambridge Guide to Prehistoric Man. Cambridge University Press, Cambridge.

Lee, C.Y. (1972). Chemistry and pharmacology of polypeptide toxins in snake venoms. Annual Review of Pharmacology 12: 265-286.

Llinas, R. (1987). 'Mindness' as a functional state of the brain. In C. Blakemore and S. Greenfield, Mindwaves. Thoughts on Intelligence, Identity and Consciousness. University Press, Cambridge, p. 339-358.

Lorenz, K. (1966). On Aggression. Methuen and Co. Ltd, London.

Margulis, L. (1981). Symbiosis in Cell Evolution: Life and its Environment on the Early Earth. W.H. Freeman, San Francisco.

Mather, J. (1986). A look at the primeval explosion. New Scientist, 16 January 1986: 48-50.

Mayr, E. (1988). Toward a New Philosophy of Biology. Observations of an Evolutionist. The Belknap Press of Harvard Universtity Press, Cambridge Massachusetts.

Meck, W.H. (1996). Neuropharmacology of timing and time perception. Cognitive Brain Research 3: 227-242.

Melbye, M. (1986). The natural history of human T lymphotropic virus - III The natural infection: the cause of AIDS. British Medical J. 292: 5-12.

Morris, D. (1967). The Naked Ape. Triad/Mayflower Books, Frogmore St Albans.

Morris, D. (1995). The human animal: a personal view of the human species. Oxford University Press, London.

Rauschecker, J.P. (1987). What signals are responsible for synaptic changes in visual cortical plasticity? In, Imprinting and Cortical Plasticity. Comparative Aspects of Sensitive Periods, John Wiley & Sons, New York, pp. 193-220.

Rauschecker, J.P. and Marler, P. (1987). Cortical plasticity and imprinting: behavioural and physiological contrasts and parallels. In, Imprinting and Cortical Plasticity. Comparative Aspects of Sensitive Periods, John Wiley & Sons, New York, pp. 349-365.

Routtenberg, A. (1980). The reward system of the brain. In, Mind and Behaviour, R.L. Atkinson and R.C. Atkinson. W.H. Freeman and Company, San Francisco, pp. 24-31.

Schmidt, G.D. and Roberts, L.S. (1981). Foundations of parasitology. The C. V. Mosby Company, St. Louis.

Schwarz, J. (1988). In P.C.W. Davies and Brown, J. (1988). Superstrings. A Theory of Everything? Cambridge University Press, Cambridge, pp 70-89.

Sutherland, S.K. (1983). Australian Animal Toxins. Oxford University Press, Melbourne.

Toffler, A. (1970). Future Shock. Pan Books, London.

Walker, G. (1991). Spider venom could help stroke victims. New Scientist, 4 May 1991: 17.

Weisz, P.B. (1973). The Science of Zoology. McGraw-Hill Book Company, New York.

West, D.J., Andrews, E.B., McVean, A.R., Osborne, D.J. and Thorndyke, M.C. (1994). Isolation of serotonin from the accessory salivary glands of the marine snail *Nucella lapillus*. Toxicon 32 (10): 1261-1264.

Wilson, P.J. (1980). Man, the Promising Primate. The Conditions of Human Evolution. Yale University Press, New Haven.

Witten, E. (1988). In P.C.W. Davies and Brown, J. (1988). Superstrings. A Theory of Everything? Cambridge University Press, Cambridge, pp 90-106.

Wortman, C.B., Loftus, E.F. and Marshall, M.E. (1992). Psychology. Fourth Edition. McGraw-Hill, Inc, New York.

www.ingramcontent.com/pod-product-compliance
Lightning Source LLC
Chambersburg PA
CBHW030424290526
45786CB00001B/129